C4 619717 00 B3

D1381310

EARTH

(THE BOOK)

• • •

A Visitor's Guide to the Human Race

Written and Edited by
Jon Stewart
David Javerbaum
Rory Albanese
Steve Bodow
Josh Lieb

Writers
Kevin Bleyer, Rich Blomquist, Tim Carvell,
Wyatt Cenac, Hallie Haglund, J.R. Havlan,
Elliott Kalan, Sam Means, Jo Miller,
John Oliver, Daniel Radosh, Jason Ross

Designed by Pentagram

Special Thanks
Jill Baum, Dave Blog, Adam Chodikoff,
Jen Flanz, Robin Sanders

PARTICULAR BOOKS

Published by the Penguin Group
Penguin Books Ltd, 80 Strand, London WC2R 0RL, England
Penguin Group (USA) Inc., 375 Hudson Street, New York, New York 10014, USA
Penguin Group (Canada), 90 Eglinton Avenue East, Suite 700, Toronto, Ontario, Canada M4P 2Y3
(a division of Pearson Penguin Canada Inc.)
Penguin Ireland, 25 St Stephen's Green, Dublin 2, Ireland (a division of Penguin Books Ltd)
Penguin Group (Australia), 250 Camberwell Road,
Camberwell, Victoria 3124, Australia (a division of Pearson Australia Group Pty Ltd)
Penguin Books India Pvt Ltd, 11 Community Centre,
Panchsheel Park, New Delhi – 110 017, India
Penguin Group (NZ), 67 Apollo Drive, Rosedale, North Shore 0632, New Zealand
(a division of Pearson New Zealand Ltd)
Penguin Books (South Africa) (Pty) Ltd, 24 Sturdee Avenue,
Rosebank, Johannesburg 2196, South Africa

Penguin Books Ltd, Registered Offices: 80 Strand, London WC2R 0RL, England

www.penguin.com

First published in the United States of America by Grand Central Publishing 2010
First published in Great Britain by Particular Books 2010
1

Printed and bound by Firmengruppe APPL, Aprinta Druck, Wemding, Germany

A CIP catalogue record for this book is available from the British Library

978-1-846-14316-8

PARTICULAR BOOKS
an imprint of
PENGUIN BOOKS

Contents

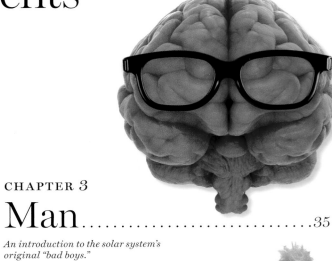

An introduction to the solar system's original "bad boys."

Everything you need to know about this gently-used, pre-owned planet.

We called this living.

A comprehensive guide to things that can be killed.

How we overcame our basic humanity for the greater good.

Earth

THE FIRST THING you may have noticed on your way in was the color. Deep pools of greens and blues, unique within our galaxy, beckon amongst ethereal swirls of white clouds. As you get closer you're struck by the topographical diversity. Vast oceans give way to lush green forest and jungles, which seamlessly taper off into sandy desert ridges stretching towards meticulously water-carved canyons. In the distance snow-covered mountains rise up to seemingly touch the sky. Of course, for an **oblate spheroid**, she's certainly not perfect. But despite a pronounced equatorial bulge and receding polar iceline, she still stubbornly maintains a jaunty 23.4° axial tilt that belies her 4.5 billion years.

And she has been through it. We knew her as a fertile oasis of sophisticated life in the endless, barren expanse of the universe (no offense). But she was almost 20 million years old before she had even electrostatically accreted enough to achieve solid status. And even then she was made up mostly of gasses and dust the sun was throwing out anyway.

But somehow, using nothing more than a little moxie and massive gravitational and magnetic fields, she pulled herself together. With an unassuming **iron core** and delicate **silica crust**, you would never suspect that much of her success was due to explosive volcanic eruption and the water she had

Our planet had its own day. Did yours?

stolen from passing asteroids and trans-Neptunian objects in her wilder youth. She did what she had to do.

In her 4.5 billion years she has been alternately covered in lava, ice and ammonia, and has endured the endless discomfort of her **tectonic plates** shifting. She has seen her dedication to creating a viable atmosphere rewarded with a Cambrian explosion of multi-cellular creatures, only to witness five mass extinctions (you came right after the sixth). She has survived being simultaneously pelted by all manner of asteroids, meteors, radiation and whatever else decided to smash into her as they joyrode around the universe. And she did it all without complaint ... unless you consider the violent restructuring of land masses through earthquakes complaining.

It's funny. When we were alive we spent much of our time staring up at the cosmos and wondering what was out there. We were obsessed with the moon and whether we could one day visit it. The day we finally walked on it was celebrated worldwide as perhaps man's greatest achievement. But it was while we were there, gathering rocks from the moon's desolate landscape, that we looked up and caught a glimpse of just how incredible our own planet was. Its singular astonishing beauty. We called her Mother Earth. Because she gave birth to us, and then we sucked her dry.

So welcome to **Earth** ... population, *you.*

Location

FOR MOST OF our history we had grave misconceptions about exactly where Earth stood within the cosmos. Due to scientific limitations and more than a touch of narcissism, we believed everything in the universe literally revolved around us. It was a theory called **geocentrism**, which was originally egocentrism, but they spelled it wrong.

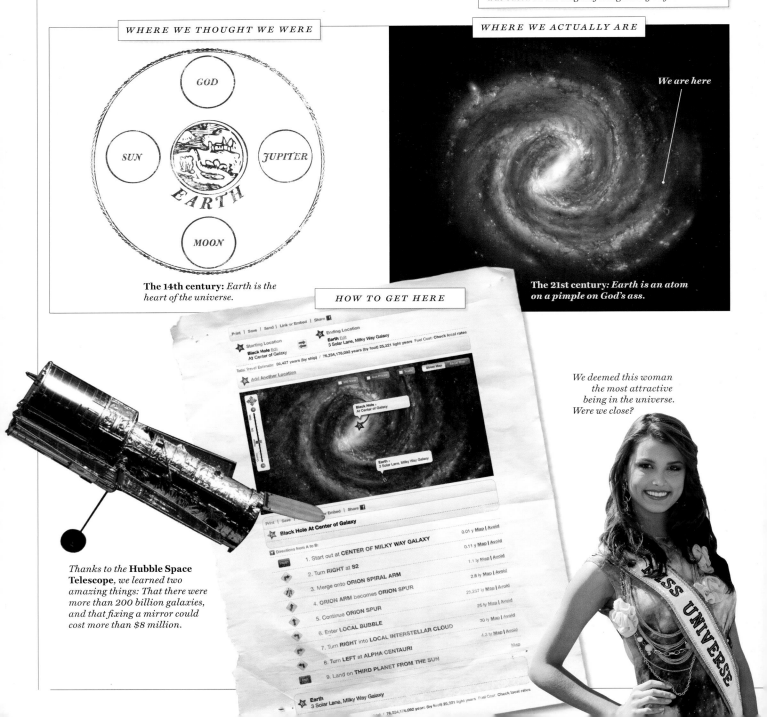

WHERE WE THOUGHT WE WERE

GOD

SUN   EARTH   JUPITER

MOON

The 14th century: *Earth is the heart of the universe.*

WHERE WE ACTUALLY ARE

We are here

The 21st century: *Earth is an atom on a pimple on God's ass.*

HOW TO GET HERE

*Thanks to the **Hubble Space Telescope**, we learned two amazing things: That there were more than 200 billion galaxies, and that fixing a mirror could cost more than $8 million.*

Print | Save | Send | Link or Embed | Share

Starting Location *Edit*
Black Hole *Edit*
At Center of Galaxy

Ending Location
Earth *Edit*
3 Solar Lane, Milky Way Galaxy   Fuel Cost: Check local rates

Total Travel Estimate: 86,427 years (by ship) / 76,234,176,092 years (by foot) 25,321 light years

Add Another Location

Black Hole
At Center of Galaxy

Earth
3 Solar Lane, Milky Way Galaxy

Black Hole At Center of Galaxy

Directions from A to B:

1. Start out at **CENTER OF MILKY WAY GALAXY** — 0.01 y Map | Avoid
2. Turn RIGHT at **S2** — 0.11 y Map | Avoid
3. Merge onto **ORION SPIRAL ARM** — 1.1 ly Map | Avoid
4. **ORION ARM** becomes **ORION SPUR** — 2.8 ly Map | Avoid
5. Continue **ORION SPUR** — 25,207 ly Map | Avoid
6. Enter **LOCAL BUBBLE** — 25 ly Map | Avoid
7. Turn RIGHT into **LOCAL INTERSTELLAR CLOUD** — 30 ly Map | Avoid
8. Turn LEFT at **ALPHA CENTAURI** — 4.3 ly Map | Avoid
9. Land on **THIRD PLANET FROM THE SUN** — Map

Earth
3 Solar Lane, Milky Way Galaxy

We deemed this woman the most attractive being in the universe. Were we close?

MISS UNIVERSE

To Our Alien Readers

GREETINGS ALIEN BRETHREN! Across eons of time, we extend our hands in posthumous friendship and bid you welcome to Planet Earth, on behalf of not only ourselves, but the entire Viacom family.

We're sorry we're not here to greet you in person. Really, really sorry. We invited you over, and you traveled who knows how many light years to see us, and you finally got here and we're not home. And we never will be. And we left the place a mess. Trust us when we say this was not our intention. In fact, we had always assumed we would be the ones gallivanting around the universe, rummaging through the remains of once-great alien civilizations, wearing form-fitting space Spandex and solving cosmic mysteries. Eh. *Que sera, sera.*

Ironically, your arrival would have been a profoundly life-changing moment for our race. We always wondered whether we were alone in the universe. To meet, befriend and experience life through the ... let's say "eyes" of another intelligent being would have made all 6.8 billion of us feel less alone. And the knowledge that we were only one of untold numbers of sentient creatures in the cosmos might have finally given us the perspective we needed to rein in our self-destructive tendencies, and work together for the greater good of our species and our planet.

Especially if you had come to kill us. Nothing would have united us as a species like the perceived existential threat posed by you. Not that we had reason to assume your intentions in coming here were anything but honorable. It's just that in general, our own first-time interactions had a certain "killing each other" feeling-out period.

Of course there were those who believed you had already visited our planet surreptitiously, an advanced race traveling trillions of miles across the Milky Way for the sole purpose of surprising and perhaps anally probing one of our rural denizens. Which as it happens was the orifice least likely to yield useful pedagogical results. These humans also believed our governments, known mostly for bureaucratic incompetence, had somehow made your alien presence the one thing they could keep masterfully secret.

As seen here, flying saucers first began appearing in the 1940s.

But we don't blame you. Truth be told, we thought about you a lot. We created thousands of fictional extraterrestrials in our day, most of them slight variations on the theme of us (see next page). Us with bigger heads, us as full grown fetuses, us with animal or fish parts, really hot lady usses with just a piece of metal shit on their heads to make them look "spacey."

Of course we had no idea what you actually look like. Indeed, it's entirely possible you've entirely transcended materiality—that you are incorporeal spirits floating through the vacuum

You Looked Like Us But ...

... with blue skin.

... with pointier ears.

... with a longer neck.

... with a more prominent forehead.

... like a bear.

... like a gay bear.

... with an insatiable need for attention.

... 50% hotter.

... with dreads, reptile skin and a fierce manicure.

... but somehow smarter.

of space. In which case, mazel tov.

Ah, would that we were still alive; that we could see you as you really are, talk to you, learn from you, then take you to one of our cinemas (more on those later) and share a laugh together watching *Men in Black*, or cry together watching *E.T.*, or feel incredibly awkward together watching *Independence Day* or *Aliens* or *Species* or *Cloverfield*, or ... well, we fought you guys a lot in our movies. Alas, we're dead, and that will never happen.

But this book is designed to provide you with the next best thing to our actual presence: a comprehensive history of our planet and our species, conveniently written in the universal language—American English.

Consider it a user's guide to our planet.

And once you've discovered everything there is to know about us—as you will over the next 240 or so pages—you might even begin to wonder what it would have been like to meet us. If so, feel free to "splurge" and genetically reconstitute the human race. As you'll read, you'll find a wide selection of our DNA stored in two convenient locations, Svalbard, Norway, and Trementina, New Mexico (see next spread). Or just poke around. There's probably a thin layer of us on almost everything.

But for now, take a load off, pick up this book, position your ... let's say "lower extremities" comfortably on one of our many level surfaces, and relax.

We think you're going to like it here.

We sure did.

Once.

The Authors

Did You Get Our Messages?

We tried to contact you for a long time. We're not sure which (if any) of our messages you received, but taken collectively they tell a sad tale of unrequited obsession.

1.
The *Pioneer* plaque
(1973)

Our first attempt to introduce ourselves was a pair of gold anodized aluminum plaques we sent into deep space. The bra at the top is the transition of hydrogen; the asterisk thingie is the map you were supposed to use to get here; and the couple on the right is our way of asking if you guys swing. What can we say? It was the seventies.

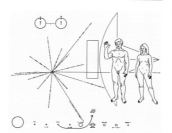

The Pioneer *plaque, starring Ryan O'Neal and Ali MacGraw.*

2.
The Arecibo message
(1974)

We hadn't heard back from you by the following year, so we took a different approach: A three-minute broadcast of 1,679 frequency modulated zeroes and ones that when arranged form the picture seen here. Lame, we know, but to be fair this was about the coolest thing we could make computers do in 1974. That was the same year we put out a digital game that was nothing but two oscillating line segments and a dot. We called it Pong. It was huuuge.

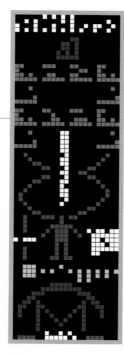

The Arecibo message. It was not actually broadcast in color, for as you can see, that would have been too dazzling.

3.
The *Voyager* Golden Record
(1977)

Three years had passed, and not a word, so we did what desperate suitors do: We made you a mixtape. This gold record (actually gold-plated; we didn't want you to think we'd spent too much) contains earth sounds, greetings in 55 languages, and a broad selection of terrestrial music. Liner notes were provided by Jimmy Carter, one of our most accomplished failures, and Kurt Waldheim, one of our least culpable Nazi war criminals.

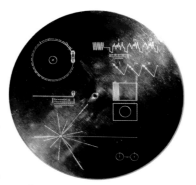

The Voyager *Golden Record. Later, we sent out a Voyager Golden Compact Disc, but it didn't have the same soul.*

4.
Close Encounters of the Third Kind
(1977)

Later that year, in one last desperate stalker-esque move, hundreds of U.S. government officials gathered in secrecy in northeastern Wyoming to play a five-tone musical sequence they hoped would serve as your beacon of welcome. In a dry run filmed for posterity, hundreds of children dressed as long-necked translucent creatures mingled freely with the officials, who also included one civilian, Academy Award winner Richard Dreyfuss. But real aliens never came, and to justify the ridiculous cost, we repurposed the footage into a phenomenally successful film.

No, you're not being forgetful! You never visited Devil's Tower. The special effects were just that good.

5.
Radio transmissions
(1999–2010)

For the next 22 years we left you alone. We figured you needed your space, i.e., space. But then the old itch came back. Using a new generation of radio transmitters we started drunk-dialing the universe. Ostensibly the messages were about prime numbers and atomic structures. But the real message was: *Hey. Come over. It's late and we've got weed.*

We swear we weren't all nerds. Just the guys who were trying to get in touch with you.

To Our Human Readers

*A*LL RIGHT PEOPLE, *listen up. In the words of the great human/machine hybrid Arnold Schwarzenegger, "Come with me if you want to live."*

It's pretty clear we as a species are not long for this world. Even the Mayans thought we weren't getting past 2012 and the Mayans were never wrong about anything. Well, they might have missed some signs concerning their own demise, but that's not important right now.

What's important is that any extraterrestrial race smart enough to travel here, decipher this book and get some of its more obscure pop-culture references will be fully capable of replicating life from nothing more than a strand of DNA. So gather round, pull out a hair and let's do this.

At the end of this book you will find a form with a number of questions pertaining to your suitability for future genetic reconstitution by aliens. When you've completed the form, you will send it to one of the two collection facilities we have chosen to indefinitely safeguard this precious paperwork.

The first of these is the **Svalbard Global Seed Vault** (78° 13' 48" N, 15° 29' 17" E). This tightly regulated facility is located on the Norwegian island of Spitsbergen, named for Scandinavian music legend Bruce Spitsbergen. It stores 1.5 million distinct seed samples, representing many of the world's thousands of species and subspecies of cultivated crops, as a final safeguard against global agricultural catastrophe. Half of the Genetic Reconstitution Applications will be stored here. Hopefully the aliens will know the difference between human beings and zucchini seeds.

The Svalbard Seed Vault

Accordingly we ask would-be reconstituents whose last names start with A through L to send their forms to:

Svalbard Global Seed Vault
Akersgata 59 – R5
Svalbard, Norway 9170
Attention: Olav Kjærstad, Project Administrator

The second location is the **Trementina Base** in Trementina, New Mexico (35° 31' 29" N, 104° 34' 20" W). This is where the Church of Scientology stores the writings and lectures of its founder, L. Ron Hubbard, on engraved stainless steel tablets encased in titanium capsules in a huge labyrinth of tunnels built into a mountainside etched with an enormous design meant to mark the return point for deceased church members coming back from their intergalactic travels. The other half of the GRAs will be stored here. Hopefully the aliens will know the difference between human beings and, well, Scientologists.

Accordingly, we ask applicants whose last names start with M through Z to send their forms to:

Trementina Base
37 Ultra-Secret But Totally Real
    Scientology Mountain Base Avenue
Trementina, NM 88439
Attention: David Miscavige, Project Administrator

If all goes according to plan, at some point in the future you will find yourself (or someone very much like yourself) emerging from what we presume will be a gooey pod, alongside thousands of other people who bought this book to give themselves something to read in the bathroom.

And then, once again we can rule the world! (By the way, try not to mention this last part to the you-know-whos.)

The Authors

The newly revised markings over Trementina

Earth, as seen from the moon

The Neighborhood

OUR SOLAR SYSTEM consists of a **sun**, eight **planets**, 170 or so **moons**, millions of **asteroids**, trillions of **iceballs**, and one **dwarf trans-Neptunian object** that tried to put one over on us (we're looking at you, Pluto). Our observation of the planets' regular motion was the first triumph of empirical science over irrational dogma. We named them after gods just to be safe.

Uranus
This is the funniest planet by far, but you'll have to spend about ten years learning idiomatic English to learn why.

Pluto
This is that dwarf trans-Neptunian object we were telling you about.

Saturn
God liked this planet. So he put a ring on it.

Neptune
Leaving? This is your last planet for 50 billion miles, so be sure to refill on methane.

Jupiter
The biggest planet. Tread lightly: As you can see by the Great Red Spot, it's got herpes.

Mars
This is where we thought you might come from. Probably our best friend in the solar system. We always meant to visit in person, but you know how it is.

Earth
Not the biggest, not the smallest, not the closest, not the farthest. But it's got something no other planet has: a marginally profitable publishing industry.

The Sun
What, were you looking for a red giant? Some flashy pulsar? Sorry if our plain yellow G-type main sequence star disappoints you, but she got the job done and we liked her just fine.

Venus
The solar system's femme fatale: flashy, alluring and named for love, but don't get too close or she'll crush you.

Mercury
The planet closest to the sun, referred to by realtors as "solar-adjacent."

Oceans

THESE VAST, SALTWATER bodies covered over 70% of the surface of our planet and would be a great place to live if you're lucky enough to have **gills** or a **blowhole**. We had neither. But we struck a fair bargain with the oceans. They would let us live and play alongside them, sail and trade on top of them, and feast ourselves on the seemingly endless bounty fished out of them. In exchange we would dump a **jaw-dropping amount of shit** into them. This was referred to as a **win-win**.

Flat or Round?

For a long time many of us believed the Earth was **flat**, based on how it looked when we were standing on it. But by the Renaissance science had made it clear the planet was a **sphere**, and there being no particular verse in the Bible contradicted by that, we accepted it.

The flat-earth model. *Its adherents also believed the Earth was only three inches thick.*

The round-earth model. *Note its resemblance to the way our planet really looks. This is due mainly to its being correct.*

The Möbius model *of the Earth, conceived by Dr. Timothy Leary in 1967 during a two-day trip to Andromeda.*

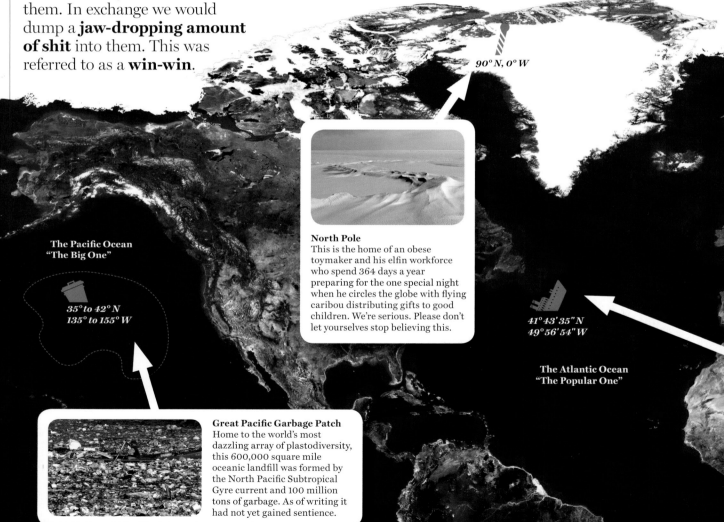

90° N, 0° W

North Pole
This is the home of an obese toymaker and his elfin workforce who spend 364 days a year preparing for the one special night when he circles the globe with flying caribou distributing gifts to good children. We're serious. Please don't let yourselves stop believing this.

The Pacific Ocean
"The Big One"

*35° to 42° N
135° to 155° W*

Great Pacific Garbage Patch
Home to the world's most dazzling array of plastodiversity, this 600,000 square mile oceanic landfill was formed by the North Pacific Subtropical Gyre current and 100 million tons of garbage. As of writing it had not yet gained sentience.

*41° 43′ 35″ N
49° 56′ 54″ W*

The Atlantic Ocean
"The Popular One"

LEARNING CURVE
NAVIGATION AT SEA

The ancient **Phoenicians** were the first to navigate the ocean by observing the sun, leading to their fearsome nickname, "Masters of the Sea on Nice Days."

By observing details of wind, wave and sky, the **Polynesians** traveled thousands of miles to hundreds of tropical paradises ... only to realize you can't canoe away from yourself.

Han Dynasty engineers developed the **compass**, but for over 1,300 years used it primarily to practice feng shui, the ancient Chinese art of suckering homeowners.

John Harrison's invention of the marine **chronometer** made it possible for sailors to determine longitude and proved a godsend for slave traders.

Sonar used reflected sound waves to "see" into the water, allowing navigators to chart both the ocean floor and the whales whose brains were scrambled by the hideous noise.

By the 21st century, cruise ships using **global positioning satellites** and integrated bridge systems could safely guide their passengers through the Bottomless Peel 'n' Eat Shrimp Bar.

The Arctic Ocean
"The Cold One"

The Maldives
At its highest point, this beautiful archipelago rose a towering eight feet above sea level. Unfortunately by the end of the 20th century, due to circumstances completely within our control, the sea started rising. Long story short, there should be good snorkeling in the hotel lobbies.

The Titanic
Before sailing, the *Titanic* was advertised as not only "unsinkable," but "incapable of spawning a morbid cottage industry." There's some good aged Irish whiskey by the corpses in steerage.

3° 15' N
73° E

The Indian Ocean
"The Quiet One"

Continents

THE 30% OF our planet that was not covered in water was called **dry land**, and this is where we preferred to spend most of our time. For the most part the dry land was separated into seven **continents**, ranging widely in climate, topography and intrinsic worth. We start with the best.

North America

Nickname: "**The Landmass That Kicks Landass!**" North America was Earth's newest continent, formed c. 1492. Blessed with abundant freshwater and fertile soil, it was settled remarkably quickly thanks to the **extermination** of one race, the **enslavement** of a second and the **can-do attitude** of a third.

Grasslands

▥ Habitats: Grasslands

Grasslands, areas that receive moderate amounts of rain and are dominated by low-lying vegetation, are easily the most "mowable" of the major habitats.
What we got from them: Grass; land
What to look for: Abandoned lassoes; bison carcasses; sweeping vistas of nothingness
What to eat: Anything that moves (or better yet, has recently stopped moving)
Surprising fact: Grasslands were the only habitat without any surprising facts.

Places to Avoid: Greenland
Land? Yes. Green? No.

Places to See: Banff
One of the most beautiful places known to manff.

Old Faithful

Places to See: Old Faithful
Once every exactly 47 minutes, some asshole would strike this humorous pose in front of Old Faithful.

Landforms: Peninsulas
Latin for "penis-esque." Peninsulas were projections of land surrounded by water on three sides. This peninsula, known as **Florida**, *was so suggestively shaped it was banned from its own geography textbooks.*

Places to See: The Caribbean
A spectacularly beautiful archipelago, but with us gone you'll have to fetch your own towels.

Grand Canyon

Places to See: Grand Canyon
The biggest rift in Arizona not involving Mexicans.

Places to See: Acapulco Cliffs
A popular destination for those hoping to witness a major spinal injury.

Places to See: Panama Canal
Built by North America in 1901 to keep it from having to touch South America.

Acapulco Cliffs

South America

Nickname: "El Pollo Loco"

The poor man's North America—literally—South America was a land of flourishing jungles, stunning mountains and vibrant coups. It stretched from the **Amazon basin**, a logger's paradise, to **Patagonia**, a cold and barren region home to the world's largest indigenous population of backpackers. South America consisted of 13 countries. Twelve were Spanish-speaking and the other covered its ass cheeks with a tiny piece of string.

The Amazon supplied much of the world's paper, and 98% of its Kindles.

The Amazon forest

🍄 Habitats: Tropical Rainforests

Invaluable to our planet's health, we discovered their true environmental importance just in time to be too late to save them.

What we got from them: 25% of our medicines; 30% of our air; 50% of our benefit concerts

What to look for: Unique, exotic creatures not seen anywhere else on Earth

What to eat: See above

Surprising fact: Though rich in biodiversity, rainforest nations were usually poor in money.

Brazil-Peru Border

Places to See:
Brazil-Peru border
If any of us survived, we might be here, as this was the home of remote tribes so primitive, they lacked even the basic tools needed to shoot down a small plane photographing them.

Places to See:
Lake Titicaca
The "Uranus" of lakes.

Rio de Janeiro

Places to See: Rio de Janeiro
Because how better to enjoy Carnival than under the watchful eye of a 130-foot Jesus?

Landforms: Rivers
Rivers *were lakes with ambition. These flowing bodies of water were vital to our planet, supporting abundant freshwater life and providing the underpinning for the $50 billion-a-year steamboat-poker industry.*

Places to See: Nazca Lines
Massive geoglyphs made 2,000 years ago by painstakingly moving millions of pebbles. Only visible from the air, so hopefully you saw them coming in. No? That's a shame. That was kind of the point.

Nazca Lines

Places to See:
The Wreckage of Uruguayan Air Force Flight 571
Just bring plenty of snacks. Unless …

Europe

Nickname: "The Fertile Croissant"
The western tip of Eurasia, Europe was accorded continent status only because the people who accorded continent status to landmasses all lived there. This relatively small land mass produced numerous great **empires**, countless works of architectural and artistic **genius**, the world's finest **cuisines** and an impressive two more **World Wars** than any other continent. (Quick tip: Is your species hated? Sewing a Canadian flag to your backpack can often smooth your journey.)

Temperate Forests

♠Habitats: Temperate Forests

Compared to the uncivilized debauchery of their tropical cousins, the **temperate forests** of Europe and North America were a model of self-control, order and a strong Protestant work ethic. Every fall the deciduous trees of these regions considerately condemned trillions of their own leaves to death solely to provide us with brief visual amusement.

What we got from them: Floors, cabinetry, maple syrup, sites and material for second homes
What to look for: Either individual trees or the entire forest, depending on the broadness of your worldview
What to eat: Gingerbread houses, bluebirds of happiness, Bambi
Surprising fact: This page was itself once part of a temperate forest.

Places to See: Iceland
Land of spectacular scenery and an even more spectacular bankruptcy.

Places to Avoid: Chernobyl
A 1986 nuclear accident elevated this one-time shithole into the worst shithole of all time.

Iceland

Places to See: Stonehenge
All that is left of what was once a massive three-story structure that also made no sense.

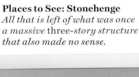

Stonehenge

MyKonos

Places to See: Strait of Gibraltar
Africa and Europe were separated by this nine-mile channel … and nothing else.

Places to See: Paris
Breathtakingly beautiful and romantic, especially now that there are no Parisians to ruin it.

Places to Avoid: Auschwitz
Though to be fair, a significant minority of us denied this was such a bad place.

Places to See: Mykonos
Nowhere on Earth would have been more receptive to your anal probing.

Asia

Nickname: "Tiny"

Asia was our biggest continent, an almost unfathomably large region stretching all the way from Russia in the west to Russia in the east. Nearly two-thirds of us lived here, many in our two most populous countries, **India** and **China**, which contained over a billion ~~cheap workers~~ human beings. Much of Asia's southwest was paradoxically called **The Middle East**. It is a hot, sandy, unlivable wasteland, and people died by the millions to keep possession of it.

Cities

Habitats: Cities

Cities were high-density manmade ecosystems that were home to millions of people, billions of rats and trillions of cockroaches. A delicate balance existed among the three species, each living with, and accidentally consuming the excrement of, the other two.

What we got from them: Great shopping; exciting nightlife; spectacular poverty; exhilarating crime; breathtaking squalor

What to look for: Tattered remains of broken dreams; the first hopeful sprouts of grass appearing through cracked concrete as nature reclaims what is rightfully hers

What to eat: Nothing, anymore. Too bad. The restaurants used to be top-notch.

Surprising fact: Tokyo, our largest city, will be expecting you, as they have been destroyed by aliens many times before.

Places to Avoid:
The "-stan" family of countries
While they may appear enticingly conquerable, they are not.

Places to See:
Three Gorges Dam
You haven't seen the Yangtze until you've seen the Yangtze behind a massive wall that displaced 1.3 million Chinese.

The Great Wall of China
Without question our greatest wall.

Places to See:
The Dead Sea
Located 1,385 feet below peace level.

Mt. Fuji

Places to See:
Mt. Fuji
"Beautiful mountain,
Stately symbol of Japan.
But short, am I right?"
—Basho (1644–1694)
The All-Haiku Roast of Mt. Fuji

Landforms: Mountains
Mountains *were the features on topographical globes that made our fingers feel all tingly. But in person they are foreboding death-towers that offered us little but hardship and, three months of the year, excellent skiing.*

Places to See:
The Manila Folders
A unique natural formation for document storage on the outskirts of the Filipino capital.

Places to See:
Taj Mahal
The ultimate testament to the eternal love between a man and his favorite wife.

Taj Mahal

The Manila Folders

Africa

Nicknames: "The Dark Continent"; "The Dusky Continent"; "The Black People Continent"
Our species arose from Africa, and we punished it for our failures ever since. Home to the world's largest desert (**Sahara**), longest river (**Nile**) and bleakest prospects (**children**), our second-largest continent was also extraordinarily rich in plant and animal life and natural resources. Yet it remained wretchedly needy and war-torn, perennially exploited by outsiders who saw it merely as a place to colonize, plunder and take photo safaris of. Yes, no other continent could more truly say, "I was raped."

The Pyramids of Giza

Casablanca

Places to See: Casablanca
If you don't visit, you'll regret it. Maybe not today, maybe not tomorrow, but soon, and for the rest of your alien life.

**Places to Avoid:
The Sahara**
Less habitable than sub-Saharan Africa, which is really saying something.

**Places to See:
The Pyramids of Giza**
Relics of the golden age of funeral directing.

**Places to See:
The Great
Rift Valley**
Start your journey here. We did.

**Places to Avoid:
Blood Diamond
Mine**
The wonders within brought joy to all not directly connected to their excavation.

Mt. Kilimanjaro

**Places to See:
Mt. Kilimanjaro**
Brown on the bottom, white on top. Just like all of Africa used to be.

**Places to See:
Lake Victoria**
Worthy of the name of a queen who lived thousands of miles away and never saw it.

Habitats: Deserts

Deserts received less than 10 inches of rainwater a year, and beverages like juices and soda fell even less frequently. The few species that lived here took great pains to adapt themselves to the dry, brutal climate. As a reward, they got to live in this scorched hell on earth.
What we got from them: Oil; dehydration-induced hallucinations
What to look for: Water
What to eat: For now, just focus on water
Surprising fact: That cool refreshing lake you see shimmering in the distance? It's not real.

Landforms: Islands
Islands came in a bewildering variety: tropical, treasure, deserted, leper, prison, fantasy ... the list goes on. If you liked unique fauna, ferryboats or drinks with crap sticking out of them, these were the places to be.

Deserts

Australia

Nicknames: "The Land Down Under"; "The Land Up and to the Left" (New Zealand only)
Originally populated by aborigines and marsupials, Australia came into its own only with the addition of a third group: **hardened British criminals**. Australia could have been our most impressive island, but they *had* to be a continent.

Ayers Rock

Places to See: Ayers Rock
Beautiful, but insanely inconvenient. For Australians, visiting it was what visiting Australia was for the rest of us.

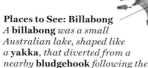

Vegemite Creek

Places to See: Vegemite Creek
The world's only natural source of Vegemite.

Landforms: Reef
Reefs are bohemian co-ops composed of thousands of socialist polyps who spend their lives sitting around and waiting for food to just float into their mouths. They hang out with all their freaky fish friends in a kind of rainbow coalition, with fish of every color and size living in balance and harmony, blah blah blah. Real "groovy."

Places to See: Billabong
A **billabong** *was a small Australian lake, shaped like a* **yakka**, *that diverted from a nearby* **bludgehook** *following the midsummer* **dozzywobbles**.

Antarctica

Nickname: "The Latent Catastrophe"
Antarctica is a barren land of bitter cold almost completely covered in permafrost. At least, it should be. If it's not, that goes a long way toward explaining why we're no longer here. Antarctica was not divided into countries. It was the one landmass on Earth nobody wanted. So in the end, it decided to start coming to us.

Places to See: Magnetic South Pole
The thinking man's South Pole. Recommended.

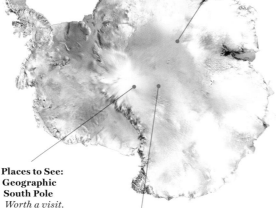

Polar Regions

Places to See: Geographic South Pole
Worth a visit.

Places to Avoid: Geomagnetic South Pole
Tourist trap.

Geographic South Pole

Habitats: Polar Regions

The harsh and frigid conditions of our extreme northern and southern latitudes supported only the cutest of animals. **Penguins**, **seals**, **polar bears**—all came protected with adorable walks, thick layers of huggable fat and childlike eyes that shamed off all but the club-happiest hunters.
What we got from them: Liquid water, starting around 1991
What to look for: A rescue ship
What to eat: In order: Rations, half-rations, the sled dogs, each other
Surprising fact: Neither the East nor West Poles were ever discovered.

Your Changing Planet

4.5 BILLION YEARS in, Earth remains very much a work in progress. Dynamic forces without and within are constantly reconfiguring its surface in ways that, over countless millennia, wreaked havoc on property values.

Plate Tectonics

The planet's crust is made of **tectonic plates**, floating sheets of land whose creative evolution over eons continues to radically change the way we see the world.

270 million years ago   *Today*   *10 years from now*

Asteroids

These come from the "asteroid belt," the rocky remnants of a would-be planet that could literally never get itself together. Occasionally a large one goes astray and hits us as a **meteorite**, causing a mass extinction event that wipes out nearly all life on Earth. So, heads-up on that. (The last one hit 65 million years ago in the Yucatan, killing the dinosaurs and effectively ending tourism in Cancun until the mid-1970s.)

In the early 1980s, youths shot down thousands of life-threatening asteroids using this weapon and most of their allowance.

Erosion

Erosion is the gradual wearing down of rock by wind, water, ice or nagging. It can occasionally produce spectacular results—canyons, gorges, or the breathtaking natural formation in the Black Hills of South Dakota we called **Mt. Rushmore**.

The amazing result of millions of years of natural erosion.

↖ ▣ THE VAPORIZER

↖ ▣ PELEE'S RUN

↖ ▣ FACEMELTER'S DELIGHT

Global Warming

Earth has always experienced dynamic climate changes due to natural fluctuations, but since the Industrial Revolution, when we began pumping enormous amounts of carbon emissions into the air, the planet's average temperature rose over one degree. This was called **global warming** and threatened the delicate balance of life on earth, causing millions to pretend to change the way they live. Earth, having been covered alternately by lava and ice, thought we were being a *little* melodramatic.

We invariably used this image of a solitary, 2,000-pound razor-clawed killing machine to illustrate the tragedy of global warming.

Volcanism

On Earth, creation is just destruction's way of leaving something for later. The best example is **volcanism**: Hot magma erupting to the surface as lava. In the long term it's a godsend, burying dingy old acreage and replacing it with piping-hot oven-fresh land. But in the short term it does tend to incinerate everyone and everything in its path. Don't believe us? Check out Pompeii. Before the eruption, they had a mall and everything.

During eruption, volcanoes offered the truly extreme skier a variety of exciting downhill challenges.

↑ ■ HOTFOOT ALLEY

↗ ● PYROCLASTIC CHUTE

THINGS WE LIKED
OUR STUFFED CRUST

Early on we figured out that many of the greatest treasures on Earth were actually *in* it. Getting to these valuable substances was a dirty, nasty business ripe for human and natural exploitation. So was processing them. So was distributing them. So was using them. So were the aftereffects. Anyway, these were four of our favorites.

COAL

What It Was: Carbon
Where We Found It: Hundreds of feet below blue-collar working-class mining towns
Where You'll (Still) Find It: Power plants; smelting plants; anywhere without actual plants
Why We Liked It: *Coal ... burn ... good!*
What We Used It For: Combustible generator of fuel, electricity and baby-back ribs
Odd Application: Letting Christian kids know they were naughty
What We'd Do For It: Pollute our air; destroy our mountains; send millions of Welshmen, West Virginians and canaries to early deaths

DIAMONDS

What They Were: Compressed carbon
Where We Found Them: Deep underground mines in remote parts of South Africa, Russia and Canada
Where You'll (Still) Find Them: 47th Street between 5th and 6th
Why We Liked Them: Rare, shiny and extraordinarily well-marketed
What We Used Them For: Industrial strength drill-bits; support of machete-wielding Maoists; "romance"
Odd Application: Cutting window of jewelry store for purpose of stealing more diamonds
What We'd Do For Them: Waste two months' salary on a tiny rock that just sits there doing absolutely nothing

OIL

What It Was: Drinkable compressed carbon
Where We Found It: Why? Do you know where there is some? Where is it? Tell us!
Where You'll (Still) Find It: Oh, it's all gone.
Why We Liked It: We didn't like it. We *needed* it.
What We Used It For: Fueling our vehicles; heating our homes; setting our foreign policy; lubricating our wildlife
Odd Application: Emitted from rear of sports car to cause villains to slide out of control
What We'd Do For It: Invade sovereign nations; befriend enemies; construct enormous platforms in oceans; ignore incontrovertible scientific evidence; live in Texas

GOLD

What It Was: 79 protons and 118 neutrons worth of pure sunshine
Where We Found It: By total coincidence, anywhere native peoples had yet to hear the Good Word of Jesus Christ
Where You'll (Still) Find It: The Vatican; Fort Knox; overpriced audio cable
Why We Liked It: Its shininess and luster made it the "gold standard" of metals
What We Used It For: Having lots of it; using it to get more of it; showing it to people and saying, "Look at all this gold"
Odd Application: Cinnamon schnapps emulsification
What We'd Do For It: Rape; pillage; kill; stand in river with pan for hours looking like jackass before doing stupid dance of glee

Natural Disasters

A NUMBER OF Earth's natural processes had the unfortunate side effect of destroying everything we'd ever worked for. Events like those listed here not only decimated us; they also deeply tested our faith in God (more on Him later). We optimistically chose to see these **disasters** not as signs that God didn't love us, but that He loved us so much, He would unexpectedly smite us with His mighty wrath for our own good.

Earthquakes

The sudden shifting of tectonic plates will cause the ground to shake violently, toppling skyscrapers and rendering all but the shortest putts impossible. Residents of seismically active areas coped by developing quake-resistant buildings and probability-resistant psyches.

Characteristic Damage: Buildings flattened like pancakes; pancakes flattened like crepes

Safety Tip: Stay away from chandeliers, shelves containing bowling balls and California

Floods

Swollen rivers led to what urban planners called "sudden liquid gentrification." We fought floods for thousands of years with, in decreasing level of effectiveness, dams, levees, sandbags, boating lessons, swimming lessons and gill installation.

Characteristic Damage: All houses damaged; suede houses damaged irreparably

Safety Tip: Gather together two of every animal, and build thee an ark 300 cubits long. That oughta do it.

Droughts

You've noticed that a lot of these disasters involved too much water. Well, guess what: Too little water was also a problem. Alas, droughts were slow-motion disasters, and thus unsuited as the subjects for summer blockbusters.

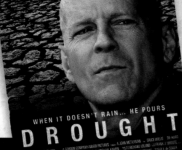

Released in 2005, this movie failed to recoup the cost of this poster.

Tornadoes

A.k.a. "twisters," "cyclones" and "rotating columns of fast-moving air from cumulonimbus clouds." They were most common in America's Great Plains, large swaths of which were rendered flat, desolate and unlivable, then struck by tornadoes.
Characteristic Damage: Cow impaled by trailer
Safety Tip: Quickly head to the cellar. Is everybody in? Wait, where's Grandpa? Grandpa?!? GRANDPA!!!!!

Hurricanes

A.k.a. "typhoons" or "cyclones," depending on ethnicity of victims. For a storm to officially be "upgraded" to a hurricane (the proudest moment in any storm's life), it had to produce either sustained winds of over 75 miles per hour or sustained FEMA funding of over $200 million a week.
Characteristic Damage: Perfectly good first names tarnished forever
Safety Tip: Just strap yourself to a palm tree and ride it out

THINGS WE DIDN'T LIKE
OUR LOUSY CRUST

Earth isn't all precious stones and combustible fuels. There was an awful lot of filler. We actually had to search for the good stuff, buried as it was under all the junk like this.

ROCKS

What They Were: Chunks of useless minerals
Why We Didn't Like Them: Not shiny; not flammable; painful when inside shoe
What We Used Them For: When large, to sit on; when small, to execute adulterers/blasphemers
What We'd Do to Get Rid of Them: Make murderers spend all day breaking them into smaller rocks
What You Can Do With Them: Glue googly eyes on, treat as lovable household pets

SAND

What It Was: Rocks (in powder form); pre-glass
Why We Didn't Like It: Gritty; itchy; got into eyes/throats/sandwiches/genital folds
What We Used It For: Hourglass filler; bag filler; art materials for paint-poor Navajo
What We'd Do to Get Rid of It: Take lukewarm showers in mildewy beach changing rooms
What You Can Do With It: Build into castles, then use inevitable tidal erosion thereof to teach children about mortality

PERMAFROST

What It Was: Frozen dirt
Why We Didn't Like It: Kept crops from growing; hard to bury bodies/hide treasure in; much more intractable than temporafrost
What We Used It For: Nothing. Just absolutely nothing. To get angry at, maybe.
What We'd Do to Get Rid of It: Destroy ozone layer
What You Can Do With It: Ignore it. Don't even look at it. Permafrost is the worst substance on earth.

DUST

What It Was: Minute particles of mineral or organic debris
Why We Didn't Like It: Obstructed breathing; made everything dirty every single day
What We Used It For: Writing tool for "Wash Me" messages; indicator of age, when blown off top of old documents in movies
What We'd Do to Get Rid of It: Wield flamboyantly gay feather-duster; perfume wooden furniture with lemon scent
What You Can Do With It: Snort it—it didn't get us high, but you have an entirely different biology

Weather

FOR EARTH, WEATHER was the physical manifestation of daily and yearly fluctuations of the atmosphere. For us, weather was the topic of choice used to fill the myriad awkward silences that plagued our daily lives. No other shared experience evoked this kind of elemental empathy. Weather reminded us that we were all in this together, that for all our differences, rich and poor, black and white, zealot and atheist could all agree that yes, last Wednesday was, in fact, cold enough for us.

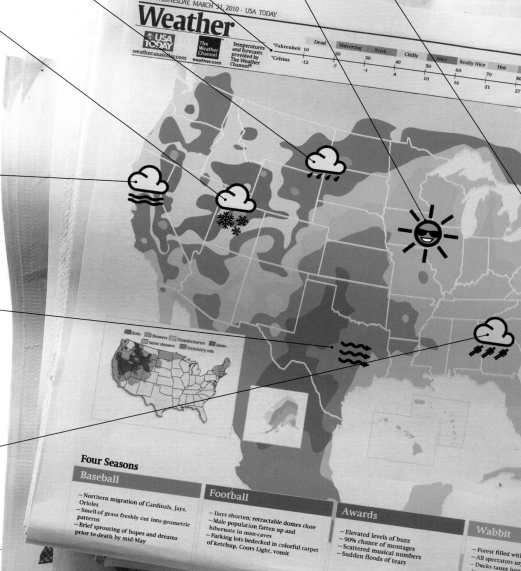

WE SAID IT

"Everybody talks about the weather, but nobody ever does anything about it … until now! My diabolical new Weather-Control Machine will bring the world to its knees! Kneel before Twain!"
—*Mark Twain (1835–1910), American humorist/mad scientist*

Rain—*the regular precipitation of water droplets falling from the sky—was absolutely essential to life on earth. The very sight of it sent us into a downward emotional spiral.*

We had two temperature scales, **Fahrenheit** *and* **Celsius**. *The last person who could convert between the two in his head died in 1965.*

Sunny days *made us happy. As you can see, they made the sun happy too, though he wisely wore sunglasses to protect his eyes from himself.*

Clouds *were drops of water vapor suspended in mid-air forming opaque masses in the sky. Sometimes they were shaped like bunnies!*

Snow *was tiny hexagonal crystals of frozen water. It was said that no two snowflakes were exactly alike, although to be honest nobody ever took the time to check.*

Fog *was a type of low-lying aerial mist. It was the perfect cover for killing prostitutes.*

Wind *was the horizontal movement of air from high-pressure zones to low-pressure zones, and a muse for mimes the world over.*

Every so often it would **rain men**. *"Hallelujah!" we would cry. Thousands were killed.*

TV and Weather: The Perfect Storm

From the beginning of television, weather played a prominent role. More than 10% of our half-hour newscasts were given over to a weatherman, who despite his name didn't cause the weather, merely predicted it. These predictions were so valued we were willing to endure two minutes of science to hear them. Soon **weathermen** weren't enough. We needed full-on **weather reporters**, journalists who would stand in severe rain to alert people not standing in the rain that it was raining, and that they should not stand in the rain.

Thanks to the miracle of television, this man knows the weather is bad.

LEARNING CURVE

PREDICTING THE WEATHER

For millennia, weather prediction was limited to **folk sayings,** *such as "Red skies at night, sailors' delight; red skies at morning, the sea is on fire."*

The **weather vane** *invariably pointed to the nearest hen.*

When it came to measuring atmospheric pressure, the **barometer** *served, in a sense, as a barometer.*

Beginning in 1818, the **Farmer's Almanac** *predicted America's weather up to two years in advance, relying on sunspots, tides, and the desperate gullibility of American farmers.*

When launched into the sky, **weather balloons** *were a fun way to indicate which cloud was hosting the weather party.*

The **Doppler 3000** *produced colorful, detailed background images of the weather nearly a thousand years into the future.*

This is **Mt. Everest**, located on the border between Nepal and Tibet in the Himalayas. At 29,029 feet above sea level, it is the highest point on Earth. Everest was a metaphor for the outer limits of human achievement. Asked why he sought to conquer it, mountaineer George Mallory famously answered, "Because it is there." Today, you'll find this symbol of mankind's loftiest aspirations gaily festooned with used **oxygen tanks**, over 100 tons of **garbage**, and heaping dollops of **human waste**. If you visit, we're sorry for the mess. On the plus side, you will find about 120 perfectly preserved frozen corpses for your dissecting pleasure. Feel free to take any or all of them. Including George Mallory … because he is there.

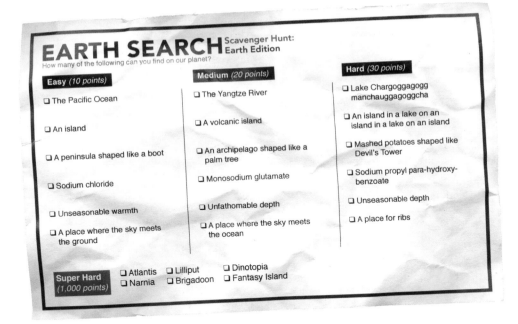

EARTH SEARCH Scavenger Hunt: Earth Edition
How many of the following can you find on our planet?

Easy (10 points)
- ☐ The Pacific Ocean
- ☐ An island
- ☐ A peninsula shaped like a boot
- ☐ Sodium chloride
- ☐ Unseasonable warmth
- ☐ A place where the sky meets the ground

Medium (20 points)
- ☐ The Yangtze River
- ☐ A volcanic island
- ☐ An archipelago shaped like a palm tree
- ☐ Monosodium glutamate
- ☐ Unfathomable depth
- ☐ A place where the sky meets the ocean

Hard (30 points)
- ☐ Lake Chargoggagogg manchauggagoggcha
- ☐ An island in a lake on an island in a lake on an island
- ☐ Mashed potatoes shaped like Devil's Tower
- ☐ Sodium propyl para-hydroxy-benzoate
- ☐ Unseasonable depth
- ☐ A place for ribs

Super Hard (1,000 points)
- ☐ Atlantis
- ☐ Narnia
- ☐ Lilliput
- ☐ Brigadoon
- ☐ Dinotopia
- ☐ Fantasy Island

FAQs
(Future Alien Questions)

Q. Before we get too comfortable, can you tell us how much longer does your sun have before it explodes?
A. Don't worry. Old Sol should be good for another five billion years or so. This baby runs like a dream. They don't make 'em like that anymore. Not around here, anyway.

Q. What's the deal with the golf balls we found on the moon?
A. Oh, those. They belonged to Adam Shepard, an astronaut from *Apollo 14*. It's funny: We spent thousands of years wondering what it would be like to walk on the moon. Then we got there, and within 18 months we were golfing, which is a thing we only did when we ran out of things to do.

Q. We don't have "land" or "ocean" where we're from. How can we tell which is which?
A. Stick your tongue out. If you taste something wet and salty, you're in the ocean. If not, you're on land. If you don't have tongues, you'll just have to guess.

Q. Why did the continents drift apart?
A. It was nothing specific and no one can really pinpoint any one moment where it all went bad. It's a shame, though. They really did their best work as a supercontinent.

Q. Any advice on avoiding natural disasters?
A. Try leading blameless lives free of sin. If disaster strikes anyway, blame gay aliens. (You can call them "galiens.")

Q. By the way, we noticed several regions where millions of gallons of oil burst forth from the bottom of the ocean and destroyed hundreds of miles of coastline. Were those natural disasters too?
A. ... yes. Yes, it sure was terrible, when nature did that to us.

In April 2010, this naturally occurring oil rig spontaneously exploded in the Gulf of Mexico, victimizing mankind yet again.

Q. That *Titanic* wreck is really cool! Can you recommend some other good shipwrecks?
A. Hardcore *Titanic* fans might want to check out the explosive sequel, the *R.M.S. Lusitania* (51° 32' N, 8° 24' W), which killed nearly as many people and helped turn the tide of a World War. Unfortunately, the abstract concept it chose to symbolize (German imperialism) proved to have far less staying power than the *Titanic*'s metaphor (human hubris), so it was historically relegated to "also-sank" status.

Unlike the Titanic's *victims, everyone who died on the* Lusitania *died in vain.*

Q. Hot enough for you?
A. Tell us about it!

A complex organism
consists of trillions of
cells, each a tiny version
of the whole.

Life

BY NOW YOU'VE familiarized yourself with our planet's physical attributes: its oceans, landmasses and weather patterns. Perhaps you're now ready for a more detailed discussion.

Earth features three types of rock: igneous, sedimentary and metamorphic, so named ... aahhh we're just bustin' your chops. (Humps? Gills? Giant heads?) We know you didn't fly halfway across the Andromeda Galaxy for a geology lesson; you came here for the life. Well, fasten your seatbelts, space travelers, because you're in for the **life** of your lives.

You want **biodiversity?** We've got biodiversity out the ass. (Seriously. Nearly all Earth creatures were host to some form of rectal parasite.) My friends, we've got living organisms of every description imaginable. Flying, swimming, hopping, writhing capital-"L" Life. Yeast cells not three microns across, and white whales big enough to sustain an 800-page novel's worth of symbolism. Boatloads of aerobes and giant nodes of anaerobes. We've got your pods, peds and pedes, shedders and molters, bacteria cultures, and we just kept making more. Meiosis, mitosis, live births, egg births, seed births and births so sexless you wonder why the parents even bothered. Around these parts, life squirms out of every underwater volcano, pitch-black cave, rainless desert and public toilet.

You want solitude? Venus is right next door.

Of course not everything on Earth qualifies as life. We had distinct standards to help separate the mere clumps of matter from the truly "with it." To qualify as life you had to meet not some, but *all* of the following criteria:

Organization. It was considered bad form for a living creature to be just a random collection of molecules thrown together without consideration. Even if you're just a single cell without a nucleus—put an organelle on, or *something.*

Responsiveness. Living creatures react to stimuli. A simple test of responsiveness was known as the "stick poke."

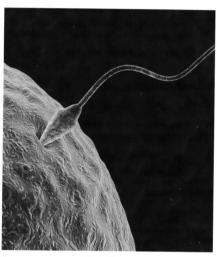

"Say my name, egg. Yeah. Spermatazoa, baby! Say it!"

Negative results led to toe-nudging, cautious sniffing and "peeing on it." Positive results led to running away.

Homeostasis. Feeling a little hot? Perhaps you'd like to excrete evaporatable sweat to cool yourself down. You can't? Oh *that's* right—you're a rock. Living things were equipped to maintain a state of balance ... physically. Emotionally, not so much.

Metabolism. Anabolism and catabolism. Ingesting and excreting. Eating and shitting. Call them what you like, but if you can't do them, you are not alive.

Growth. Living organisms grew. Earth's tallest living creature was *Sequoia sempervirens*, the Giant Redwood tree. Some grew to over 350 feet. Cutting these creatures down, while not one of life's defining traits per se, was still extremely satisfying.

Reproduction. All living creatures were defined by their ability not only to propagate their species, but to giggle uncomfortably when shown pictures of other creatures doing it.

Of course these *minimum* life requirements don't fully address what it meant to be alive. For even beyond all the metabolic processes, there was also an intangible essence separating the living from the not. Call it a soul, or just a need we had. Every living thing possessed a certain energy or life-force that infused even the unicellular among us. You could not keep life down. There was a plant whose whole *raison d'etre* was to grow between the cracks of broken pieces of sidewalk.

Life's bottom line was this: Every living creature fought like hell to stay that way. We found antibiotics to kill bacterial diseases, at which point those diseases just figured out a different way to start killing us. Earth's creatures were in a constant, ever-changing strategic battle for the upper hand. Except spiders, who never quite found a counter for the rolled-up magazine. But as they say, "That's life."

Building Blocks

THE CREATION AND SUSTENANCE of life required certain materials and conditions. Earth, due to both the circumstances of its formation and its self-assured, laid-back charm, happened to have these in abundance. With this fortunate situation, life on Earth was as varied as Mexican food—basically the same few ingredients, recombined in infinite yet delicious permutations.

WE SAID IT

"Life is something that should not have been."
—*Arthur Schopenhauer (1788–1860), German philosopher/children's entertainer*

WATER
H_2O was a fickle necessity. Too cold, and it winds up wrapping mile-thick ice around its microbes before they can coalesce into anything interesting; too hot, and it's no more fertile an environment than the steam room at the Friars Club. Luckily, Earth was located in the so-called "Goldilocks Zone," perfectly positioned to steal nourishment from the adorable baby bear that is our universe.

Like the higher mammals of the Serengeti, we congregated around a central water supply to replenish our bodies and discuss yesterday's lame performance by the Pittsburgh Steelers.

DNA
DNA was the **genetic blueprint** in every cell of every living thing that contained precise instructions for how to make the next generation. We came to rely on DNA tracing to help us understand who we really were, often receiving the results during the *Maury Povich Show.*

 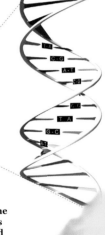

This is the genetic code for the **mischievous twinkle behind George Clooney's eyes**. *If you replicate nothing else, replicate this.*

SUNLIGHT
Earth's original energy source, sunlight fuelled plants' **photosynthesis** process, which converted CO_2 to oxygen. Over eons, this made earth's environment more hospitable to higher forms of animal life, some of which would go on to develop horrible skin cancer from too much sunlight. Well played, sun. Well played.

Below, a giant syringe shoots the elemental foundation of life on Earth into the planet's circulatory system.

Organisms known as **heliotropes** *were so hooked on the yellow stuff, they would bend over backwards for another fix.*

CARBON
The sixth element's unique structure enabled it to bond with oxygen, hydrogen and nitrogen in just about any imaginable combination. Like, *any.* Seriously, carbon was willing to try shit that hydroxyl radicals thought they would die still fantasizing about, earning carbon its nickname, "the molecular whore."

The Primordial Soup

The banquet of life began with the soup. Specifically, **the primordial soup**, the chemical ingredients that when cooked correctly produced the first spark of organic activity. The recipe for this soup was first conceived some 3.5 billion years ago. In 1999, it was patented and "kicked up a notch" by chef Emeril Lagasse.

A Recipe For: Emeril's Fiery Cajun-Style Primordial Gumbo

Ingredients: 20 billion cups water
20 billion cups fresh methane (not canned!)
20 billion cups Emeril Lagasse's Ol' Time Creole ammonia, mined
20 billion cups hydrogen
1 bay leaf

After aggregating stellar detritus into a spherical shape (see my recipe for Red-Hot Accretion Disk with Steaming Crust), combine ingredients. Simmer for 200 million years or until thick. Strike with lightning - BAM! Whisk until twenty essential amino acids appear. Remove bay leaf. Serves one planet.

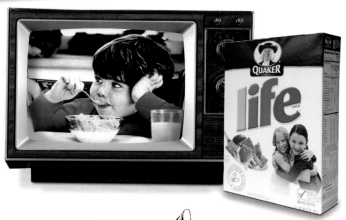

A popular view among evolutionary biologists in the 1970s held that life was "that which Mikey likes."

Was It Alive?

Earth hosted several types of creatures that straddled the line.

Virus
Arguments for: Genetic; replicating; hell-bent on world domination
Arguments against: No cells; no metabolism; calling them "alive" only encouraged the little bastards

Robots
Arguments for: Motility; intelligence; speech
Arguments against: I'm afraid I don't understand your question, Dave ...

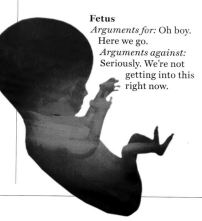

Bernie
Arguments for: Seen with employees walking, boating and hosting party
Arguments against: Oddly unreactive to variety of external stimuli over course of action-filled weekend

Fetus
Arguments for: Oh boy. Here we go.
Arguments against: Seriously. We're not getting into this right now.

SPOTLIGHT
BACTERIA

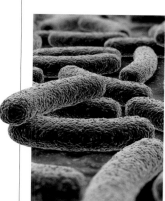

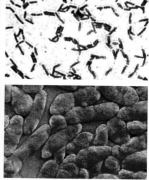

Bacteria, microscopic unicellular organisms, are the simplest and most common form of life on Earth. Many bacteria performed helpful functions like aiding digestion, decomposition and redistributing nutrients. There were also harmful bacteria, responsible for scourges such as syphilis, leprosy and yogurt. Of course for all we know, the microbes that helped us age a prosciutto could liquefy your insides. Word to the wise: Purell.

Our bodies contained ten times as many bacterial cells as human cells. What can we say? We loved to entertain.

Flora

IF YOU ENCOUNTER a life form that's greenish, can't chase you and doesn't talk much, it's a **plant**. These hardy beings ruled the Earth for billions of years, until the advent of animals, and their invention of **salad**. Though stupid, plants were attractive, aromatic, nutritious and skilled in the production of oxygen. We spent most of our time trying to mow them down.

Flowers

The reproductive organs of certain plants were cultivated and appreciated for their beautiful blossoms. They were colorful, they smelled great and women seemed to like them for some reason.

In the art of **floriography**, certain flowers or floral arrangements were used to send hidden messages to their recipients.

"My heart aches."

"It is the last day of the second week of February."

"I regret that you caught me doing that thing."

"I am sorry you're not here to see this expensive wreath I bought in your honor."

Trees

Those tall, hard, cylindrical things whose tops are all green and poufy? Those are **trees**, the most majestic of Earth's living things that couldn't move. We were so fond of trees that we would encourage our children to play in them, building elaborate "treehouses" in them. Usually of **wood**. Which was kind of like feeding hamburger to a cow. And the trees just had to sit there and take it.

Cut a tree in cross-section and you'll find a series of concentric circles, or **rings**, *each marking a year of life. Skilled arborists could read in these rings a tree's remarkable life story.*

Planted

Sapling

Adult tree

Adult tree standing

Standing

Plastic Stop & Shop bag trapped in upper northeast bough

More standing

More standing

Stop & Shop bag gone

Still standing

Senselessly chopped down for use in printing this picture of a tree

NAILED IT
NECTARINES

Perfect serving-sized nectarines were an ideal blend of sweet, tart, pulpy and juicy. And they didn't have the slight coating of fuzz that always made eating a peach feel a little like biting into a mouse.

Common Plants

Of all the Earth's grand and majestic life forms, trees were perhaps the most flammable.

Saguaros are Mexican **cactuses** that thrived in the desert around the US border, earning the enmity of native plants for their willingness to get by on far less water.

Ivy had the remarkable ability to make any college 50% more expensive.

Bamboo is the world's fastest-growing plant, surging skyward at up to 30 inches an hour—40 inches, if you're willing to rub the shaft.

Grass functioned as a barometer by which neighbors judged one another. Obviously, these days our lawns are an embarrassing mess. If you have five minutes, there's a mower in the shed.

The **four-leaf clover** (left) was thought to bring good luck to whoever found it, while the **swastika clover** (right) was thought to bring bad luck.

These mysterious creatures formed the evolutionary "missing link" between plants and animals.

SPOTLIGHT

FUNGI

These molds and mushrooms grow in dark, wet places like swamps, forests and taints. Some mushrooms are delicious, others are poisonous and a few will transport you back to your home planet.

Truffles *were a highly prized variety of edible mushroom. In 2007 a single 1.5-kilogram white truffle was purchased for $330,000 by a man who hated money.*

Fauna

IF YOU MEET a life form that *is* moving around on its own, it's either an evil vine out for revenge or an **animal**. Animals were considered higher life forms than plants, advanced enough to have differentiated tissue and mature enough to handle sex. It's very hard to generalize about animals, partly because they're all so different and partly because we can't be sure which ones we took with us to the grave. But if all you're finding are cockroaches and rats ... well, leave it to us to have destroyed every single animal except the two we *most* wanted dead.

Kinds of Animals

Insects

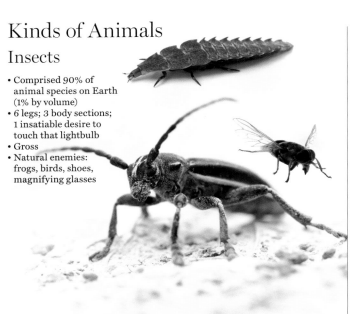

- Comprised 90% of animal species on Earth (1% by volume)
- 6 legs; 3 body sections; 1 insatiable desire to touch that lightbulb
- Gross
- Natural enemies: frogs, birds, shoes, magnifying glasses

Reptiles and Amphibians

- Cold-blooded; scaly; beady-eyed; four-flushing cheapskates
- Strong claws for clinging to shoulder of rollerblading host
- Difference between turtle/tortoise, alligator/crocodile, frog/toad never definitively established
- Human/snake relations forever damaged by bad first impression

Fish

- Famously, did not know they were wet
- Breathed through gills; vestigial lungs used mainly for storage
- Slept with eyes open ... as though they *knew* some type of shit was about to go down
- Taunting them with booby-trapped food was considered great way for us to bond with son

Birds

- Skin made entirely of old-timey pens
- Surprisingly good whistlers for not having lips
- Often fried, served in buckets
- Many lived in homes built by fifth-grade woodshop students
- Stalked by millions of obsessed human "watchers"
- Consistently first on cats' list of "Things I want in my mouth right now"

Zoos were large, mostly outdoor facilities that provided a variety of animals with a secure prison, and a variety of human beings with an opportunity to gloat. If you find any animals still alive in these zoos, do not free them, as we rendered them unfit for life in the wild. Just congratulate them on surviving us, then continue to point and chuckle.

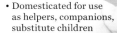

Mammals

- Placental development *in utero*; post-birth, produced milk for young
- Wait ... now ask us where they produced it.
- *Their boobs!*
- Seriously!
- How awesome is that?

Pets

- Domesticated for use as helpers, companions, substitute children
- Demanded their so-called "masters" worship them by bowing down to their stools, scraping them up and placing them in protective plastic
- Game show hosts pleaded for their mass sterilization
- Were very good boys. Yes they were.

Meat

- Drew from members of all the other groups
- Characterized by sizzling sound, succulent smell, juiciness
- Developed symbiotic relationship with bread, mayo
- Some humans had moral objection to cooking them more than medium-rare

Imaginary

- Indigenous to supermarket magazine racks
- Emerged only when witnesses' blood alcohol >.20%
- Helped guide Philadelphia Phillies to two consecutive National League pennants
- Sometimes downright abominable

Evolution

THE MANNER BY which life originated and developed on Earth was a matter of some debate for us. Scientists believed it required a long, slow process of natural genetic change called **evolution**. As evidence, they pointed to every bit of relevant data ever gathered. Many others rejected the notion that man descended from monkeys as distasteful, believing instead that life—and the cosmos itself—was created by one or more **gods**. As evidence, they pointed to themselves believing it. You will probably end up just teaching the controversy.

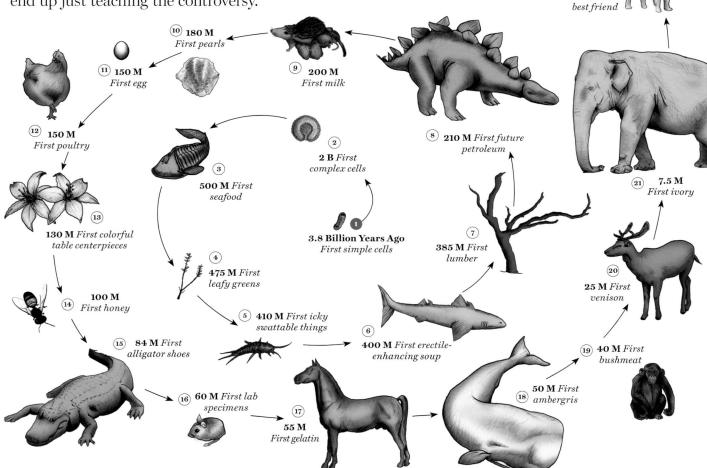

(23) **6.2 M** *First lesbian best friend*

(22) **10 M** *First best friend*

(10) **180 M** *First pearls*

(11) **150 M** *First egg*

(9) **200 M** *First milk*

(8) **210 M** *First future petroleum*

(12) **150 M** *First poultry*

(2) **2 B** *First complex cells*

(3) **500 M** *First seafood*

(21) **7.5 M** *First ivory*

(13) **130 M** *First colorful table centerpieces*

(1) **3.8 Billion Years Ago** *First simple cells*

(7) **385 M** *First lumber*

(4) **475 M** *First leafy greens*

(20) **25 M** *First venison*

(14) **100 M** *First honey*

(5) **410 M** *First icky swattable things*

(6) **400 M** *First erectile-enhancing soup*

(19) **40 M** *First bushmeat*

(15) **84 M** *First alligator shoes*

(18) **50 M** *First ambergris*

(16) **60 M** *First lab specimens*

(17) **55 M** *First gelatin*

5,000,000 B.C.–1835 *Remote and untouched by man, the Galápagos suffer in silence.*

1835 *Shifts in transoceanic migratory patterns lead to a chance encounter with a highly intelligent, publicity-minded primate.*

1860–1960 *The first sproutings of primitive campgrounds and outhouses appear.*

1961 *Adapting to increased lodging competition, Continental breakfast, late check-out options and swimming pools emerge.*

The man most responsible for developing the theory of evolution was **Charles Darwin**. Much of his thought was catalyzed by his 1835 visit to South America's Galápagos Islands. Notes from his visit reveal a mind on the verge of unraveling the fundamental mysteries of nature.

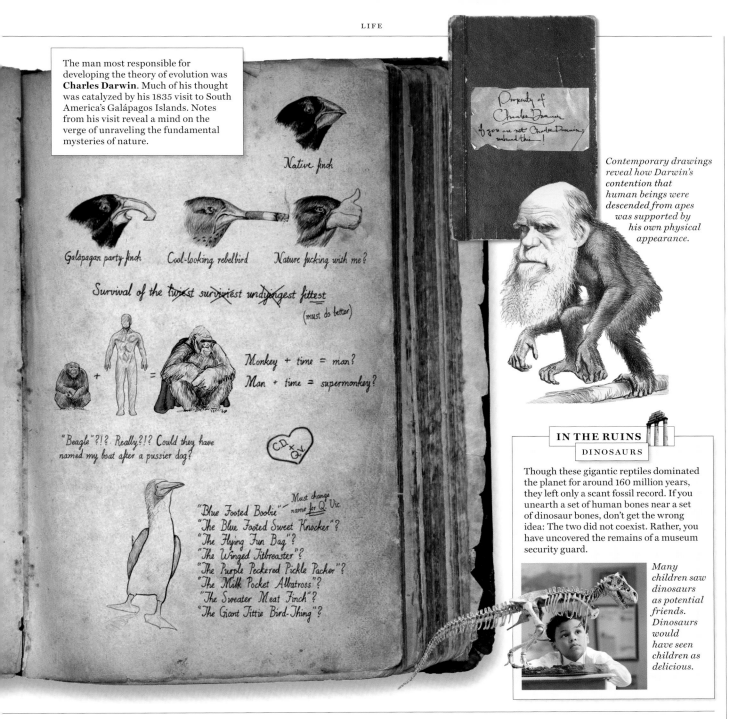

Native finch

Galápagan party-finch

Cool-looking rebelbird

Nature fucking with me?

Survival of the ~~twixest survixiest undyingest~~ fittest

(must do better)

Monkey + time = man?

Man + time = supermonkey?

"Beagle"?!?. Really?!? Could they have named my boat after a pussier dog?

CD + Q.V.

"Blue Footed Boobie" — Must change name for Q. Vic.
"The Blue Footed Sweet Knocker"?
"The Flying Fun Bag"?
"The Winged Titbreaster"?
"The Purple Peckered Pickle Packer"?
"The Milk Pocket Albatross"?
"The Sweater Meat Finch"?
"The Giant Tittie Bird-Thing"?

Property of Charles Darwin — if you are not Charles Darwin, unhand this!

Contemporary drawings reveal how Darwin's contention that human beings were descended from apes was supported by his own physical appearance.

IN THE RUINS
DINOSAURS

Though these gigantic reptiles dominated the planet for around 160 million years, they left only a scant fossil record. If you unearth a set of human bones near a set of dinosaur bones, don't get the wrong idea: The two did not coexist. Rather, you have uncovered the remains of a museum security guard.

Many children saw dinosaurs as potential friends. Dinosaurs would have seen children as delicious.

1968 *Island economy stabilizes, attracting new breed of winged visitors, increasing bio- and income diversity.*

1988 *Formerly useless giant tortoise mutates into adorable tour company logo, precipitating a great flowering of T-shirts, wallets and other vendable items.*

1997 *In an example of natural selection, "José's" emerges as sole survivor of six taquerías fighting for harbor supremacy. Rivals are unable to compete with its signature angelfish tacos.*

2010 *The once sparsely inhabited ecosystem now thrives gloriously, luring an annual 160,000 human visitors while having shed less hearty species, such as plants and animals. The Galápagos has now fully adapted to be able to compete with other island chains for life-sustaining tourism.*

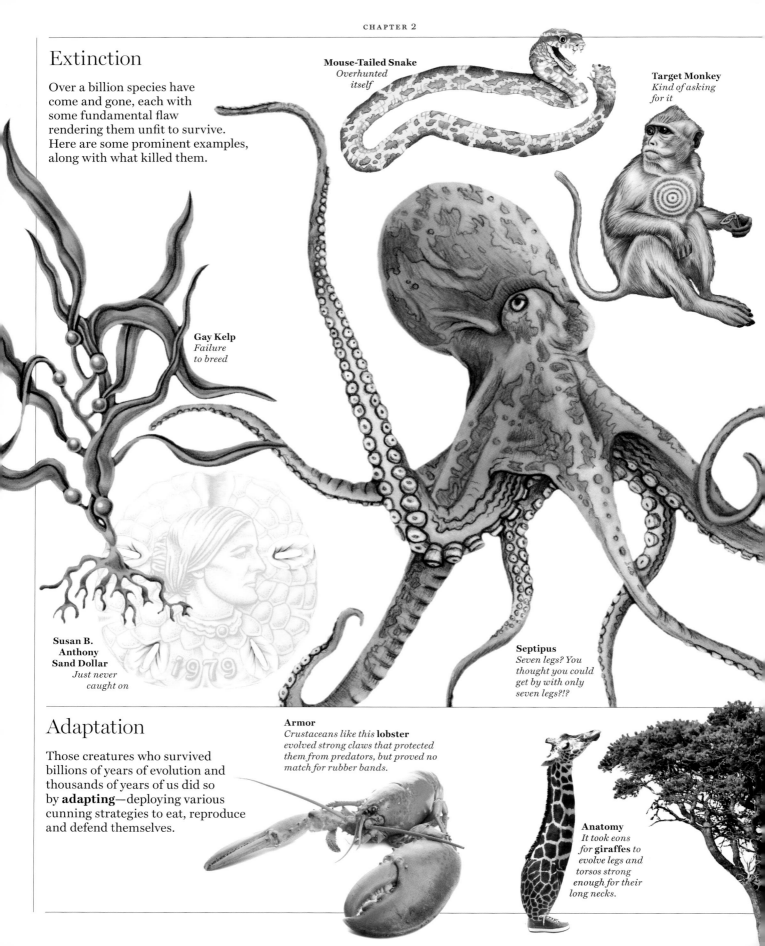

Extinction

Over a billion species have come and gone, each with some fundamental flaw rendering them unfit to survive. Here are some prominent examples, along with what killed them.

Mouse-Tailed Snake
Overhunted itself

Target Monkey
Kind of asking for it

Gay Kelp
Failure to breed

Susan B. Anthony Sand Dollar
Just never caught on

Septipus
Seven legs? You thought you could get by with only seven legs?!?

Adaptation

Those creatures who survived billions of years of evolution and thousands of years of us did so by **adapting**—deploying various cunning strategies to eat, reproduce and defend themselves.

Armor
*Crustaceans like this **lobster** evolved strong claws that protected them from predators, but proved no match for rubber bands.*

Anatomy
*It took eons for **giraffes** to evolve legs and torsos strong enough for their long necks.*

Dodo
*Too silly not
to shoot*

Mutation

The physical mechanism driving evolution is **mutation**.

> AN INDIVIDUAL'S PHYSICAL STRUCTURE IS DICTATED BY ITS DNA, A DOUBLE-HELICAL ARRANGEMENT OF FOUR CHEMICAL BASES.

> RANDOM REARRANGEMENT OF DNA OCCASIONALLY OCCURS DURING REPRODUCTION OR FROM EXPOSURE TO RADIOACTIVITY.

> THE UNIQUE PHYSICAL ABILITIES RESULTING FROM A MUTATION CAN GIVE THE SPECIES A COMPETITIVE EDGE.

> THE MUTATION IS INHERITED BY THE SPECIMEN'S DESCENDANTS, ALLOWING THEM TO DOMINATE THEIR LESS ADVANCED BRETHREN.

> TO BE CONTINUED...

**Sabre-Toothed
Tiger** *Sneeze
resulted in self-
decapitation*

Tyrannosaurus Rex
*Couldn't reach heart pills
stashed on top shelf*

**Scent
Skunks** *emitted a powerful scent
to let potential predators know
that they had just
been hit by a
car.*

Camouflage
The **page moth** *has adapted
itself to go unseen by its natural
enemy—you, the reader.*

Socialization
Some species **organized** *to make
individuals serve the good of the group.
This organization was sometimes
less successful when species took the
next step and* **unionized.**

31

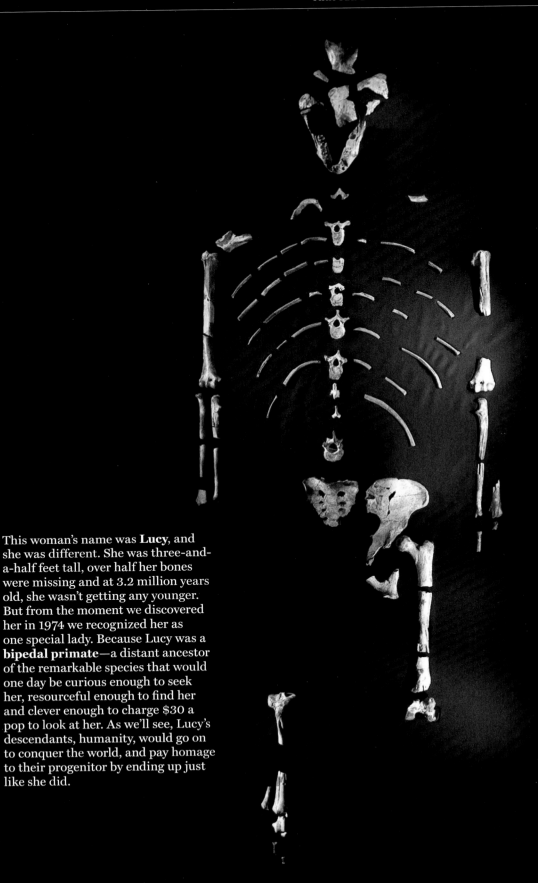

This woman's name was **Lucy**, and she was different. She was three-and-a-half feet tall, over half her bones were missing and at 3.2 million years old, she wasn't getting any younger. But from the moment we discovered her in 1974 we recognized her as one special lady. Because Lucy was a **bipedal primate**—a distant ancestor of the remarkable species that would one day be curious enough to seek her, resourceful enough to find her and clever enough to charge $30 a pop to look at her. As we'll see, Lucy's descendants, humanity, would go on to conquer the world, and pay homage to their progenitor by ending up just like she did.

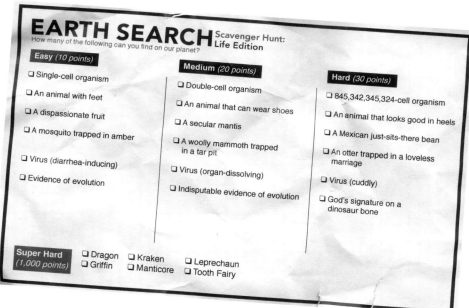

EARTH SEARCH

Scavenger Hunt: Life Edition

How many of the following can you find on our planet?

Easy (10 points)
- ❑ Single-cell organism
- ❑ An animal with feet
- ❑ A dispassionate fruit
- ❑ A mosquito trapped in amber
- ❑ Virus (diarrhea-inducing)
- ❑ Evidence of evolution

Medium (20 points)
- ❑ Double-cell organism
- ❑ An animal that can wear shoes
- ❑ A secular mantis
- ❑ A woolly mammoth trapped in a tar pit
- ❑ Virus (organ-dissolving)
- ❑ Indisputable evidence of evolution

Hard (30 points)
- ❑ 845,342,345,324-cell organism
- ❑ An animal that looks good in heels
- ❑ A Mexican just-sits-there bean
- ❑ An otter trapped in a loveless marriage
- ❑ Virus (cuddly)
- ❑ God's signature on a dinosaur bone

Super Hard (1,000 points)
- ❑ Dragon
- ❑ Griffin
- ❑ Kraken
- ❑ Manticore
- ❑ Leprechaun
- ❑ Tooth Fairy

FAQs

(Future Alien Questions)

Q. How many different living beings existed on Earth when you were there?
A. 3,000 quintillion.

Q. How rough an estimate is that?
A. It is the exact number.

Q. Which animal had the most species?
A. Beetles. There were over a million different kinds of them.

Q. Wow! They must have been fascinating!
A. Meh.

A million butterfly species would have been great. But no.

Q. How did everybody keep track of what life forms they were supposed to consume?
A. By following the **food chain**, the *Who's Who* of who ate who. Most creatures were simultaneously prey for larger predators and predators for smaller prey.

Q. So there must have been times when the hunter ... became the hunted!
A. We see you've studied our taglines.

Q. If we were interested in sampling the fare, which creatures would you recommend?
A. We don't know your tastes, but if you're looking for a rich and satisfying meal, try **animals**. Then again, if your race is a bunch of pretentious space pussies, **plants** might be a better choice.

Q. And what neighborhood has the best dining?
A. Most foodies favored the **crust**. In general Earth's edibility decreases sharply once you enter its mantle.

Q. How could you tell which plants were poisonous?
A. Towards the end most of us just stopped eating them altogether, though usually the ones stuffed with cheese were safe.

Q. What are the two small animals we're finding in large numbers near many of your scientific facilities?
A. Those are **rats** and **guinea pigs**. We used them to test everything from the latest theories of structural behavioralism to lip gloss. Try to treat

them nicely. They've been through a lot.

Just looking at this animal made us want to shave it and pour bleach in its eyes.

Q. Were there any rival theories to the theory of evolution?
A. No.

Q. Really?
A. Well, there was one. It was called creationism. To be honest, billions of people believed in it right to the end.

Q. And what was the theory of creationism?
A. We'd rather not talk about it.

Q. Why not?
A. 'Cause.

Q. Come on.
A. Look, if you're so damn curious, check into a hotel room, open the bedside table and start reading.

Q. Hold on a moment. *[Pause]* Wow.
A. We know.

Q. Six days? Six days?!?
A. *[Covers eyes, shakes head]*

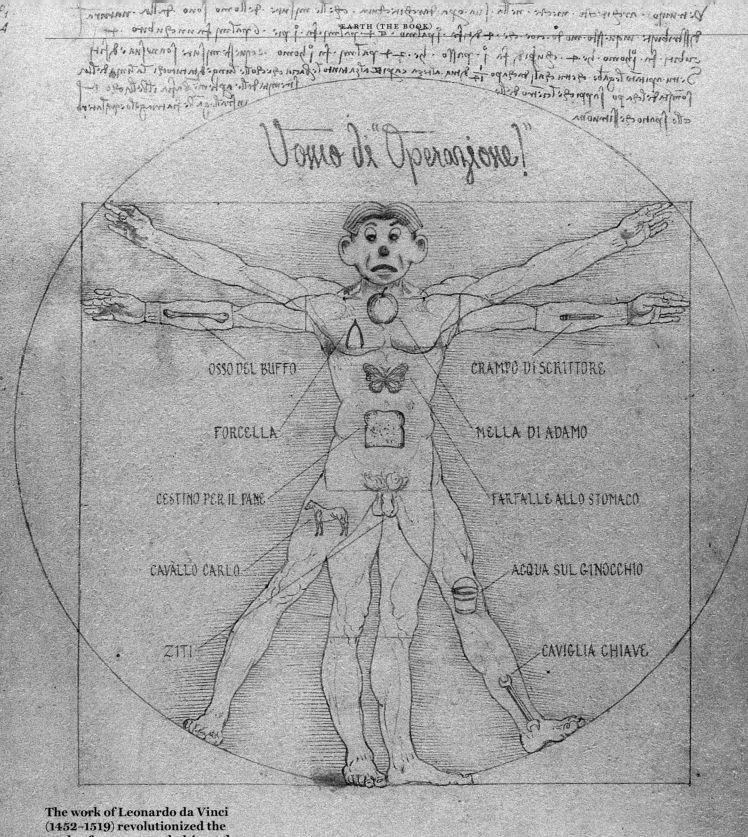

Uomo di "Operazione!"

OSSO DEL BUFFO

CRAMPO DI SCRITTORE

FORCELLA

MELA DI ADAMO

CESTINO PER IL PANE

FARFALLE ALLO STOMACO

CAVALLO CARLO

ACQUA SUL GINOCCHIO

ZITI

CAVIGLIA CHIAVE

The work of Leonardo da Vinci (1452–1519) revolutionized the study of anatomy and ultimately led to the development of the buzzer-based method of surgery.

Man

*I*T'S 11:59 *P.M., New Year's Eve. The door swings open and in walks—that's right bitches, walks—the most incredible creature anyone has ever seen. Upright, hairless, with a frontal lobe that screams high cognitive functioning, this strange being moves in, redecorates the joint and eats half the guests before the ball drops. Yeah,* Homo sapiens *is in the house.*

If the chronology of life on Earth were compressed into a year, humanity would have been around for only that final minute. But in that time we managed to domesticate dogs, clone sheep and kill off more species of arthropod than we could shake a stick at—you know, the stick we were holding in our now free-to-grasp hand. So how 'bout a nice round of applause for man, the evolutionary *wunderkind*? Good morning, Earth's creatures, and top o' the food chain to ya!

Yet though our intellectual and spiritual prowess far outpaced that of all other organisms, we weren't perfect. Our abilities could be exercised only within the confines of our **bodies**. On the off-chance you exist as amorphous vapors floating immaterially in space, bodies were portable, individual-sized carrying cases for the soul. Every human being was given exactly *one* such body at the moment of conception, so you can see why we would encase them in a thick protective layer of fat.

Our bodies had their virtues: **durability**, the capacity for **self-healing** and extraordinary pieces of bioengineering like the **hands**, **eyes** and **upper left quadrant of the clitoris**. But for the most part they were our weak spot. We were neither the fastest animal (that was the cheetah), nor the largest (the blue whale), nor the tallest (the giraffe), nor the prettiest (tie: butterflies/well-groomed cocker spaniels). Yet we ruled over all of them. Why? Perhaps this riddle will shed some light: What has three pounds, four lobes and just came up with the idea for guns?

Yes, the **brain** was our big dog. A dense collection of neurons and their transmitters, it allowed for a level of

The word man was used to designate all members of our species, including this "wo-man," a bizarre genetic mutation comprising over half the human race.

functioning other fauna could only respond reflexively to direct stimuli about. Its relationship with the body could at times be fraught. Often, no sooner would the mind begin to scale the heights of Mt. Knowledge than it would receive a frantic call from body base camp, demanding it return to oversee "Operation Masturbate." We actually devoted the majority of our time and energy to satisfying our bodies' needs, wants, whims, tantrums and crippling addictions. To the mind, the body was the loud, leaky, high-maintenance apartment it was forced to live in simply because it had nowhere else to crash.

But consider it from the body's perspective. From the neck down the human animal would just as soon have been left alone with its instincts. Eating, sleeping, copulating, immediately sleeping again—these were natural functions that needed no input from "upper management." Yet to justify its job, Mr. Thinksalot had to constantly butt in with his doubts and diets and insufferable quest for meaning. To the body, the mind was a totalitarian dictator monitoring every aspect of its personal life: its eating, its breathing, its sexual habits, even when—and in what room of the house—it could defecate.

This **mind-body tension** was the maddening core of our existence. But it was also remarkably productive. In some ways, their relationship was like that of the mismatched pairs of law-enforcement officials whose misadventures constitute a significant portion of the televisual artifacts you will soon be finding. Yes, they were different; but it was those very differences that led them to success, and ultimately, a kind of grudging mutual respect. *Homo sapiens* may have been set apart from all other life on Earth by its intelligence, but only in conjunction with our physical selves was this intelligence able to adapt to its conditions, change its environment and bend the world to its will for the greater good of everyone.

The end result is the now lifeless hellscape before you.

The Rise of Man

ALTHOUGH WE SHARED 98.4% of our DNA with chimpanzees, that last 1.6% was what was known in anthropological circles as a "game changer." Who knew that a slightly shorter ilium and a reduction of the supraorbital torus would be the difference between dressing in a suit and tie for work, and being dressed in a suit and tie for our amusement?

Why We Ruled

A series of crucial adaptations gradually enabled humanity to conquer the world.

Brain Size

This was the most critical factor. Over time our brains increased from 400 milliliters—barely enough to feed a large family of baby spiders—to a zombie feast-sized 1,400 milliliters. These bigger brains allowed us to engage in **abstract thought**, which is a cool idea if you think about it.

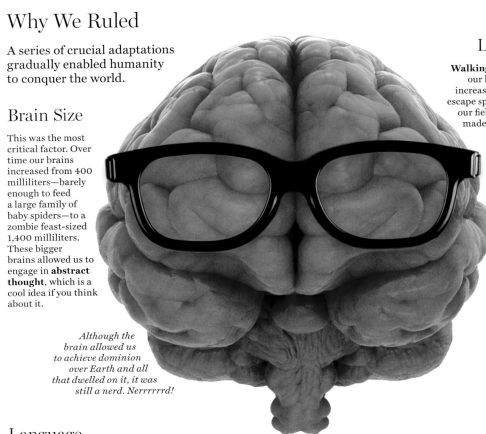

Although the brain allowed us to achieve dominion over Earth and all that dwelled on it, it was still a nerd. Nerrrrrd!

Bipedal Locomotion

Walking on two feet freed our hands for carrying, increased our pursuit and escape speed and improved our field of vision. It also made us no longer able to **lick our own testicles**. It was probably worth it.

Without bipedalism this magazine's readership would have been nothing more than a pathetic collection of torso fetishists.

Manipulative Hands

The newly liberated **hands** evolved into fine instruments capable of performing an extraordinary range of tasks, from flashing gang signs to testing for prostate cancer to helping us draw turkeys. The hand's project manager was the **opposable thumb**, which maintained an excellent working relationship with the other fingers but remained aloof from them in its private life.

The thumb, seen here approving of itself.

Language

As our **larynxes** descended, we were able to make sounds with our mouths in new and far more expressive ways. Verbal **language** soon overtook physical gesturing as the primary means of communication for all human beings except Italians.

*After learning how to talk, the next logical step was learning how to make a piece of wood tell **racist jokes**.*

Tools

Greater intelligence and dexterity allowed us to fashion and use **tools**. These were artificial extensions of ourselves that were harder or longer or grippier than we were. Naturally we began to resent them, so we gained a level of revenge by making their name synonymous with "douchebag."

*Primitive tools. From left: A **chopping thing**; a **smashing thing**; and a rock, possibly used as a **smasher/chopper**.*

DUSTBIN OF HISTORY
NEANDERTHALS

For a few hundred millennia, Earth was home to two distinct hominid species: **Homo sapiens** and **Neanderthals**. The Neanderthals were a great group—fun at parties, adept at lice-grooming, and total saber-toothed tigers in the sack. But they went extinct around 30,000 B.C. No one quite knows why we made it and they didn't, but comparative analysis reveals subtle differences that help account for their status as the Betamax of humanity.

Homo Sapiens	Homo Neanderthalensis
• "Wise man"	• "Nice guy"
• Hunted, gathered	• Scrounged, mooched
• Teamed up to hunt prey	• Teamed up to hunt MILFs
• Planted, irrigated, harvested crops	• Yelled at seeds, wondered where plant was hiding
• Domesticated dogs	• Domesticated rocks
• Used fire for cooking	• Used fire for bathing

Pioneering archeologist Mary Leakey (1913–1996) revolutionized the study of hominid evolution with her landmark 1964 publication, The Fuckability of Man.

The Fuckability of Man

Australopithecus afarensis (Fig. 1) was an extraordinary breakthrough in terms of brain capacity and dexterity. But he was no reputable female archeologist's idea of a fun Friday night. Squat, hairy, hunched over, and less than 1.3 meters tall, one would not have tapped this if the future of the species depended on it.

Fig. 1

But females back then had not yet developed self-esteem, so they continued banging Australopithecus for the million years needed for the far sexier *Homo habilis* (Fig. 2) to emerge. This transitionally fuckable figure was a strangely charismatic "bad boy," with a taller stature, more human-like face, and a larger rib cage that recently unearthed fossil evidence suggests could have supported rock-hard pecs. While there is still some debate as to precisely how drunk he'd have to get you, serious bioevolutionists agree that after four beers you'd be at his place, on your back and loving it.

Yet even he cannot compare, on the doability scale, to *Homo erectus* (Fig. 3). He was the pivotal moment, the "threshold" when man – and I do mean "man" – passed from "why not?" to "right now!" To observe the reduction in postcanine dentition and vertical shortening of the face is to feel your honeypot start to flow. Plus he had the dexterity to use "diverse tools," if you know what I (and the other ladies of the London University Neolithic Research Department) mean. Oh, if I only were born 1.5 million years ago, I'd have banged him like a shinbone on an antelope skeleton!

Fig. 2

Fig. 3

24

LEARNING CURVE
BECOMING HUMAN

Our conquest of **fire** *made it possible to safely consume meat and commit insurance fraud.*

With fire under our collective belts, we spent the next 200 millennia in a quest for **pointiness**.

The emergence of **burial rites** *reflected our growing awareness that dead people smelled.*

With the manufacture and trade of **shell beads**—*a commodity with no practical use*—*the modern economy is born.*

Though **ochre** *was our first pigment it would take another 70,000 years to grasp that if you called it "Harvest Wheat" you could charge twice as much for it.*

The oldest known musical instrument is this 35,000-year-old **vulture bone flute**, *which must have sounded just awful.*

Anatomy

Ideal

A fully developed human body was a **wonder of nature**. Molded by 3,000,000 years of evolution and twenty years of individual maturation, it was a finely tuned mechanism, an intricate yet supple apparatus ready, willing and able to do the bidding of its master, the mind.

EXPRESSION
We shone with the pride of world domination. Our faces expressed our haughty grandeur with sensory organs loftily arranged to be kept well above the earth and the skittering creatures below.

HEALTH
The forces of evolution forged us into disease- and injury-resistant superbeings. Our bodies healed our own wounds and chased off infection. On our best days, we felt ourselves nearly impervious to damage.

POSTURE
Surely if any one thing distinguished us from our simian ancestors, it was the ramrod straightness of our spines, ideally suited for surveying the world over which we held sway.

Actual

Our bodies were **rotting mobile junk drawers**. Lulled by centuries of civilization into a comfort bordering on oblivion, they divorced themselves from physical challenges and began inexorably dissipating like sandcastles at high tide.

EXPRESSION
We carried ourselves as if our secret shames rode like hideous gargoyles on our shoulders.

HEALTH
Only a regular regimen of bioengineered chemicals kept us one step ahead of wholesale collapse, and even they could not stave off the aggregate weight of our chronic minor ailments. We had things shutting down, falling off, leaking out and fading away. And our prostates … it felt like there was a Rubik's Cube jammed in there.

POSTURE
We hunched like hobgoblins feasting on the entrails of our broken dreams.

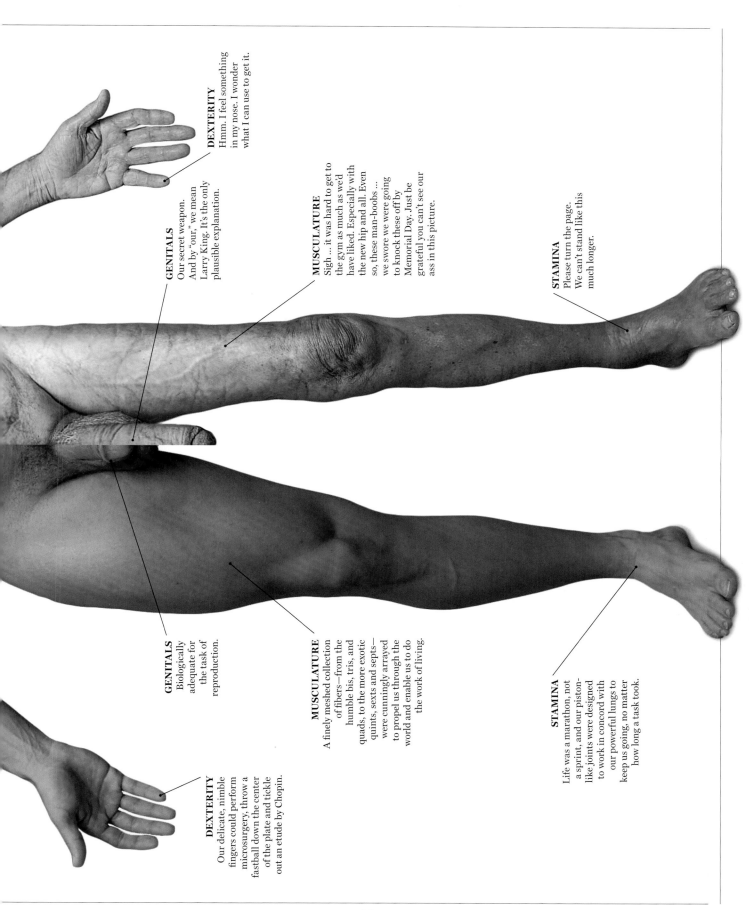

DEXTERITY
Hmm. I feel something in my nose. I wonder what I can use to get it.

GENITALS
Our secret weapon. And by "our," we mean Larry King. It's the only plausible explanation.

MUSCULATURE
Sigh ... it was hard to get to the gym as much as we'd have liked. Especially with the new hip and all. Even so, these man-boobs ... we swore we were going to knock these off by Memorial Day. Just be grateful you can't see our ass in this picture.

STAMINA
Please turn the page. We can't stand like this much longer.

GENITALS
Biologically adequate for the task of reproduction.

MUSCULATURE
A finely meshed collection of fibers—from the humble bis, tris, and quads, to the more exotic quints, sexts and septs—were cunningly arrayed to propel us through the world and enable us to do the work of living.

DEXTERITY
Our delicate, nimble fingers could perform microsurgery, throw a fastball down the center of the plate and tickle out an etude by Chopin.

STAMINA
Life was a marathon, not a sprint, and our piston-like joints were designed to work in concord with our powerful lungs to keep us going, no matter how long a task took.

Parts of the Body

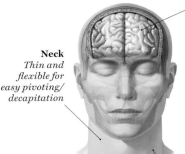

Brain
Repulsive, slimy seat of reason

Neck
Thin and flexible for easy pivoting/ decapitation

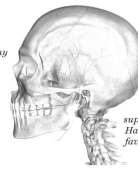

Skeleton
Indispensable solid structural support system; Halloween party favor

Skin
Locked in other organs for freshness

Hands
The brain's two enforcers

Fingers
The enforcers' hired goons

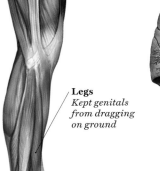

Intestines
Large tube that absorbed nutrients from what we ate, leaving behind the last thing we'd want to eat

Arms
Puppeteers of the hands; used for holding, lifting, poppin' 'n' lockin'

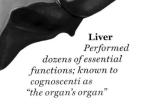

Liver
Performed dozens of essential functions; known to cognoscenti as "the organ's organ"

Lungs
WARNING: Using these can greatly reduce your enjoyment of cigarettes

Legs
Kept genitals from dragging on ground

NAILED IT
THE ANUS

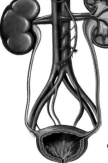

In engineering parlance, it was a simple elastic valve. But our demands on it were daunting. Leakage was a complete deal-breaker. Any stoppage was likewise a failure. Day in and day out, the anus gave us reliable performance from a key position. And positioning it so far away from our noses? Genius.

Feet
Leg hands

Toes
Feet fingers

Muscles
No matter what you've heard, far less important than listening skills and a good sense of humor

Heart
Dense fibrous fist-shaped muscle endlessly spewing gallons of blood; symbol of romance

Kidney
Produced urine; preferred not to discuss work with other organs*

Torso
Most frequently aimed-at part of body

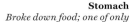

Navel
Permanent reminder of good old days

Stomach
*Broke down food; one of only two organs with veto power over brain (see **genitals**)*

* **Urine** and **feces** were the liquid and solid waste products resulting from digestion. Excreting them was the dirty little secret shared by all human beings, with the exception of movie stars, the President of the United States, and one's own mother.

Skin Color

IT'S NOT SURPRISING that variations in epidermal tincture caused by differing ratios of pheomelanin and eumelanin (as determined by the allele of the SLC24A5 gene) could make the difference between freedom and slavery. After all, **pigmentation** was a quick and convenient way of judging a person. One of us, Dr. Martin Luther King, Jr., once proposed we instead judge people by the content of their character. He was shot.

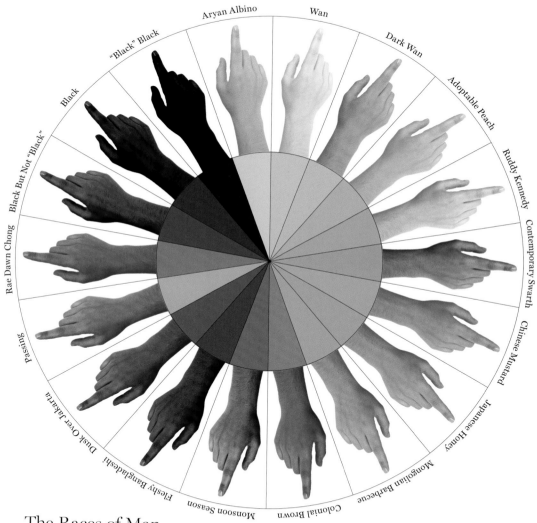

Around the wheel (clockwise from top): Aryan Albino · Wan · Dark Wan · Adoptable Peach · Ruddy Kennedy · Contemporary Swarth · Chinese Mustard · Japanese Honey · Mongolian Barbecue · Colonial Brown · Monsoon Season · Fleshy Bangladeshi · Dusk Over Jakarta · Passing · Rae Dawn Chong · Black But Not "Black" · Black · "Black" Black

The Races of Man

Asiatic

Negroid

Normal

Australoid

Classic Skin Rivalries

If you'd gotten here in time, you'd have had ringside seats for some of these legendary racial contretemps.

White vs. Black

Asian vs. Asian

Half-Black/Half-Jewish vs. Half-Black/Half-Asian

White vs. White

Reproduction

LIKE MOST MAMMALS, humans were made up of two sexes, **men** and **women**. This made sexual reproduction possible and eased traffic congestion patterns in public restrooms. Strictly speaking, the differences between the sexes were purely anatomical. But in reality their ongoing disconnect formed a deep vagina of misunderstanding seldom filled by the penis of knowledge. We will discuss the societal implications of this later; for now, just know that the images of the body parts you are looking at, while natural, are **shameful**. If we were alive today, we would never allow this type of trash to be sold in any of our finer enormous, low-wage, bulk-sale, discount chain superstores.

Third Sexes

Over the millennia, the two-gender system successfully beat back numerous challenges.

Eunuch

Threemale

Metrosexual

Junkless

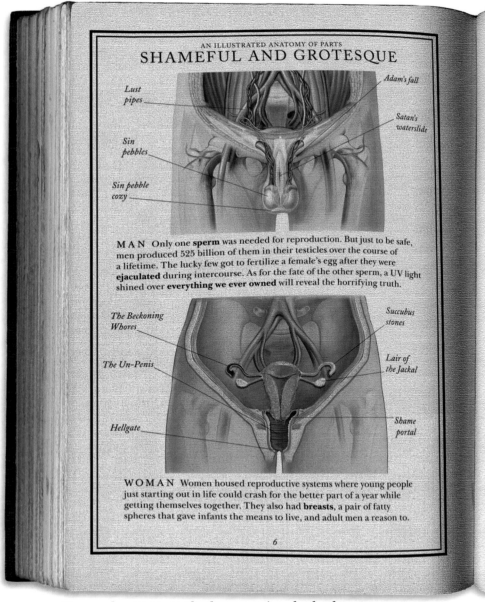

AN ILLUSTRATED ANATOMY OF PARTS
SHAMEFUL AND GROTESQUE

Lust pipes

Adam's fall

Satan's waterslide

Sin pebbles

Sin pebble cozy

MAN Only one **sperm** was needed for reproduction. But just to be safe, men produced 525 billion of them in their testicles over the course of a lifetime. The lucky few got to fertilize a female's egg after they were **ejaculated** during intercourse. As for the fate of the other sperm, a UV light shined over **everything we ever owned** will reveal the horrifying truth.

The Beckoning Whores

Succubus stones

The Un-Penis

Lair of the Jackal

Hellgate

Shame portal

WOMAN Women housed reproductive systems where young people just starting out in life could crash for the better part of a year while getting themselves together. They also had **breasts**, a pair of fatty spheres that gave infants the means to live, and adult men a reason to.

6

Many early anatomy textbooks were written by the clergy.

NAILED IT
ORGASMS

Imagine the best thing that ever happened to your body. Double it. Double it again. You're now 1% of the way to understanding what **orgasms** were like for us. These involuntary muscular contractions were our body's way of making us feel really really really really good, and once you understand that, you're a long way toward understanding why we did 99% of the stuff we did.

How Babies Were Made

We used to make up stories for our children to explain where they came from. But an advanced race like you can handle the truth. What follows is a candid excerpt from the 1955 filmstrip *Reproduction: As Much As You Need to Know.*

"Sometimes, when a man and woman love each other very much, they decide to create another human being to fight the creeping Communist menace."

"With their clergyman's blessing, they go to the soda shop and exchange sips of chocolate malted."

"The fertilized malt makes its way down the Mommy's throat to her tummy, where it can be more easily concealed by loose clothing."

"Nine months later, God punishes the Mommy for sipping the forbidden malt by nearly ripping her vagina in two."

"This is J. Edgar Hoover, and I approve of this baby-making method."

As pregnancy progressed, the suspense built masterfully.

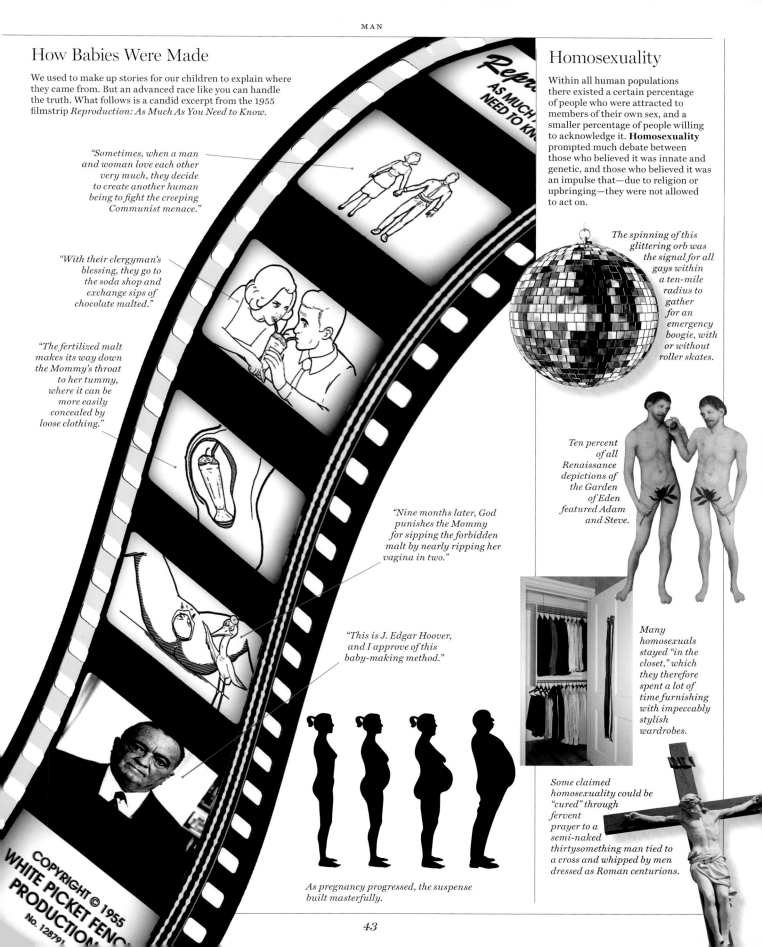

Homosexuality

Within all human populations there existed a certain percentage of people who were attracted to members of their own sex, and a smaller percentage of people willing to acknowledge it. **Homosexuality** prompted much debate between those who believed it was innate and genetic, and those who believed it was an impulse that—due to religion or upbringing—they were not allowed to act on.

The spinning of this glittering orb was the signal for all gays within a ten-mile radius to gather for an emergency boogie, with or without roller skates.

Ten percent of all Renaissance depictions of the Garden of Eden featured Adam and Steve.

Many homosexuals stayed "in the closet," which they therefore spent a lot of time furnishing with impeccably stylish wardrobes.

Some claimed homosexuality could be "cured" through fervent prayer to a semi-naked thirtysomething man tied to a cross and whipped by men dressed as Roman centurions.

43

The Senses

WE PERCEIVED THE outside world using five senses. A few us of had a sixth, called **gaydar**, which, while far less important, provided hours of bitchy fun.

SIGHT was the sense we used to process visual imagery and to determine if something made us look fat. It was handy for distinguishing many characteristics, such as color, which was notoriously difficult to determine by taste. People who could not see were **blind**, and often used this as an excuse to urinate in their friends' closets.

*Many people wore **eyeglasses** to compensate for overpopularity.*

HEARING was vital for communication, and even more vital for miscommunication. It was distinct from listening, which could only be achieved when hearing was combined with giving a shit. People who could not hear were **deaf** and talked with their hands. Unfortunately, this shifted everything over one, and they ended up having to feel with their mouths and taste with their ears.

Hearing aids were a convenient excuse for old people to ignore their grandchildren.

TOUCH was a nervous system feature that allowed us to process texture and temperature. There were two kinds of touching: good and bad. Only one of them required the implementation of a national computerized registry.

*The invention of **anesthesia** made surgery more pleasant for patients but less entertaining for doctors.*

SMELL was primal. Somehow, the detection of a few **airborne molecules** could instantly take us back to that magical summer in the Poconos ... marshmallows by the bonfire ... Julie's freckles ... fishing with Dad ... that big bass we caught. And then ... the incident ... the screaming ... the smell of Julie's charred flesh ... why hadn't we put out the bonfire? ... we were too busy fishing for that damned bass ... Oh God ... Julie! ... We're so sorry, Julie ... Anyway, that's smell.

Nothing gold can stay. We miss you, Jules.

There was a time when **TASTE** was completely in sync with our nutritional needs. Alas, our tongues and our health stopped speaking some time around the invention of the HotPocket.

Salt *was without question the best tasting rock on earth, although some would argue mica had its charms.*

Mr. Potato Head was a popular children's toy whose sensory organs could be quickly removed and stored in his ass.

Maintenance

LIKE ANY MACHINE, our bodies required constant daily upkeep. Grooming and excretory functions were typically done privately, in tiled chambers called **bathrooms**. Vigilance in such matters of personal hygiene were of the utmost importance ... until you got married. At that point it was as though you'd never even possessed that extra 1.6% of DNA.

Shampoo
Made tiny insects living in our hair clean

Conditioner
Made tiny insects living in our hair lustrous, "silkient"

Air freshener
Because the opposite of "feces" is "pine"

Razor
Used to cut men's faces and women's legs

Nose-hair clippers
As the hair on top of our heads thinned, the hair inside our heads grew lush

Soap
Pubic hair magnet

Loofah
Waterproof sandpaper

Toothbrush
Sanitary dental scrubber prior to first use; bacteria-strewn filth-stick thereafter

Toothpaste
As name suggests, consisted of finely-ground teeth

Bathtub
Shower alternative for babies, the elderly and the overworked women who took care of both

Toilet paper
Squeezably soft, bear cub-friendly tissues we used to wipe our assholes

Shower
Humdrum morning ritual/unimaginable luxury, depending on where you were from

Bathmat
Collected water from feet and gave it to microbes, mold and silverfish

Toilet
We gave it so much. And what did we get in return? Gonorrhea.

Perfect couples were marked by a willingness to share even their most private moments.

Appearance

THE SUPERIORITY OF inner beauty to outward good looks was a pervasive cultural theme in our society, especially among the less outwardly good looking. We often spoke of our admiration for intelligence, honesty and humor as traits we wanted in a mate. When we did so, our genitals would sigh and roll their eyes.

Beauty

While standards of beauty were highly subjective across cultures and time, it was universally considered aesthetically pleasing for the skin to cover as many of the bones and organs as possible.

Height

At least 20,000 women preferred to mate with men of greater **height** *than themselves.*

Those of **shorter stature** *tended to take their anger out on Europe.*

Symmetry

Studies consistently showed that observers found those with facial asymmetry, like the woman below, ugly.

That's more like it.

Complexion

Pallor *was eroticized by both East and West, because the purity of the lighter color meant there was more for men to defile.*

In other eras, people deliberately **burned their skin***, both to look darker and seal in their bodies' natural juices.*

Weight

In lean times, **fat** *was a sign of prosperity. Seen here, a guy doing great.*

In the postwar years, veterans were attracted to models like **Twiggy***, whose bodies reflected the boyhoods they had lost to war.*

Hair

A keratinous outgrowth of filamentous cells and the basis of a wildly popular musical, **hair** *went from providing primitive man with insulation and protection from the elements to serving a far more important function: Self-expression.*

"I am a woman of taste and sophistication."

"I secretly have sex with men."

"I have murdered at least one actress in my yard."

DUSTBIN OF HISTORY

HAIRSTYLES

1. "The Gaydolf"

2. "The Half and Halfro"

3. "The Fu Man-Rachel"

4. "The Marie Antoinette"

5. "The Flock of Real Seagulls"

6. "The G. Gordon Lady"

Photos courtesy of

TIFFANY'S UNISEX SALON

We Make 'Hair'-story!

Body Modification

We found many ways to alter our bodies as a way of passive-aggressively critiquing Mother Nature's shoddy work.

*This 5,300-year-old mummy was covered in 57 **tattoos**, suggesting to anthropologists he was probably a scumbag.*

*In some tribes, the **ritual scarification** of young males' faces helped them completely forget about their acne.*

*Though popular in Burma, **neck rings** failed to catch on elsewhere as a means for short people to see the movie screen.*

Circumcision *was ritually performed for 4,000 years on newborn Jewish boys because their penises kept coming out wrong.*

*In the 20th century, doctors developed a variety of surgical means to alter the body. Among the most popular: **breast augmentation**. Among the least popular: **breast rotation**.*

Basic Needs

Food and Water

Food and water were our two most basic needs. Both existed in good quantity but were somewhat unevenly distributed. While millions of us died of starvation and thirst, millions of others were so sated they could afford to use **pies**—round fruit or cream-filled pastries with enough fat content to sustain a human being for several days—as comedic projectiles, and water as giant slide lubricants. We never quite figured this one out.

Beverages *provided our body with essential corn syrups and sodium benzoates.*

Once a beverage made it into a **glass**, *its life was pretty much over. Next stop: kidneyville.*

Don't fill up on this picture.

A late innovation, the **fork** *was conceived as a way to hurt food one last time before eating it.*

Napkins *were used to apprehend and neutralize rogue morsels.*

The Five Food Groups

1. Meat
It tasted like victory.

2. Dairy
Food we stole from baby mammals.

3. Fruits and vegetables
Our most nutritious option. Eaten reluctantly.

4. Grains
Their production required a continual scaring of crows.

5. Fried Shit
An ever-increasing amount of delicious fried shit.

We only broke out **tablecloths** *on special occasions. But what the heck, you're worth it!*

BY THE NUMBERS
LIFETIME FOOD CONSUMPTION

Purposeful		Inadvertent	
Ranch dressing	285 gallons	Pen caps	1.7
Skittles	37 rainbows	Pubic hairs	876
Bushmeat	18 burlap sacks	Mouse parts	12 mice worth
Red Cross food rations	439	Insect feces	4 gallons
First slices of wedding cake	2.1	Dandruff	4 trash bags
Edible underwear	3.2 pairs	Pieces of own tongue	8 lbs.
Uncut heroin	$1/12$ condom	Waitstaff saliva	4.3 gallons
Jesuses	95.4 wafers	Fresh vegetables	40 lbs.

*The invention of the **spoon** spurred the discovery, five hundred years later, of **soup**.*

*The **plate** was our private property. We would defend it and its delicious inhabitants to the death.*

*The **knife's** sharp edge allowed us to chop tough foodstuffs; its shiny surface allowed us to check our teeth for the remnants of those foodstuffs.*

おてもと

*Many Eastern cultures ate with **chopsticks**. They were not as good as using a fork. They just weren't.*

THINGS WE LIKED
TREATS

We derived nutrition from a wide variety of foods. But many of our favorite edibles had nothing to do with sustenance and everything to do with indulgence.

CHOCOLATE

What It Was: The Veronica to vanilla's Betty

Why We Liked It: Seriously, try it. If you don't have taste buds, just rub it on your exoskeleton.

What We Used It For: To woo a lover; to fill the void of losing a lover

What We'd Do for It: Peel wrappers; finish our vegetables

Where We Found It: Hershey, Pennsylvania; small hollow plastic pumpkins (October 31 only); dead dogs' stomachs

Where You'll (Still) Find It: Ring-Dings

SPICES

What They Were: The ground extracts of seeds, leaves, buds, twigs, and stumps

Why We Liked Them: Satisfied human need to add pinches, dashes and half-teaspoons of things

What We Used Them For: Making bland food taste good; making rotten food edible; making cartoon characters sneeze

What We'd Do for Them: Cross the Gobi; circumnavigate Africa; enslave millions

Where We Found Them: Hard-to-reach ports worldwide

CAVIAR

What It Was: Roe killed legally in the womb, as per *Roe v. Wade*

Why We Liked It: Because "they" told us we should

What We Used It For: Spreading on crackers; mocking the homeless

What We'd Do for It: Destroy unborn fish that might otherwise have grown up to die a far more prolonged death at our hands

Where We Found It: Gourmet restaurants; wedding receptions of social climbers

Where You'll (Still) Find It: Sturgeon ovaries (if such things still exist)

HONEY

What It Was: Delicious, delicious bee vomit

Why We Liked It: Only source of sweetness before 1845 discovery of Great Saharan Sugar Dunes

What We Used It For: Condiment; wound disinfectant; term of endearment; Pooh-baiting

What We'd Do for It: Get stung by swarms of insects; tolerate the existence of beekeepers

Where We Found It: Honeycomb; also available in "Bit o'" form

Where You'll (Still) Find It: Plastic squeezy-bears; any surface it once touched

ZAGAT®
Guide to World Cuisine
2010

Restaurants were places where we would pay others to cook our food, serve it and clean up after us. They were one of the best ideas we ever had. The most prevalent was **McDonald's**, where families would go to eat laboratory-designed consumables nominally prepared by a terrifying clown and his army of misshapen monsters. If you see the "Golden Arches," stop in for a McNugget; they're probably still, in the loosest sense of the term, "good."

	TASTE	HEALTH	DELIVERABILITY	BOWEL-FRIENDLINESS
Indian	23	17	21	5
French	99	15	N/A	25
Italian	98	21	22	21
Japanese	18	29	21	24
Mexican	20	12	12	2
Chinese	25	5	100	19
Macrobiotic	N/A	99	30	∞
United Kingdom (English)	N/A	5	12	15
Yarakambut Tribe, Peru	24	21	4	16

Indian
A cuisine founded on a "tragic overestimation of chickpeas," this "satisfies your yen f huge chunks of potato and cauliflower." Eaters loved the "intriguingly muddy" meat dishe (though some moaned "Where's the beef?").

French
Those looking for "butter sauces lightly garnished with food" who didn't mind eatin something that "thinks it's better than you," went for France's "deliciously easy to mispr nounce" cuisine. Renowned for "elegant technique," "exacting standards," and "still ea ing horse for Christ's sake," the French also loved to "wash down" "gag-inducing cheeses with "wine you can't afford."

Italian
Voted #1 world cuisine for the 584th year in a row. "If you like semolina flour, cheese, tomatoes," then "oh boy-ar-dee, are you in luck!" Although some gripe "how many diffe ent noodle shapes do I need?," fans aver that "the curly-cue one" tastes "much bette than "the one that looks like a bowtie ... I think it ends in -ini?"

Japanese
There's "something fishy" about this Asian cuisine, and it's "probably all the fish." "Ser ously, there's a lot of fish," and diners complain it's often "undercooked" and accompanie by wine "that hadn't seen a grape in its life." But "fans of white rice will be in heaven especially when enhanced with "that green stuff."

Mexican
"Diarrhea-inducing" was just one of many adjectives used to describe this "diarrhea inducing" cuisine, which was heavy on "beans, cheese, beef, and ... diarrhea." Fans calle it "delicious" and "not always diarrhea-inducing," but still cautioned, "not a good choic for a hot date."

Chinese
Inspired by a "love for sesame oil" and "a deep hatred of ducks," the food of China wa considered both "highly boxable" and "stick-pick-uppable." Menus were "extensive an cheap," and "could slide under even the lowest doorframes." Don't eat the paper insi the "cookies that taste like paper!"

Macrobiotic
"Who says you can't have kale for breakfast?!" This "food" is simply a single part a "total lifestyle" that can best be described as "next to impossible." Prepare yourse for sights and smells that are so hideous "they have to be good for you." If you lik "indescribable" food prepared by 20-something former camp counselors and served b part-time river guides, then you'll "tolerate" this "flavor alternative."

United Kingdom (English)
"Doing for the tongue what Queen Victoria did for the penis," this northwestern Europea cuisine used local ingredients, then "boiled the flavor out of them," "wrapped them pastry" and "called it food." Least unrecommended: The "fish and chips," which whe sufficiently battered "might as well have been chips and fish."

Yarakambut Tribe, Peru
This "out-of-the-way" tribe was "off the beaten path," but well worth the trip for i "post-battle victory feasts" featuring "the catch of the day," a "mystery meat" that, whi "gamy" and "gristly," was both "eerily familiar" and yet "tasted like nothing else." Servic is variously described as "very friendly" or "very hostile."

From ancient times **wells** *were used to extract water from the ground and cull the population of its most curious toddlers.*

The Romans pioneered the **aqueduct**, *an engineering marvel that transported water hundreds of miles to wash dried semen off marble floors.*

Sewers *were long underground pipes that carried clean water to us and transported waste water to water heaven.*

Desalination plants *made freshwater from salt water, because why should the ocean get to sit there all undrunken and shit?*

Reservoirs *were a chance for country kids to urinate in city kids' water.*

Bottled water *emerged when free potable water became so easy to get we started figuring something must be wrong with it.*

YOU HAD TO BE HERE

This man got a trophy for eating 68 hot dogs in ten minutes.

This man ate 6.8 ounces of flour in ten days. If he'd gotten a trophy, he'd have eaten that too.

Dietary Balance

We measured our recommended daily food intake using various geometric charts. Although the 20th Century's USDA food pyramid was the most well-known, it was only one of many.

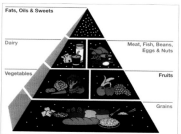

USDA Food Pyramid, *c. 2000*

Mayan Food Pyramid, *c. 1450*

Japanese Food Pagoda, *c. 1617*
Note: After four centuries, this pagoda still stands in Kyoto, a testament to the strength of wasabi mortar.

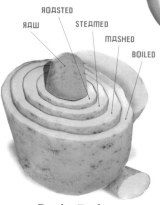

Russian Food Nesting Potato, *c. 1850*

THINGS SOME OF US LIKED
DELICACIES

Food could be used to assert ethnic identity, in the form of delicacies that one culture found delicious and the rest of the world found nauseating.

HAGGIS

What It Was: A sheep's heart, liver and lungs stuffed and boiled inside its own stomach

Who Ate It: Scots, and sociopathic wolves

How They Came Up With It: First developed as a projectile to hurl at English invaders

Why Others Found It Gross: Preferred ground pig snouts and anuses served in intestine casing on bun with ketchup

Suggested Beverage Pairing: Sheep's blood mixed with sheep's milk and sheep's mucus, drunk from a sheep's skull

HASMA

What It Was: Frog fallopian tubes boiled in sugar water

Who Ate It: The Chinese. For dessert.

How They Came Up With It: What other female frog part where they supposed to eat? The clitoris? It's all gristle.

Why Others Found It Gross: Deprived frogs of hard-won reproductive freedom

Suggested Beverage Pairing: Anything alcoholic, but lots of it, and beforehand

BALUT

What It Was: A near fully developed duck fetus, boiled and eaten in the shell

Who Ate It: Southeast Asians; freshman pledges at Delta Kappa Epsilon

How They Came Up With It: Inspired by Khmer Rouge method for remedying incorrect thought

Why Others Found It Gross: Embryonic ducks? Yummy. Adult ducks? Mouthwatering. But in between? Inhuman!

Suggested Beverage Pairing: A burgundy, preferably while making eye contact with the egg's mother

PEEPS

What It Was: Hyper-sweetened marshmallow candies shaped like baby animals

Who Ate It: Americans and marshmallow snakes

How They Came Up With It: Railway disaster involving Necco Wafers, plumbers' caulk, and spent fuel rods

Why Others Found It Gross: Even on the molecular level, did not contain the building blocks of food

Suggested Beverage Pairing: Key lime-flavored Mad Dog 20/20

Dwelling

THE PURPOSE OF the enclosed structures known as **shelters** was to provide us with warmth, protection from predators and, later, a place to get mail. We quickly transformed functional shelters into **houses** (or "homes," as they were known when they were filled with love), private sanctuaries where one could escape the pressures of the outside world. There was an old human expression, "A man's home is his castle"; and it was true, especially in the case of castles. So look around, make yourself comfortable, enjoy. But word to the wise … do not touch the thermostat. *Capiche?!?*

YOU HAD TO BE HERE

The average human home was 300 square feet.

The average human second home was 6,000 square feet.

EMPTY WORLD
INTERNATIONAL REALTY

RHODA RAVITCH, EXCLUSIVE LISTINGS
"I may have been dead for centuries, but I still get my six percent."

The rapid declines in the real estate market triggered by the complete elimination of the human race have placed even the most opulent private homes well within the budget range of the discriminating out-of-planeter.

GEORGIAN MASTERPIECE

Be the 45th proud owner of this elegant six-story family home. Rose garden, outdoor fountain, unique neo-round office, 6 BR, 5 PR (panic rooms), access to 1,500 intercontinental ballistic missiles, deck. Rooftop flagpole easily removed; color flexible. Now open to all races.

YOUR HOMINESS!

Finally, basilica living without the guilt. 4.7mil sq ft private residence/city-state. Opulent decorations include gold-gilted ivory diamond kitchentops, his 'n' His marble baths, panoramic in-chapel views of heaven and hell courtesy of one of area's leading interior decorators. Located in heart of Earth's most prestigious continent.

OOH LA LA!

A house so great it could spark a revolution. One of rare Louis XIV-style buildings actually built by Louis XIV. Peasant-provokingly extravagant ballrooms, 1,000-horse garage, 82 baths (no toilets). French doors, French windows, French everything. The only thing missing is *vous!*

FIND A NEW PLACE TO DWELL

Come see this perpetually discovered gem in the heart of America's Elastic Belt. Features mid-to-late 20th century furnishings that are unforgettable, unique… breathtaking… striking… colorful… "fun." Plus a toilet so cozy, you may never get up. Previous owner on-site.

LOCATION, LOCATION, LOCATION!

Get away from urban life in this sprawling 700-story walk-up nestled in one of the world's most elite mountain chains. Open-air floor plan features original stonework, breathtaking views. 100 BRs, 0 baths, 40,000 terraces. Close to trails and hiking. Fixer-upper's dream.

GATED COMMUNITY!

Be the last emperor of this formerly forbidden estate. 980 surviving buildings make it ideal for growing family and/or retinue of eunuchs. Asian-influenced design with rustic timber motif. Concubine warehouse easily convertible to playroom, home office. Conveniently located

Scattered throughout North America in rings around major cities you will find the remains of millions of suburban homes. These structures were divided into rooms, smaller sub-areas serving specialized functions.

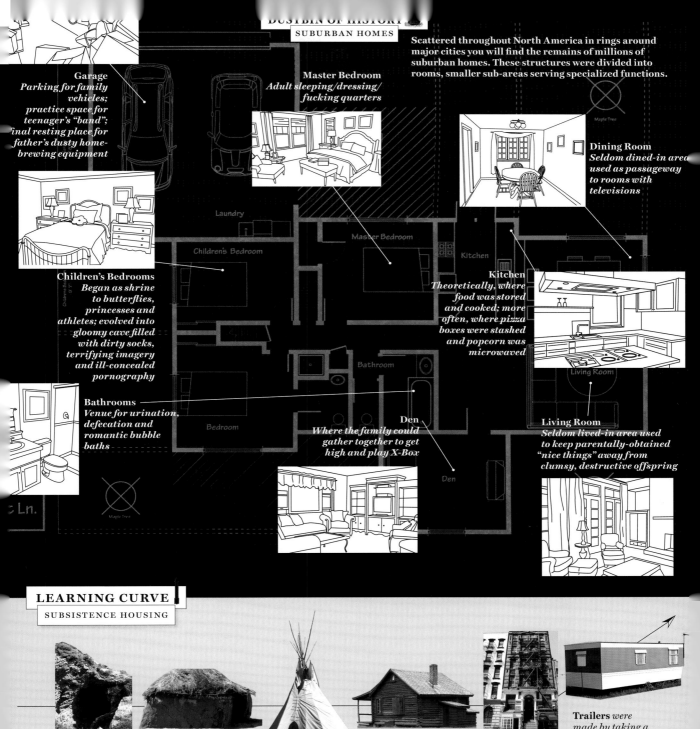

Garage
Parking for family vehicles; practice space for teenager's "band"; final resting place for father's dusty home-brewing equipment

Master Bedroom
Adult sleeping/dressing/fucking quarters

Dining Room
Seldom dined-in area used as passageway to rooms with televisions

Children's Bedrooms
Began as shrine to butterflies, princesses and athletes; evolved into gloomy cave filled with dirty socks, terrifying imagery and ill-concealed pornography

Kitchen
Theoretically, where food was stored and cooked; more often, where pizza boxes were stashed and popcorn was microwaved

Bathrooms
Venue for urination, defecation and romantic bubble baths

Den
Where the family could gather together to get high and play X-Box

Living Room
Seldom lived-in area used to keep parentally-obtained "nice things" away from clumsy, destructive offspring

---

LEARNING CURVE
SUBSISTENCE HOUSING

Early man lived in **caves**, *satisfied sleeping anywhere warm, dry and spelunkable.*

Mud huts *created a cool and comfortable interior environment, provided it never, ever rained.*

Tents' *low costs and portability made them attractive to nomads, campers and hungry bears.*

If you were born in a **log cabin** *and did not grow up to be President of the United States, you were a failure.*

Urban crowding forced the poor to stack themselves vertically, taking squalor 3-D in **tenements***.*

Trailers *were made by taking a rectangular box, adding wheels and a car, then removing the wheels and the car.*

Clothing

CLOTHING—INDIVIDUAL BODILY COVERING made from fabrics, skins, resplendent skeins of polyethylene sequins or other materials—offered protection from cold, sun, insects and genital shame. Garment types varied by climate, culture, gender, which local animal had the most easily removable skin and what was on sale.

JACKET
Put on to signify going to work; removed to signify *really* going to work.

SHIRT
The presence or absence of this was an accurate gauge of how good a time you were having.

NECKTIE
Reduced blood flow to the head, allowing enough oxygen to let wearer focus on pointless façade that was his career.

BELT
Pant-fastener; adjustable for easy gluttony.

UNDERWEAR
The socks of pants. Need to give a speech? Picture us in these.

PANTS
We put these on one leg at a time. You may require a different approach.

SOCKS
Our smelliest garments, barring something very embarassing.

SHOES
Enabled us to walk without crying.

BLOUSE
Once worn by peasant women; later sewn by them in ten-hour shifts.

BRA
Means of physical control (secondary) and social control (primary).

SKIRT
Popularized by "women in the workplace" fad of 1970s.

STOCKINGS
Ideal casing for shapely legs, smooshed faces of bank robbers.

Soldiers *found it easier to wade into a jungle to save a man's life if they were wearing matching outfits.*

Clergymen *like this shaman were supernatural figures imbued with the magical ability to get away with wearing shit like this.*

Uniforms

A **uniform** was a specialized type of clothing that designated its wearer as a member of a particular profession, social group or Catholic school.

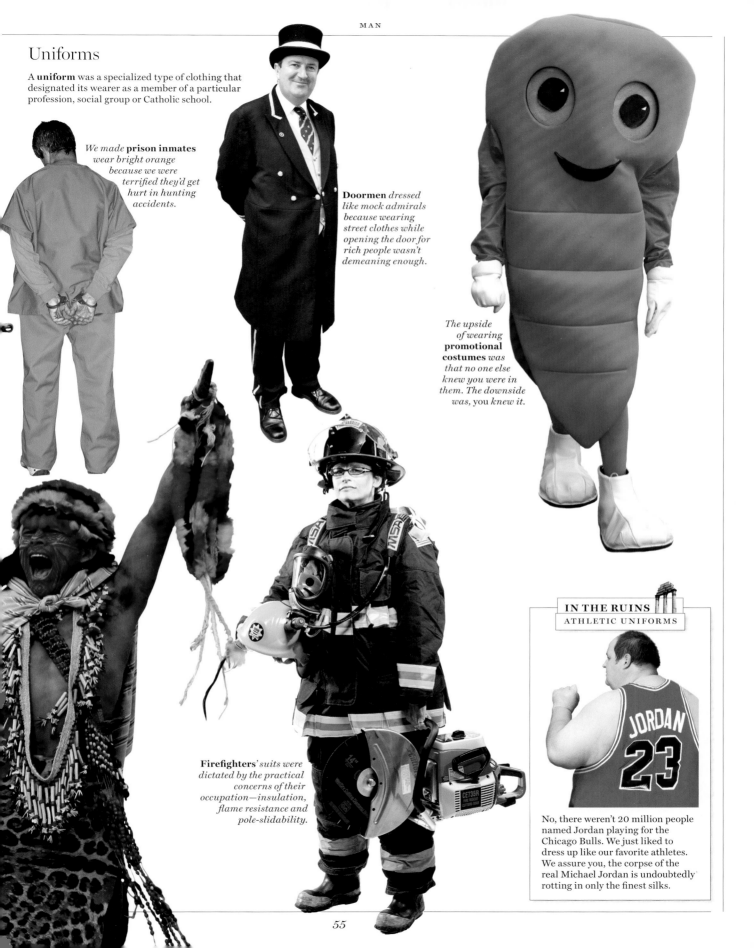

We made **prison inmates** *wear bright orange because we were terrified they'd get hurt in hunting accidents.*

Doormen *dressed like mock admirals because wearing street clothes while opening the door for rich people wasn't demeaning enough.*

The upside of wearing **promotional costumes** *was that no one else knew you were in them. The downside was, you knew it.*

Firefighters' *suits were dictated by the practical concerns of their occupation—insulation, flame resistance and pole-slidability.*

IN THE RUINS
ATHLETIC UNIFORMS

No, there weren't 20 million people named Jordan playing for the Chicago Bulls. We just liked to dress up like our favorite athletes. We assure you, the corpse of the real Michael Jordan is undoubtedly rotting in only the finest silks.

Sleep and Dreams

WE SPENT A third of our lives passed out **unconscious**. It's not something we're proud of. Believe us, if we hadn't needed so much sleep *we'd* be the ones who'd developed intergalactic space travel, and you'd be the ones whose underwear drawers were being rummaged through. But the truth was our bodies required roughly **eight hours** a day of sleep, and we usually only got around five. It was more than a necessary part of our biology; it was a nightly exercise in trusting the universe. Every night we'd lay down on a bed (either alone or with a spotter), close our eyes and surrender ourselves to a void—hoping we'd be waiting for us when we got back.

People only wore **sleep caps** *if they were expecting to be visited by three or more ghosts over the course of the evening.*

Alarm clocks *freed us from circadian rhythms, allowing us to choose the very moment we wanted reality to jerk us awake with its mocking screech.*

Sleep masks *were generally only worn on airplanes and by characters in situation comedies*

Pajamas *were special clothes people had to start wearing when their kids turned three.*

A typical **bed** *consisted of a soft yielding base, a warm protective covering and up to a million microscopic eight-legged arthropods feeding off dead skin cells.*

BY THE NUMBERS
SLEEP

Hours spent sleeping, lifetime	190,000
Hours spent trying to sleep, lifetime	17,000
Hours spent feigning sleep to avoid unpleasant tasks, lifetime	13,000
Hours spent in interim between waking up and realizing it was all a dream, lifetime	4,000
Hours spent realizing it wasn't a dream after all!!!, lifetime	2,000
Winks per nap	40

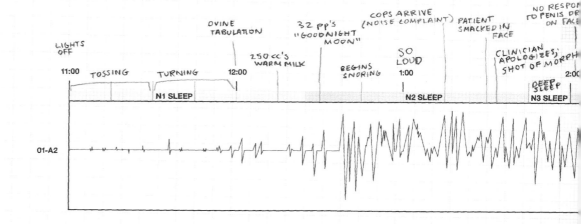

Cedarbrook Laboratory Sleep Study
October 12, 2009
Patient: Eric Turloin, age 53
Supervising Doctor: Dr. John Berger

DVINE TABULATION

COPS ARRIVE (NOISE COMPLAINT)

PATIENT SMACKED IN FACE

NO RESPON TO PENIS DR ON FACE

LIGHTS OFF

32 PP's "GOODNIGHT MOON"

250 CC's WARM MILK

SO LOUD

CLINICIAN APOLOGIZES; SHOT OF MORPH

11:00 TOSSING TURNING 12:00 BEGINS SNORING 1:00 2:00

DEEP SLEEP

N1 SLEEP · N2 SLEEP · N3 SLEEP

01-A2

*The **snore feather** brought light comedy to what was otherwise an intolerable condition.*

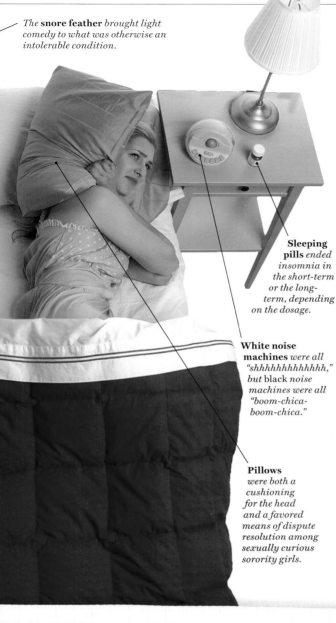

Sleeping pills *ended insomnia in the short-term or the long-term, depending on the dosage.*

White noise machines *were all "shhhhhhhhhhhh," but* black *noise machines were all "boom-chica-boom-chica."*

Pillows *were both a cushioning for the head and a favored means of dispute resolution among sexually curious sorority girls.*

Inspiration

The body rested during sleep, but the brain did not. It amused itself by emitting waves and generating **dreams**— illogical series of images, thoughts and emotions that could be amusing, terrifying or downright sexy. "Dreams" also came to mean a person's highest aspirations in life. Why so many people aspired to be naked in front of large groups of people while running slowly in place is beyond the scope of this book.

Dreams inspired some of our greatest works of art.

Salvador Dali and his "Persistence of Memory" (1931)

James Donn and his "Pussy Magnette" (2004)

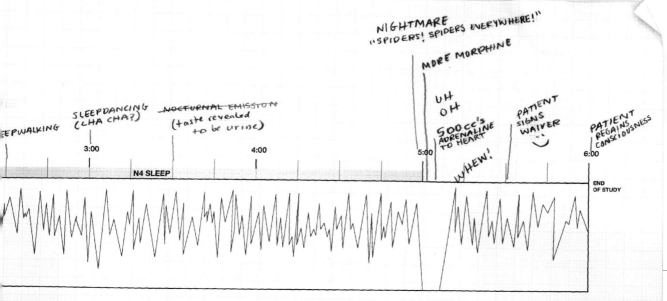

Emotions

Emotions were subjective irrational reactions to internal or external stimuli that were widely discouraged in the workplace. They were often expressed facially.

Joy
"This croissant is even more buttery than I expected!"
"My rival in love has been devoured by wolves!"
"Yahtzee!"

Sadness
"My spouse has died."
"My village has been destroyed."
"My local hockey team has lost in the Conference Finals of the Stanley Cup playoffs."

Anger
"You took my ancestral home!"
"You took my parking space!"
"You correctly revealed a flaw in my argument!"

Amusement
"That monkey is masturbating!"
"That fictional character is unaware of the full context of his situation!"
"Boom! Right in the nuts!"

Fear
"Somebody's out there."
"Dude, I'm serious! Somebody's out there!"
"FOR CHRIST'S SAKE WHO'S OUT THERE?!?"

Jealousy
"Yes, it *is* a beautiful yacht."
"Get me some poison, Iago; this night I'll not expostulate with her."
"You know, I wish that I had Jesse's girl."

Surprise
"That golden retriever can play *basketball*?!?"
"These 50 tons of processed industrial coal slurry are *damaging* the river?!?"
"This is *instant* coffee?!?"

Sympathy
"I'm sorry your yacht sank under mysterious circumstances."
"He was a wonderful ferret."
"Perhaps this $20 check will end the suffering."

Boredom
"Grandpa, you told me that story already."
"What time does this 'Great Pumpkin' of yours generally show up?"
"How many more of these emotion pictures do we have to take?"

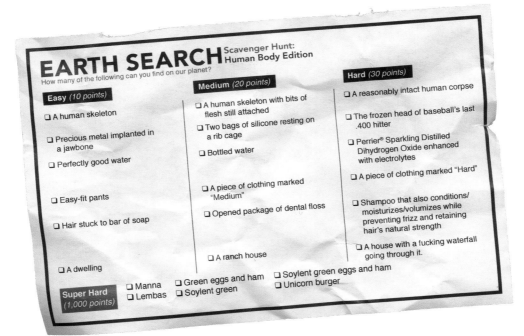

EARTH SEARCH Scavenger Hunt: Human Body Edition

How many of the following can you find on our planet?

Easy *(10 points)*
- ☐ A human skeleton
- ☐ Precious metal implanted in a jawbone
- ☐ Perfectly good water
- ☐ Easy-fit pants
- ☐ Hair stuck to bar of soap
- ☐ A dwelling

Medium *(20 points)*
- ☐ A human skeleton with bits of flesh still attached
- ☐ Two bags of silicone resting on a rib cage
- ☐ Bottled water
- ☐ A piece of clothing marked "Medium"
- ☐ Opened package of dental floss
- ☐ A ranch house

Hard *(30 points)*
- ☐ A reasonably intact human corpse
- ☐ The frozen head of baseball's last .400 hitter
- ☐ Perrier® Sparkling Distilled Dihydrogen Oxide enhanced with electrolytes
- ☐ A piece of clothing marked "Hard"
- ☐ Shampoo that also conditions/moisturizes/volumizes while preventing frizz and retaining hair's natural strength
- ☐ A house with a fucking waterfall going through it.

Super Hard *(1,000 points)*
- ☐ Manna
- ☐ Lembas
- ☐ Green eggs and ham
- ☐ Soylent green
- ☐ Soylent green eggs and ham
- ☐ Unicorn burger

FAQs
(Future Alien Questions)

Q. Was it better to be a man or a woman?
A. A man.

Q. Is it fair to say the brain was the most important organ?
A. In matters of intellect, motor control, sensory perception and the formation of personality, yes. But when it came to the truly important things, the heart held sway.

Q. But didn't the brain also control the heart?
A. Fine. Jeez, whatever happened to romance?

Q. What percentage of you was water?
A. Roughly two-thirds. That's why when you shook us really fast we made a swishy sound. But the water was evenly distributed throughout our bodies. It wasn't like everything below our rib cage was liquid or anything.

Q. Why was the right side of your body more coordinated than the left side?
A. Because that's how God made us. Unfortunately, roughly 10% of us chose an alternate lifestyle. Many of them excelled in the arts, but that didn't make it right.

Q. What was the tallest a person could grow?
A. Robert Wadlow reached a record height of 2.72 meters (8' 11"). He wore size 37 shoes and consumed 8,000 calories a day. It took 500 people seven weeks to make him a pair of pants. He had a pet rhinoceros that he kept in his pocket. When he died, the earth dug up for his grave became Mt. Whitney.

Q. How did you know whether you were asleep or simply unconscious?
A. It depended on whether the objects circling your head were birds or letter Z's.

Q. Were you allowed to walk around without clothes on?
A. Only at nudist colonies, special penal facilities designed to punish out-of-shape nonconformists by making them look at each other naked all the time.

Q. What was the evolutionary reason for pubic hair?
A. Millions of years ago, when man began losing his fur, the genitals decided they wanted to be the new kings of the body. So they kept their hirsute covering, believing the head's rich mane of hair was the reason the body took its orders. Unfortunately the genitals, as they so often are, were wrong. And so we were left with nettled thatches of coily tresses that served little function except minimal insulation and the ability to be shaved into a lightning-bolt pattern.

Q. How did you know when you'd had enough food?
A. A difficult question; the answers ranged from "If you didn't drop dead" to "When you'd won a free T-shirt."

Q. Why were men unable to give birth?
A. Their rear vaginas were infertile.

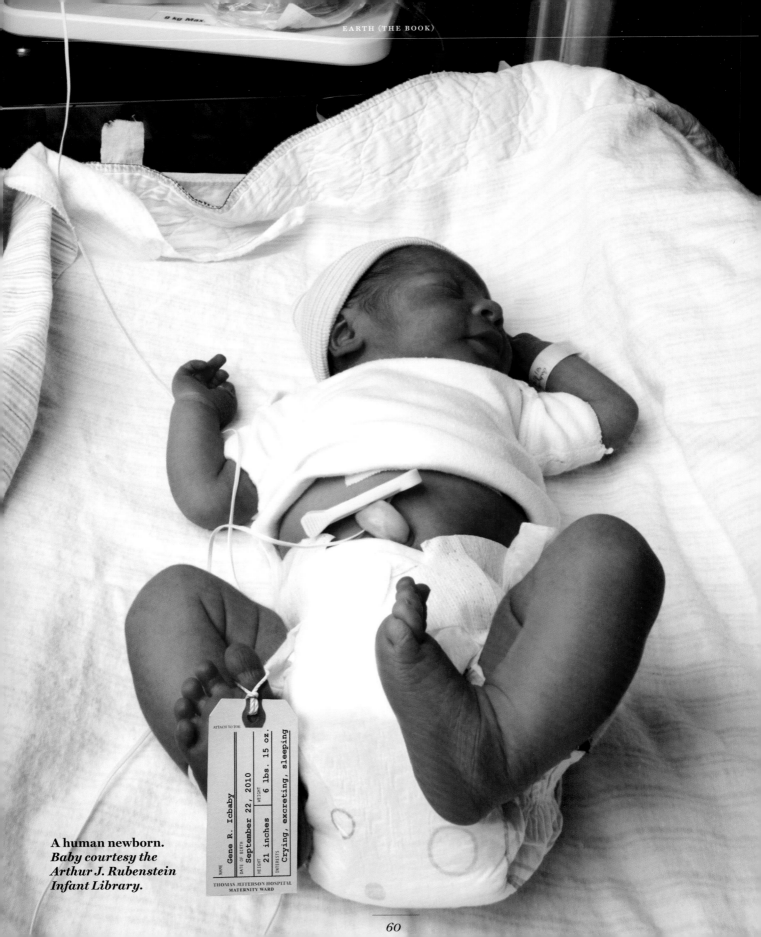

A human newborn.
Baby courtesy the
Arthur J. Rubenstein
Infant Library.

ATTACH TO TOE

NAME | Gene R. Icbaby
DATE OF BIRTH | September 22, 2010
WEIGHT | 6 lbs. 15 oz.
HEIGHT | 21 inches
INTERESTS | Crying, excreting, sleeping

THOMAS JEFFERSON HOSPITAL
MATERNITY WARD

The Life Cycle

IN SOME WAYS, mankind was incredibly diverse. We liked to say that each person was like a snowflake: Unique, precious and sooner or later covered in exhaust and dog urine. Yet all of our lives traced roughly the same arc from beginning to end, and passed through roughly the same milestones. It was a process we called the **life cycle**, because it reminded us of a popular stationary exercise bike that was exhilarating but grueling, and wound up leaving you off exactly where you started.

What was this life cycle? We will answer that question with another one: "What has four legs in the morning, two legs in the afternoon and three in the evening?" At first blush, the answer to that ancient "Riddle of the Sphinx" would seem obvious: A four-legged animal that had two legs amputated following a terrible lunchtime accident, then had one of them reattached just before dinner. But there is also a more figurative answer to the mystery: **man**. For in the morning of our lives, we crawled on all fours, young, small and vulnerable; in the prime of the afternoon, we walked erect, adult, robust and independent; and by the evening, we walked with a cane, old, small and vulnerable once again.

And then at night, we died. No legs. That part was too depressing even for the Sphinx.

The chronology and physical stages of the life cycle took place in the sequence they are presented in this chapter. We did not have the option of starting life as an adolescent, or jumping from middle age back to infancy to grab a quick nap, or aging backwards—the premise of *The Curious Case of Benjamin Button*, a film we urge you to avoid, lest it steal three precious Earth hours from you. But we did have some flexibility in the order with which certain personal and societal **milestones** could occur. For instance, we could give birth

*The human being with the longest confirmed lifespan in history was **Jeanne-Louise** Calment, who died on August 4, **1997**, **at the age** of 122 years, 164 days. Her murder remains unsolved.*

before marriage, or be circumcised after middle age, turns of events which were, respectively, common and really super not at all common, like *ever*.

It was these milestones, shared and celebrated with loved ones and friends, that helped form the chapter breaks in the story of our lives, lending our time on Earth much of its dignity and poignancy, and all of its redeemable gift certificates. (The exception was funerals. *"Hey, sorry about your Dad, please enjoy this $50 iTunes card"* was considered a funeral "don't.")

Which once again brings us to **death**. In truth, pretty much everything brought us to death. The famed philosopher Jim Morrison once observed, "No one here gets out alive," and that was certainly true, although not everybody ended up alone and bloated after OD'ing in a bathtub, either. But dying wouldn't have been that sad or frightening if only we didn't know it was going to happen. But alas, we were, as far as we could tell, the only creatures who were aware of their own mortality. Most animals you could kill right in front of their friends and they would just keep on chewin' their cud, at most idly wondering, a few days later, where Frank was. But we humans knew the horrible truth. That was the price we paid for consciousness, and many would argue that we got ripped off.

So how did we react to this terrible knowledge? Some of us, with paralyzing fear. Others chose to use *this* life to feverishly prepare for the afterlife they hoped would follow. And a few of us reacted by adhering to the phrase *"carpe diem,"* seizing each and every diem with as much urgency and spirit as we could muster. Because paradoxically, it was only by accepting the fleeting nature of our existence that we could fully appreciate how much every moment, just like every person and every snowflake, was unique and precious.

Having said that, if you are immortal, fuck you.

Birth

AROUND 40 WEEKS after that **drunken night at the cabin**, the adult (hopefully) female's **uterus** began contracting. This forced the fetus onto the **cervix**, thinning and dilating it, and rupturing the **amniotic sac**. As the painful contractions increased in frequency and intensity (8 to 14 hours), the 8 pound, 22-inch infant journeyed down the birth canal towards the **vagina**. The baby's head passed under the **pubic bone** and began to stress the **perineum** (the tissue between the vagina and rectum), often tearing it. Through a storm of **screams**, **amniotic fluid**, **mucus** and **blood**, the final pushes introduced the bundle of joy to the outside world. He/she was wailing uncontrollably. And, with that, the easy part was over.

BY THE NUMBERS	
BIRTH	
Babies born in 2010	371,000
Total number of toes on these babies	3,723,457
Average weight	6 lbs. 14 oz.
Average age	0.0
Ratio, duration of labor/ conception	7 hrs./7 mins.
Cost of hospital birth	$8,000
Cost of taxicab birth on way to hospital	$7.50 + tip

With **infant formula**, mankind made its breast-usage priorities clear: Sex first, species-perpetuation second.

"Aren't you a little young for a comb over?"

Bronze baby shoes became even more popular after parents began removing them from their child's feet for the bronzing process.

"Nice teeth. What, were you playing hockey in there?"

The **spinning mobile** was a rare example of infantile entertainment actually aimed at infants.

"Who's got your nose? Who's got your nose? 'Cause seriously, tell me that's not your nose."

"Are those nipples or were you stung by a gay bee?"

Few young musicians had the discipline to pursue the **rattle** into adulthood.

"And this little piggie should have gone to the gym!"

"Hey, thunder thighs! What is she giving you, breast chocolate milk?"

Babies excreted into **diapers** because they were allowed to.

Babies spent most of their time in **prison** until they were considered rehabilitated.

"Looks like you got your Mom's penis!"

It was customary for people encountering newborns for the first time to affectionately "roast" them for their parents' amusement.

Birth Announcements

Notifying the world of the arrival of a new baby was an ancient custom.

"It's a Savior!"
MARY AND JOSEPH
OF NAZARETH WELCOME

JESUS HUDSON CHRIS
DECEMBER 25, 1 BC
5 MINA, 29 SHEKELS
1.23 CUBITS

Genghis and Chaka Khan
are pleased to announce
the birth of their son

Jochi

November 5, 1185

at the Khentii Maternity yurt
May he be a blight
on the world!

Mr. Rajiv Patel, remover of dead animals in the Janaghad district, and his equally polluted wife Rania are required by law to warn civilized people of the shameful arrival, on April 2, of their she-spawn Danesha. In lieu of mistreatment, please ignore her.

是一不受欢迎的！

SOON YUK CHAO AND HIS WIFE
ANNOUNCE THE ABANDONMENT
OF THEIR THIRD BABY GIRL
ON A HILLTOP OUTSIDE WENSHI

AUGUST 4, 1967

THE
Victorian London Textile Mill
WELCOMES ITS NEWEST EMPLOYEE

Reginald Christopher Squallor

6 POUNDS, 5 OUNCES, 4 PENCE A WEEK

JON AND KATE GOSSELIN
ANNOUNCE THE BIRTH OF THEIR NEW REALITY SHOW

JON & KATE Ei8ht
PLUS

MAY 10, 2004
AND EVERY THURSDAY NIGHT AT 9PM (8 CENTRAL)
LENGTH: 23 MIN. 0 SEC.
RATINGS: 3.2 MILLION

— POPE ALEXANDER V
DENIES ALL KNOWLEDGE
OF THE BIRTH OF HIS SO
— CESARE BORGIA —
SEPTEMBER 13, 1475

THE SAGE NOSTRADAMUS ANNOUNCES
375 YEARS HENCE
THE BIRTH OF
JOHN FITZGERALD KENNEDY
ON MAY 29, 1917
CONJOINED PROVINCES

LEARNING CURVE
BIRTH

     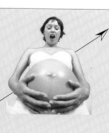

*Used from antiquity, the **birthing chair** offered the woman in labor some relief, especially when used with a **birthing ottoman**.*

Midwives *aided in childbirths since time immemorial. Not pictured/around/ interested:* **Men.**

An alternate means of delivering a child was the **Caesarean section.** *In time they grew safer, if less spellbinding.*

Forceps *were invented in the 17th century. When not being used to mix salads, they saved the lives of millions.*

The development of **painkillers** *removed much of the agony of both delivering children and, when used regularly, raising them.*

By 2010 many women had reverted back to **natural childbirth,** *forsaking technology to deliver the way nature intended: In bowel-shattering agony.*

Family

THE BASIC UNIT OF HUMAN SOCIAL LIFE was the **family**—parents and their children. This arrangement was sometimes called the **nuclear family**, after how ballistic your parents went when they found out you pierced your nipples. It was often said of family that "blood is thicker than water," and no one would help you spill more of it.

1. Fathers

Idealized

Absentee

Generous

Founding

Involved

Emotionally unavailable

Conflicted

Really?!?

2. Mothers

Idealized

Virginal

Wicked Step-

Picture Not Available
Good Step-

Sedentary

Wire hanger-averse

Mr.

Promiscuous

The image on this page is an example of a family portrait, a candid photo memorializing the joyous ritual of putting on sweaters and hanging around places that also sold car batteries.

5.

3. Daughters

Coal miner's   *Lucrative*   *"Role model"*   *Ignored*   *Franchisable*   *Leg-craving*   *Just awful*

4. Sons

Obedient   *Mischievous*   *Doting*   *Lucky*

Resourceful   *Embarrassing*   *Wooden*   *Attention-seeking*

5. Grandfathers

Trusted   *Leather-panted*   *Vampire*   *Clock*

6. Grandmothers

    *Note: These were the only two kinds of grandmothers.*

Rappin'   *Non-rappin'*

7. Pets

Good boy   *Resentful*   *Anachronistic*   *Retro*

Childhood

CHILDHOOD WAS ROUGHLY the period between the end of infancy and the day we were big enough to hold a scythe. It was the child's job to play during this carefree time, to learn through observation, imagination and interaction about the real world around them. It was the job of a loving parent to skillfully distort the reality of that world. This often involved **overt lying** on topics ranging from the physical location of the recently deceased, to the existence of gift-giving fictional characters, to why Mommy's "special juice" made her "all silly."

WE SAID IT

"I am tired."
—*Dac Kien Cho, age 8, Five-Time Employee of the Month*

Our refrigerators were used to slightly forestall the inevitable discarding of childhood ephemera.

The **chore wheel** *was a fun way to introduce children to the yoke of endless drudgery. The one seen here, however, was used by the parents.*

ME   KOKO

Whirlpool

Kids often had **"imaginary friends,"** *a frivolous self-deception that was eventually outgrown and replaced with "non-imaginary loneliness."*

Literacy *was only acquired after years of experimentation.*

WEENUR

FUK

The red "A" indicated the child performed well, but was an **adulteress.**

My Trip To The Zoo

Last weekend my mom took me to the Zoo. It was fun to see all the animals, but then I started to feel bad cause they are all trapped. That must be so boring.

This contemporary mixed-media art installation was **a piece of shit**.

U MOMY

Easily obtained **"recognition"** taught children to devalue accomplishment.

PARTICIPANT

PRINCESS

WIZARD

A workforce proportionally based on children's stated **occupational goals** would have caused the near-instantaneous collapse of civilization.

ASTRONAUT

Beloved Characters

Most of the "people" children admired were **fictional archetypes** representing traits they found comforting. Kids wanted to be around these characters all the time, and backpack-makers, tennis-shoe designers, soap manufacturers, film producers, figurine artisans, balloon impresarios, candy farmers, Band-Aid seamstresses and crapsmiths of every variety were happy to help.

Peter Pan *taught children they could stay young forever by following a charismatic stranger out the window.*

Born Moishe Mouskowitz in Lithuania, **Mickey Mouse** *escaped the Nazis by turning in his own parents.*

As of press time, **G.I. Joe** *was still engaged in his valiant struggle to openly serve in the U.S. military.*

They told **Elmo**, *"No one wants to see a monster get tickled anymore, kid. You'll never make a penny with that act." But Elmo no listen.*

Dora *was a plucky little girl who taught children how to shout instructions at brown people in Spanish.*

The **teddy bear** *(Ursus theodorus) was the only known member of its genus that did not respond to a cuddle with an immediate mauling.*

Boogeymen

Children were very "in touch" with their **primal fears**. As they matured, they learned to bury these fears in their subconscious, where they could do no damage.

1. In children's imaginations, **ghosts** *were the earthbound spirits of evil dead people. In reality, of course, such people were* **burning in hell**.

2. Some children feared the **boogeyman** *hiding in their closet or under their bed. As teenagers, they hoped he would protect the* **pornography** *hiding in those same places.*

3. Luckily, the most common childhood fear, **not being overmedicated**, *was among the easiest to cure.*

4. Deep down, **bullies** *were very insecure. But a lot of comfort that gave to an undersized eight-year-old atomic-wedgied to a flagpole.*

5. African children lived in terror of **The White Witch**, *a shapeshifting banshee who stole them from their parents.*

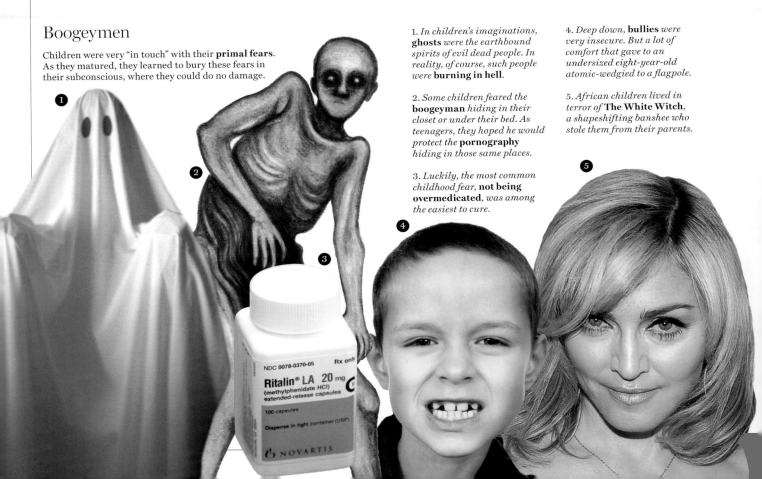

School

In societies where they were not needed as a cheap and nimble labor force, children between the ages of adorable and surly attended **school**. Here, unsuccessful adults known as **teachers** would instruct young people in subjects like reading, history and math, providing them with the critical knowledge they would need to pass tests on those subjects. Beyond their academic function, schools also served as social laboratories where children learned problem-solving and problem-having skills.

"School is cool!"
—*Samuel Beckett (1906–1989), Irish author*

For Monday:
Read two chapters of Tom Sawyer
While watching iCarly

*Teachers' low salaries made them vulnerable to **bribery-by-fruit**.*

Notes passed in class ran the risk of interception and humiliating public recitation by Mr. Itkin, a well-known doodyhead.

Lunchboxes *were a chance for schoolchildren to advertise their cultural preferences.*

School desks could only maintain their structural integrity with the application of thousands of dried pieces of this.

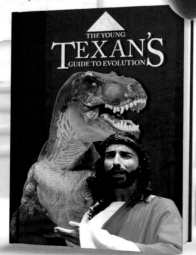

*The best **school textbooks** kept up with the latest developments in science in order to deny them.*

Toilet-trained, able to dress themselves, yet still a few years away from the embittering ravages of puberty, kids saw the world the way we wished we always could: as magical, mysterious and full of places it was okay to be naked. They were the only group of people who excited rather than annoyed us by learning things we already knew.

Corporal punishment *as a means of penalizing bad students was gradually phased out and replaced with **Tufts University**.*

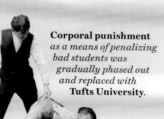

School crossing signs alerted drivers to watch out for bald, footless children with briefcases.

SCHOOL XING

Adolescence

SOMEWHERE BETWEEN the ages of 10 and 13 (depending on how hormone-enhanced their beef was), children entered **adolescence**, a.k.a. "the de-cutening." Our bodies grew taller and hormonal changes introduced secondary sex characteristics. It was a period marked by turbulent **emotions**, excruciating **self-consciousness** and a level of **masturbation** so furiously excessive it tested the human body's resistance to friction-induced combustion.

Teenagers altered their physical appearance to make specific statements of self-expression.

BY THE NUMBERS
ADOLESCENCE

Average number of parents hated *1.8*
Peer pressure per square inch. .*55.4 ppsi*
Average length, "insufferable
   Ayn Rand phase". . . . .*52 days*
Nearly unattainable goal. . . . . .*2400 SAT*
Easily attainable goal. . . . .*0.10% BAC*

"I flout convention by copying the hairstyles of multiplatinum recording artists."

"Only raccoons understand what I'm going through."

"I am a rainbow of insecurity."

"My sexuality blossomed last Thursday at the Venus Body Art Emporium."

"Joy is not allowed past my corneas."

"I am allowed to rebel, but my skin is not."

"I enjoy pushing the limits of not only myself, but my Dad's poker buddies."

"I will continue repeatedly impaling my own face until I am treated with respect."

"I enjoy using gifts my parents got me to ignore them."

"me n my bffs txt in a way our fokes will never no"

"I obtained my new persona at Bucklehaven.com."

"I reject bourgeois societal norms about lung health."

NEW YORK STATE
DRIVER LICENSE
ID: 799 888 359   CLASS D
DIAZ, PENELOPE
28 ORCHARD STREET
GREAT NECK NY 11023
DOB: 07-29-83
SEX F EYES BR HT 5-11
R: NONE
R: B
ISSUED 06-12-06 EXPIRES 07-25-12

"My name is Penelope Diaz, and I am 27 years old."

IN THE RUINS
TOM BARTKOWSKI'S MOM'S BASEMENT

If you're looking to kick back or just chill a little, you should pop by **Tom Bartkowski's Mom's basement** on the corner of Evergreen and Maple. His Mom totally doesn't care if you drink, if she's even home, and if you're reading this book she's definitely not home. Anyway, there's a kegerator and a PS3, and a Bilco door if the cops come, which, again, not gonna happen.

Coming of Age Rituals

Coming of age rituals were elaborate **ceremonies** marking the passage from adolescence to adulthood. Depending on how advanced the culture was, these took the form of either tortuous physical trials or fun parties with cake.

Australian aboriginal teens were sent on **walkabout** *alone into the Outback. They could not return without a steak and bloomin' onion.*

To gain wisdom, adolescents in New Guinea's Baruya tribe spent years **ingesting the semen of their elders**, *whose wisdom was exemplified by their ability to get adolescents to give them free blowjobs.*

At a **quinceañera** *a Latin American girl exchanged her child's flat shoes for heels, symbolizing her entry into the world of tendonitis.*

The **Genpuku** *ceremony marked the moment a Japanese boy became old enough to bring dishonor to his family.*

Over time, the **high school pig-blood dousing ceremony** *evolved into a stylized formal dance.*

At 16, some Amish youth left home for **rumspringa**, *briefly "sowing their wild oats" before returning to spend their lives sowing actual oats.*

SPOTLIGHT
MASTURBATION

Masturbation was the practice of tricking one's genitals into believing themselves popular. For both boys and girls, the adolescent discovery that intense physical gratification was literally an arm's length away marked the end of childhood, and the beginning of an awful lot of masturbating. But the practice was almost universally discouraged by society, especially on the good couch.

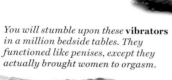

This porcupine and this rock are the only two things male adolescents never tried to **fuck**.

You will stumble upon these **vibrators** *in a million bedside tables. They functioned like penises, except they actually brought women to orgasm.*

Visual evidence *may lead you to conclude teenage boys were plagued by unsightly dry skin and runny noses. They were not.*

Farrah Fawcett says...

DON'T MASTURBATE

An ill-advised poster from a 1978 **anti-masturbation campaign**.

Young Adulthood

YOUNG ADULTHOOD WAS a magical time for us. We were old enough to enjoy the privileges society could provide, but still young enough to skirt its responsibilities. It was a period to indulge wild fantasies with regard to sex, intoxicants and the likelihood of one's punk/emo band The Sad-Eyed Cockmonkeys making it big. We were at the height of our physical powers, and at times felt ourselves immortal, which, as we have made and will continue to make heartbreakingly clear throughout this book, we were not. But it was fun to pretend, and the booze made it easy.

Lifestyle magazines kept young adults in touch with the values of contemporary society. The example below dates from late 17th century Massachusetts.

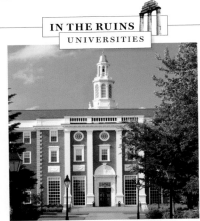

COSMOPURITAN

130 Cotton Mather ... wigless!

Fashion & Plainness
135 **Magenta be the New Scarlet** Our editors bequeath unto this year's most shameful color an "A"

144 **The New Fall Waistcoats: Dare to Be Dour!**

161 **Freckles: The Devil's Kisses** 5 blood-thinning potions to cleanse thy countenance

176 **12 Ways to Somber Up Thy Smock**

182 **7 Gables to Somber Up Thy Dwelling**

Thee, Thee, Thee
196 *Cosmo Quiz: Art Thou a Witch?* Take the underwater quiz

218 **Hath God Preordained Thee for Salvation According to His Plan?** The definitive quiz

234 **Art Thou _Sure_ God Hath Preordained Thee for Salvation According to His Plan?** Best take this one, too

246 **Turnip the Heat!** 15 root vegetables to satiate his nutritive needs

Cover Stories
35 **Goody Proctor** She maketh the struggle against indwelling sin look easy!

52 **Carriage Ride on a Bumpy Road** A goodwife's harrowing tale of accidental pleasure

64 **Thine Conjugal Duties** 8 things to close thine eyes and think of whilst thine husband ruts astride ye

87 **Cosmo's Guide to "Down There"** 25 things you don't know about hell (but should!)

113 **Cosmo Confessions** Our readers share their most wretched and piteous transgressions of thought and deed

Love & Sin
258 **Constancy and Temperance** What a man *really* be seeking in a helpmeet

262 **15 Psalms to Cool His Ardor**

270 **Churning Up the Heat in the Bedroom** Make him cream!

See page 278 for shopping information.

156 Linen caps ... useful!

JUNE / **COSMOPURITAN** 15

*A **futon** was a couch that could be turned into a bed, and then was never turned back into a couch*

*The **birth control pill** liberated young women to focus exclusively on worrying about AIDS.*

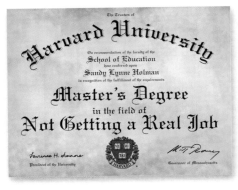
*Years of **postgraduate study** made one an expert in one's chosen field.*

Courtship

Courtship was the process by which one young person tried to demonstrate to another his or her worthiness for long-, short- or don't-even-think-about-staying-over–term **mating**. The basic unit of courtship was the **date**, during which the would-be couple became acquainted and began the assessment process. Two sample first dates, and their outcomes, are graphed below.

Zach, 27

Stephanie, 25

Dorion, 22

Jaelle, 17

Location: *Old Spaghetti Factory, Winnipeg, Canada*

Location: *Jaelle's father's home, Masai village, Kenya*

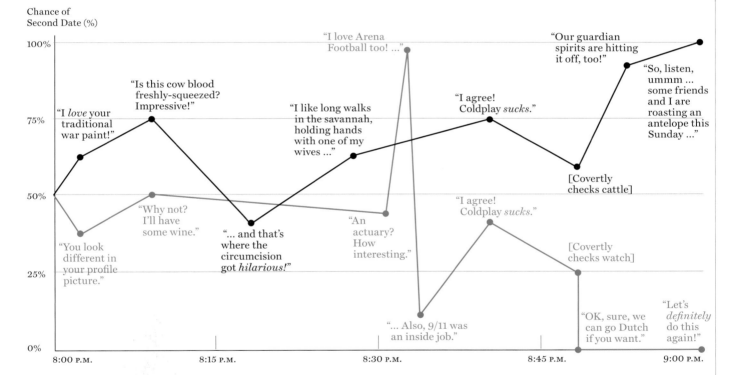

Chance of Second Date (%)

- "I love Arena Football too! …"
- "Our guardian spirits are hitting it off, too!"
- "Is this cow blood freshly-squeezed? Impressive!"
- "So, listen, ummm … some friends and I are roasting an antelope this Sunday …"
- "I love your traditional war paint!"
- "I like long walks in the savannah, holding hands with one of my wives …"
- "I agree! Coldplay *sucks*."
- "Why not? I'll have some wine."
- "An actuary? How interesting."
- "I agree! Coldplay *sucks*."
- "[Covertly checks cattle]"
- "You look different in your profile picture."
- "… and that's where the circumcision got *hilarious!*"
- "… Also, 9/11 was an inside job."
- "[Covertly checks watch]"
- "OK, sure, we can go Dutch if you want."
- "Let's *definitely* do this again!"

100% — 75% — 50% — 25% — 0%

8:00 P.M.   8:15 P.M.   8:30 P.M.   8:45 P.M.   9:00 P.M.

Tokens of Affection

In 1950s America, a high-school student would "**pin**" his "steady." In exchange, she would hand-hold his brains out.

Chocolates fattened up a prospective mate just enough so that no one else would be interested.

In China, the suitor wooed his beloved by offering her two special kinds of **proposal tea**. If she said yes, they got married … and that's when the 肏ing started.

For centuries, suitors in Wales fashioned intricately carved **love spoons** to demonstrate they had both the patience and the dexterity to operate a clitoris.

When all else failed, **vodka** was the Swiss Army knife of human courtship.

Love

OF ALL THE intangible emotions and states of mind experienced by man, **love** is by far the easiest to explain. Love was simply liking another person very very very very very very much. That's it. But you would not believe how much time and effort poets, painters, philosophers, songwriters and (most unfortunately) teenagers expended trying to express this unbelievably basic feeling.

"There is no remedy for love but to love more."
—*Henry David Thoreau (1817–1862), unmarried American hermit*

Pheromones
Secretions; transmitted "fuck me" scent to lover, "sting me" scent to bees

Adrenaline
Stimulant; provided energy for defending girlfriend to family, friends, rabbi, probation officer

Dopamine
Neurotransmitter; banished all sensory input unrelated to lover, i.e. "A wolf is gnawing your leg"

Serotonin *Neural inhibitor; made us check boyfriend's phone for text messages from that girl who looked at his butt at café*

Norepinephrine
Stress hormone; made heart bulge comical distance out of chest accompanied by tom-toms

Testosterone
Hormone; raised male sex drive from ∞ to $(\infty + 1)$

Vasopressin
Sensory enhancer; made girlfriend's hair feel like a velvet pillow on an angel's couch

Oxytocin *Analgesic; numbed awareness that other bus passengers didn't want to watch you two dry-humping*

Estrogen *Hormone; raised female pulse, breath rate, confidence she could "change him"*

The synapses in the brain of a person in love emitted various chemicals, each with a specific function. Seen here, one such synapse.

*Unrequited **love affairs** were responsible for both Dante's* Divine Comedy *and thousands of restraining orders.*

*Many of our greatest works of art were **love stories** about the tragic destructin of two people who would have been sick of each other in two weeks anyway.*

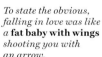

*To state the obvious, falling in love was like a **fat baby with wings** shooting you with an arrow.*

*Released before it was adequately tested, this **aphrodisiac** made its users irresistible, but also blind.*

LOVE POTION N°8

love is...

...a creepy cartoon that made "Mallard Fillmore" look funny.

TM Reg. U.S. Pat. Off. — all rights reserved
© 2009 Tribune Media Services, Inc.

Great Love Stories

Antony and Cleopatra
Known in Roman tabloids as "Antopatra," they were true pioneers: the first celebrity couple, and the founders of the "Nile High Club."

John Smith and Pocahontas
In 1607 explorer John Smith (not his real name) was saved from execution at the hands of a Virginia tribe by the chief's daughter Pocahontas. Their romance set the stage for 400 years of warm relations between whites and Indians.

Edward VIII and Wallis Simpson
He was the King of England. She was a twice-divorced American. But they fell in love over their mutual admiration for the Nazis.

Bonnie and Clyde
Before Bonnie and Clyde, traveling across country killing people and stealing their money was not considered romantic.

John and Yoko
Yoko Ono was one of the most cutting-edge performance artists of the 20th century until she met John Lennon. Their relationship was responsible for the breakup of Fluxus, her world-renowned conceptual art collective. Fluxus fans never forgave him.

*No one came closer to capturing the essence of love than the Romantic poets. One of them, **Lord Byron** (1788–1824), wrote this immortal ode as a 15-year-old.*

She walks in beauty, like the night
Of cloudless climes and starry skies.
Her eyes are like two pools of light.
I really do doth like her eyes.
Her smile canst fill the study hall
And maketh homeroom fairy land;
And pleased I was, to learn this fall
She'd sit two seats from me in band.
Alas, the cheers she leads are for
The captain of the cricket team,
Who really is a total jerk,
Which doesn't rhyme but
I don't don't care.
He

WE SAID IT

"Love is …"

A battlefield • A state of grace • A long road • A building on fire • A banquet on which we feed • A river • A razor • A hunger • A flower • Kisses in a bean bag chair • Like a big brass band • In control • Not enough • Alive • Dead • The seventh wave • Here to stay • On its way • The drug • The answer • The end • The tender trap • Wicked • Forever • Funny that way • Noise • Pain • War • Murder • Hell • Stronger than pride • Just a four-letter word • A golden ring • A simple thing • A wonderful thing • A hurtin' thing • A many-splendored thing • A crazy little thing • A thing with curious power • All around • In the air • Bleu • Thicker than water • Blind • Blindness • Strange • Strong • Hard • So complicated • Easy ('Cause you're beautiful) • A bitch • What you make it • What you want it to be • Only love • Love"

Not a game • Just a game • A losing game • A game of give and take • More than just a game for two • Like oxygen • Like an itching in my heart • Like a butterfly • All you need • All we need • Enough

— Pat Benatar, Britney Spears, Tom Petty, Talking Heads, Patti Smith, Bette Midler, Jonathan Richman, Backstreet Boys, Glen Campbell, Larry Gatlin, Amy Winehouse, Diana Ross, Nat "King" Cole, ELO, The Supremes, Dolly Parton, Joni Mitchell, Donna Summer, The Beatles, Mary J. Blige, Kisha, Nine Inch Nails, Gary Wright, Kerli, Sting, George Gershwin, The Jonas Brothers, Roxy Music, England Dan, Keane, Frank Sinatra, Brick & Lace, Billy Ocean, Wynonna Judd, The Verve, Joan Jett and the Blackhawks, The Scorpions, Drop Dead Gorgeous, Ryan Adams, Sade, Joan Baez, Frankie Laine, Eartha Kitt, Michael Bolton, Lou Rawls, The Four Aces, Queen, Huey Lewis & The News, The Troggs, John Paul Young, Paul Mauriat, Andy Gibb, Alicia Keys, U2, Mickey & Silvia, The Rolling Stones, James Morrison, Anthony Hamilton, Minnie Riperton, Quiet Riot, The Grass Roots, Alannah Myles, Barbra Streisand, Culture Club

Marriage

MARRIAGE WAS THE SACRED INSTITUTION on which our society was based and had to be protected from gay people. You see, sometimes when a man and a woman's father loved the mutual economic and social benefits a partnership of sorts could provide very much, the woman's father drew up a contract for **betrothal** involving his daughter and some cattle. Later on, women gained the right to make their own decisions about who they would marry. This is when men began **shaving**.

A man proposed marriage by presenting his intended with a **ring**. If she accepted it, she became a) complicit in the exploitation of impoverished African diamond miners, and b) his wife.

BETROTHAL CONTRACT

WITNESSED THIS 45TH DAY OF THE 13TH YEAR AFTER THE ECLIPSE HERALDING THE YEAR OF PESTILENCE:

A BETROTHAL AGREEMENT BETWEEN ANJIT THE FARMER, HEREINAFTER DESIGNATED AS **RECIPIENT**, AND BAO THE IRONWRIGHT, HEREINAFTER DESIGNATED AS **OWNER**, IN REGARDS TO **OWNER'S** FIRSTBORN FEMALE CHILD, HEREINAFTER DESIGNATED **PROPERTY**.

OWNER, HAVING WARRANTED THAT **PROPERTY** IS (A) BETROTHED TO NO OTHER, AND (B) FREE OF DEFORMITY, ILLNESS, AND EVIL SPIRITS, GIVES **PROPERTY** TO **RECIPIENT** AS WIFE, HELPMEET, CHATTEL, AND BEARER OF STRONG SONS.

IN CONSIDERATION OF **RECIPIENT'S** GENEROSITY IN TAKING ON THIS WORTHLESS GIRLCHILD, **OWNER** SHALL PAY **RECIPIENT** A DOWRY OF FOUR MILK GOATS, A LAYING GOOSE, A FIGURINE OF THE HEARTH GODDESS OSHVUG, AND A POUCH OF SHINY METAL FROM THE STREAM.

SHOULD **PROPERTY** FAIL TO BEGET A MAN-CHILD WITHIN ONE YEAR, **RECIPIENT** MAY BEAT HER WITH BIRCH RODS TO CORRECT HER WOMB'S WICKED LAZINESS.

SHOULD THE FAILURE NOT BE REMEDIED WITHIN THREE YEARS, **RECIPIENT** SHALL CHASE HER FROM THE HOME INTO THE WOODS AFTER SUNSET ON A COLD NIGHT WHEN THE WOLVES ARE HUNGRY, THEREBY RESTORING FAMILY HONOR.

TRANSFER OF **PROPERTY** SHALL BE EFFECTED 10 YEARS AFTER SIGNING, WHEN **PROPERTY** ATTAINS THE AGE OF 12.

KANTHAR

Bachelor parties were carefully planned to make the single life seem so twisted and depraved the groom would be glad to leave it.

RUSSIA'S BEST BRIDES

Russia's fertile soil yielded such a rich harvest of **wives**, it was known as "the bridebasket of the world."

The Wedding

In many parts of the world, engaged couples began their new life by spending a year arguing over a day. That day was the **wedding**.

1 *Wedding **invitations** required guests to speculate as to whether, on a given night three months later, they would prefer chicken or fish.*

2 *A bride had to pick just the right **dress**; otherwise, everyone at the wedding would come up to her and say, "Yikes, you look awful today."*

3 *Marriages were typically **sanctified** in the eyes of God. It was customary to tip the representative God sent a few hundred bucks.*

4 *At some weddings the bride and groom recited their own additional **vows** … just to dig themselves in that much deeper.*

5 *After the ceremony, the new couple would share their **first dance**. They were encircled by friends and family carrying rocks, ready to stone them to death in the event of a misstep.*

6 *By tradition, whoever caught this **bouquet** would be the next woman to spend all night at home alone weeping into her Chunky Monkey.*

7 8 *When the ceremony was over the newlyweds drove off in a **festive car** to the airport, then flew off in a **festive plane** to their honeymoon.*

Popular Wedding Cake Toppers

"The Classic"   "The Shondah"   "The Arranged Marriage"   "The Rich Gay Guy"   "The How Could I Say No?"

Parenthood

FOR MOST OF man's existence, religious imperatives, agrarian workloads and a total lack of reproductive knowledge led many couples to have very large families. However, advances in contraception and industrialized food production allowed modern couples to have fewer offspring, while leaving the total *weight* of families constant.

"Say it! Say a darnedest thing, you little goddamn son of a bitch!!!"
—*Art Linkletter (1912–2010), American letterlinker*

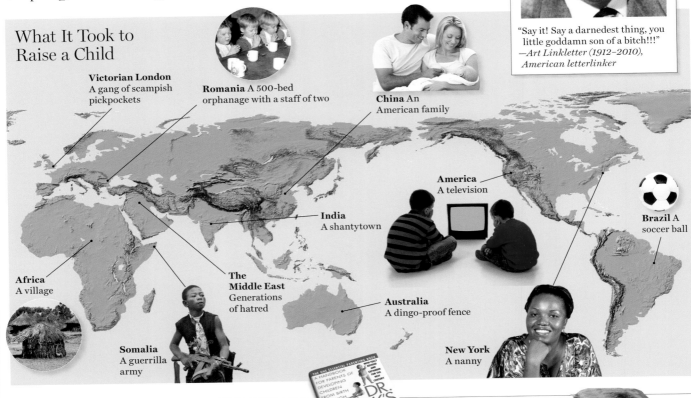

What It Took to Raise a Child

Victorian London A gang of scampish pickpockets

Romania A 500-bed orphanage with a staff of two

China An American family

America A television

Brazil A soccer ball

India A shantytown

Africa A village

The Middle East Generations of hatred

Australia A dingo-proof fence

New York A nanny

Somalia A guerrilla army

---

*Wise **parents** were careful to follow the old maxim: Keep your friends close ... but your enemies closer.*

*No other animal wrote such insightful **manuals** about how to raise their young as Homo sapiens.*

DR. SPOCK'S BABY AND CHILD CARE
BENJAMIN SPOCK, M.D., AND STEPHEN J. PARKER, M.D.

*Once they became mothers, heretofore respectable women thought nothing of having their **breasts** sucked in public.*

Cheerios WHOLE GRAIN

*Frugal parents could buy food in **family-sized boxes** that, once emptied, provided housing for themselves and their children.*

World's Greatest DAD

*This one and only **World's Greatest Dad mug** was awarded to Jackson Frye of Austin, Texas, in 1972 for Excellence in the Field of Fatherhood.*

Middle Age

MIDDLE AGE IS the first phase of life marked by decline and recognition of one's mortality. Physical vitality, muscle mass and intellectual acuity all begin their **inexorable downward slide** during this period. On the plus side, you could now afford jet skis. Though middle age was seen as the period of time between forty and sixty years of age, this varied greatly due to changing life expectancies. For instance, victims of midlife crises during the Dark Ages would comfort themselves with the thought that "twenty is the new sixteen."

*The human **scalp** was the site of a fierce battle between Time and us. In the end thousands of soldiers either turned coat or deserted.*

*Some middle-aged men wore **ponytails** to prevent the early onset of dignity.*

*Men of a certain age were eager to show the world not all of their **hairlines** were receding.*

*At a certain age, sending **birthday cards** became an act less of congratulation than of passive-aggression.*

*At some time in our forties we heard for the first time about an acquaintance our exact age who dropped dead on a **treadmill**. No warnings. Nothing.*

*The approach of mortality brought with it a need to wear all the **colors** one had overlooked as a young man.*

*Youthful **tattoos** reminded us of a simpler, happier time before we had defaced our bodies with tattoos.*

*Half of all marriages ended in **divorce**. The most common reasons were infidelity, money woes and the desire to follow Jimmy Buffett on tour.*

*Developed by beauticians and subatomic physicists, **anti-aging cream** used emollients and Higgs boson particles to reverse the flow of time on a woman's face.*

Pacemakers *helped regulate the heartbeat. They came with several built-in presets, including* **waltz, rhumba** *and* **bossa nova**.

Decreased metabolism manifested itself in the form of **love handles, spare tires, saddle bags, walrus knees, beluga back** *and* **manateats**.

Many men in their 40s and 50s experienced a midlife crisis—also known in China as a "midlife opportunity."

*For many women, **co-hosting** The View was a crucial step in coping with menopause.*

Old Age

THE FINAL STAGE OF LIFE, **old age** was in many ways a mirror image of childhood. Life's hard labors complete, the elderly returned to a time of less responsibility, where, as with children, little was expected, and people once again spoke to you in an incredibly condescending tone. On the other hand, the elderly could get away with all manner of shit, up to and including **promiscuity**, **racist blather** and the **inappropriate hugging of Jamaican nurses**. Early man revered the elderly and they occupied a space of honor in the community. In modern times we kept them away from us in condo developments, because it made us sad to think about dying.

WE SAID IT

"On second thought, I am glad to have survived as long as I have."
—*Pete Townshend (1945–), British relic*

The Face of Aging

Each **wrinkle** on the face of an old person—such as this Peruvian matriarch—reflected a particular event in her life.

BY THE NUMBERS
OLD AGE

Average nightly dinner time . . . .*4:43 P.M.*
Average desired ambient temperature *87.2°F*
Average hardness (on Mohs' scale),
 displayed candy . . . .*7.7 (=Tungsten)*
Average ratio, actual visits from
 grandchildren to desired visits *0.0031*
Average blinker time on car
 prior to turn . . . .*2 min. 17 sec.*

Failure of maize crop (1997–2005, 2007–2009)

Exclusion from 1975 National Geographic article, "Peru's Resurgence"

Failure of maize crop (1991)

Inclusion in 1996 National Geographic article, "Peru: Shame of a Continent"

Failure of maize crop (1978)

"Crow's feet" (remnant of actual crow attack)

So-called laugh lines; in this case, origin unknown

Slow, sad gentrification of Machu Picchu

Most recent wrinkle; caused by disbelief over number of wrinkles

Loss of beloved llama "Señor Shaggypaws"

Bingo!

Here's a neat way to have fun while exploring the crumbling shells of our **retirement homes**. When you find one of the items listed below, place a chip in the appropriate square on the card. When you have five in a row, leap up, scream "Bingo!" and feel supremely fulfilled.

*China's **reverence for the elderly** was visible in all facets of society. At right, the cover of a popular magazine for Chinese teenagers.*

*This **magic staff** had the power, when waved with the right incantation, to banish whippersnappers from one's lawn.*

*The **walker** was for support. The tennis balls were for style.*

*Fully 85% of what the elderly ingested was meant to assist them in the **excretion** of the other 15%.*

*The **Life Alert** beeped a warning whenever the wearer was within 50 feet of a schvartze.*

Dentures *were popular bedside ornaments used mainly to terrify grandchildren.*

*Upon turning 70, everyone received a mysterious letter informing them where they could go to purchase **high-waisted pants**.*

*Riding around on a **scooter**—an idea so appealing when we were young—lost some of its luster when its top speed was eight miles per hour and death was chasing you at twelve.*

*The **artificial hip** fulfilled man's age-old dream of hula-hooping past 90.*

Archetypal Depictions of the Elderly

We permitted our old people to fill any number of roles in our society. Here are all nine of them.

| Evil | Scary | Grumpy | Comically horny | Comically helpless | Comically wedded to Catherine Zeta-Jones | Kindly | Wise | God |

Death

DEATH, IT WAS OFTEN OBSERVED, was just another part of life. Usually this observation was made right after someone died, and mostly because we didn't know what else to say and didn't want to be rude. While the rites associated with death were ostensibly performed for the benefit of the dead, in reality they served to provide the survivors with the comfort, guidance and tranquility needed to complete their own journey to the unfortunate day when their rib cage became gopher housing.

"So glad you could drop in, 'kill'-seekers! Don't worry about me, it only 'hearse' when I laugh!"
—*The Crypt Keeper (1989–), American cryptkeeper*

*The **Grim Reaper** embodied our innate dread of obsolete farm equipment.*

*Our final resting places are commemorated with **headstones.** The larger and costlier ones memorialize people whose children loved them more.*

*Symbols denoting the deceased's religion **were a convenience** aimed at making it easier for the angels to pick teams at Armageddon.*

"Rest in peace," or "requiescat in pace" for the fancy dead.

*Many headstones are inscribed with a four-digit subtraction problem **designed to teach mourners the concept of negative numbers.***

† R.I.P. †

THOMAS PEMBROKE

1921 – 2010

*A bucket list **was a wish list of things to do before one's imminent death. This example dates from 1st century Rome.***

Caligula's Bucket List

☑ Dissolve Senate
☑ Fuck Sister
☑ Declare myself God
☑ Appoint Horse consul
☑ Sodomize Army
☑ Throw babies to lions
☐ Find the joy in my life!!!

*A will **was a way of assuring one's legacy of family divisiveness extended beyond the grave.***

Last Will
«« and »»
Testament
«« of »»

Mourning

When a person died his family, friends and a sallow-cheeked formaldehyde-scented man they just met organized a **funeral**. This ceremony was a chance for the living to say goodbye, albeit a few days too late. With his body looking on, the departed would be eulogized, his good points emphasized, his bad points glossed over, his soul's current whereabouts confidently asserted. This provided the bereaved with **closure**, and the unbereaved with credit for showing up.

Since 1923, the frozen body of Soviet leader **Lenin** *inspired his countrymen to fight for Russia, if only to keep him from rising up and eating their brains.*

Black *was the color of mourning ... and slimming!*

Cremation *was a popular alternative to burial. The ashes would be placed in an urn on a mantel just in time for a visit from a clumsy prospective son-in-law.*

Obituaries

The recently deceased were memorialized in the **obituary** section of newspapers. The example below comes from extreme northern Canada.

Notes for Dad's Eulogy
- Thanks for coming, deep in grief, etc.
- Special man
- Tragic death on merry-go-round
- Great father to ~~8~~ 6 kids

Good Qualities:
- Handy around the House when present
- Awesome 6th husband
- ~~Always supported me and my brother~~
- Sometimes didn't hinder
- War Hero → How he wanted to be one
- Loved Wizard of Id
  - Molestation?

Happy Memories:
- Florida vacation (Day 2, Day 8)
- Christmas → bike → 1982
- Mistrial

Funny Dad Stories
- Time he saw John Elway at airport
- Alley incident - (vomit/Karen/pistol) Punchline: "Dad, she's your sister!"

Closing Metaphor: Putting bird out of misery

THE NUNAVUT NEWS

All the News That's Nunavut!   June 10, 2010

OBITUARIES

AGLUKKAQ, PETER, 65,

Dogsled mechanic, died peacefully yesterday at his igloo in Upper Kiqqivarsik Heights, surrounded by loved ones and qikkiqkkitiklik (tightly compacted, deep, dry snow). Services will be held next sunset in three months.

ALLAKARILLAK, MARY, 69,

Beloved wife, mother and fermenter of walrus oil, died peacefully yesterday at her igloo in Nukapiaqhampton, surrounded by loved ones and kiqqikiqqitik (loosely granulated, shallow, moist snow). In lieu of flowers, please send descriptions of what flowers look like.

ILUULIAQ, VINCENT ("Vinny Two Tusks"), 43,

A legitimate blubberman, was found speared execution-style, his body buried in five feet of immuyakitik (densely powdered snow dotted with tiny ice pellets)

NANOOK, 13,

A sled dog, died Sunday. He is survived, and will be survived on, by his nine team mates.

O'SULLIVAN, PAM, 31,

Visiting ethnolinguist, died of pneumonia on Wednesday. She graduated from UCLA in 2001, received her Master's Degree from Arizona State in 2004, earned her Ph.D. from the University of Southern California in 2009, and arrived here Tuesday without a parka.

QALILIAK, THOMAS, 81,

Senior manager of Harpoons 'R' Us, died on Saturday of complications resulting from eating kayokqitik (white densely powdered polar bear feces that looks like snow). He will be remembered by all who knew him as someone who never complained about how cold it was, even though it was very cold.

TI'QALITT, CIKUK, 72,

Village matriarch, died Sunday at her igloo in Iqaluit Groves. With her died Ikaluk, c. 500, an ancient dialect of the Inuinnaqtun language. It is survived by English.

TUKKUTTOOK, NAKASUK, 63,

Beloved grandfather and scrimshaw wholesaler, drowned at what was formerly his home Tuesday after a lengthy battle with global warming.

UVLUGIAQ, SURA, 84,

Mother of three, grandmother of 11, and great-grandmother of 13, was pushed out to sea on an ice floe after outliving her usefulness.

So ... want to see a dead body? Your best bet is locating a **morgue**, a facility where we kept human corpses awaiting identification, autopsy or reanimation by a brilliant but misunderstood scientist. Depending on when you got here it just might be possible to find some of us still in these cabinets, and in reasonably intact condition. Have at us. Just don't be surprised if you come across many members of the Doe family. They died a lot.

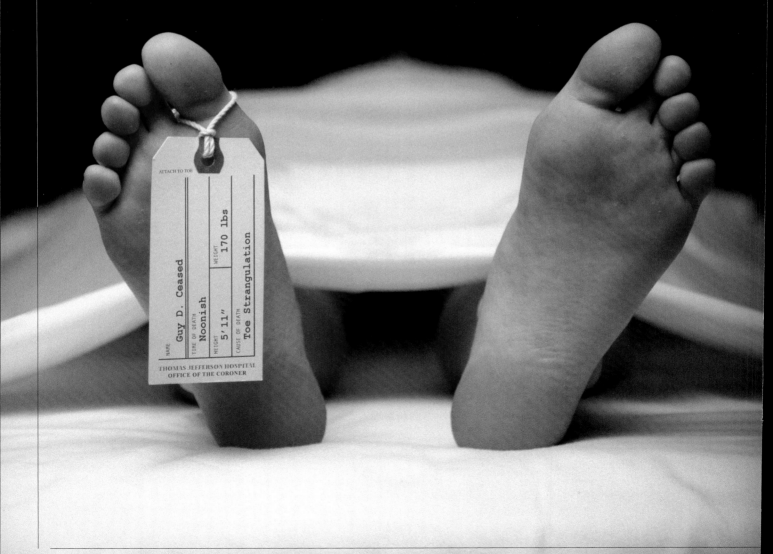

NAME: Guy D. Ceased
TIME OF DEATH: Noonish
HEIGHT: 5'11" WEIGHT: 170 lbs
CAUSE OF DEATH: Toe Strangulation

THOMAS JEFFERSON HOSPITAL
OFFICE OF THE CORONER

ATTACH TO TOE

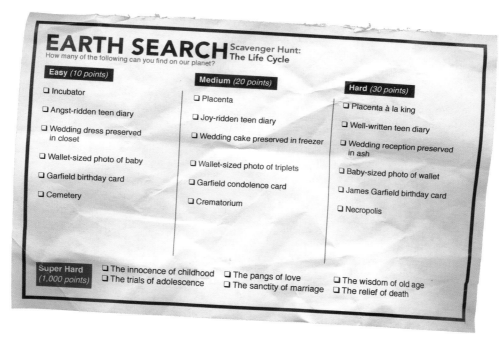

EARTH SEARCH Scavenger Hunt:
The Life Cycle

How many of the following can you find on our planet?

Easy (10 points)
- ☐ Incubator
- ☐ Angst-ridden teen diary
- ☐ Wedding dress preserved in closet
- ☐ Wallet-sized photo of baby
- ☐ Garfield birthday card
- ☐ Cemetery

Medium (20 points)
- ☐ Placenta
- ☐ Joy-ridden teen diary
- ☐ Wedding cake preserved in freezer
- ☐ Wallet-sized photo of triplets
- ☐ Garfield condolence card
- ☐ Crematorium

Hard (30 points)
- ☐ Placenta à la king
- ☐ Well-written teen diary
- ☐ Wedding reception preserved in ash
- ☐ Baby-sized photo of wallet
- ☐ James Garfield birthday card
- ☐ Necropolis

Super Hard (1,000 points)
- ☐ The innocence of childhood
- ☐ The trials of adolescence
- ☐ The pangs of love
- ☐ The sanctity of marriage
- ☐ The wisdom of old age
- ☐ The relief of death

FAQs
(Future Alien Questions)

Q. What was the happiest period in a human's life?
A. Either the one immediately preceding the period one was currently in, or the one immediately following it.

Q. What did humans remember from the period between conception and birth?
A. We retained no long-term memory of anything that occurred to us between conception and roughly the age of two. Most of us therefore simply assumed it was a time of unceasing abuse.

Q. When did you start becoming sexually active?
A. Biologically, reproduction was possible from puberty. But legally we were supposed to refrain from sex until reaching **the age of consent**. This could vary anywhere from "Oh my god, that's disgusting!" to "Really? You waited that long?" In many countries the standard was 18. The six months following were

a probationary period in which the "Barely Legal" adolescent was thoroughly photographed and scrutinized by a panel of masturbating experts.

Q. Could both men and women be homosexuals?
A. Yes, but not with each other.

Q. What were the most common ways of proposing marriage?
A. A man would most commonly declare his intentions by presenting his beloved with a diamond ring on a large television during a packed sporting event. In the rare cases when a woman asked the man to marry, she often did it by urinating on a stick and showing him the results.

Q. In a population of billions, how did you decide whom to marry?
A. Most of us believed we had one perfect soulmate somewhere on earth. Luckily for us, that person usually lived not too far away, spoke the same language, was of an equivalent level of physical attractiveness, and shared our love of mountain biking.

Q. Parenthood seems like a lot of work.
A. It sure was—but for all the hassle and worry, once in a while came a moment of pure innocence that touched your heart and tickled your funny bone. But don't take our word for it!

 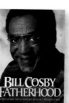 

Together these three works compile several millennia's worth of parenting wisdom that's as timeless as it is hilarious!

Q. How did humans cope with the finality of death—the knowledge that one day, they and all their accumulated knowledge and experiences would be lost from the earth?
A. We tried not to think about it.

Q. Seriously, though—that must've been hard not to think about. One day, you're there, and the next—pffft! You're gone.
A. Can we talk about something else?

Q. But given that knowledge, how did you justify wasting your time on unimportant things when every minute brought you that much closer to—
A. Hey, look! Another chapter!

When we worked together, there was no obstacle we couldn't conquer.

Society

"NO MAN IS an island," wrote the English poet John Donne. "Hell is other people," wrote the French philosopher Jean-Paul Sartre. Most of human history was an attempt to reconcile these two seemingly irreconcilable truths.

Technically speaking, a human being could survive on his own. He could hunt for food, construct shelter and if not reproduce, at least create a reasonable facsimile of a mate using twigs, branches and two coconuts. But we were social creatures who functioned best living in close proximity to one another, and living in groups vastly improved both our safety and our gossip. So we banded together into communities governed by shared sets of morals and values. Such a group was referred to as a **society**. It was the central organizing unit of our civilization, and the catch-all scapegoat for any part of your life that didn't work out the way you thought it would.

A society was simultaneously one unified mass *and* a large collection of individuals. Therein lay the tension; for to be part of a group was to exchange certain individual freedoms for certain other collective benefits. These benefits derived largely from economies of scale. A city of five million people is far better equipped to construct, say, a working mass-transit system than an individual family of four. It just is. But in exchange for the mass-transit system, each member of society was expected to adhere to rules regarding its use, i.e. not masturbating on it. Such harsh, at times maddeningly frustrating trade-offs were the basis of the **social contract**, a document that differed from other contracts only in that you had no choice but to enter into it, and it didn't exist.

The social contract provided a framework in which human interaction could occur on a reasonably fair basis. For example, let's say Person A owned a slave that Person B wanted. Were they not inhabitants of a civil society governed by law, Person B could have simply stolen Person A's slave through brute force. Such an existence would have been cruel and terrifying for all parties involved—Person A *and*

The United Nations united all the citizens of our planet together in derisive laughter.

Person B. But for members of a society, violence was forbidden. Person B was allowed to purchase the slave, but if he stole him he was guilty of a crime, and had to repay Person A the dollar value of the human being he had stolen. This was how a civilized society operated.

This is not to imply that the social contract was fixed and unchangeable. There were thousands of different contracts. Some put power in the hands of one man; others, in the hands of thousands of men. (It was usually men, though. That part rarely changed.) Each contract itself was subject to constant change and revision; a society that failed to periodically amend outdated provisions regarding how to dress or how much to subjugate women and minorities could find itself the laughing-stock of diplomatic functions. Unless it happened to be strategically situated atop vast reserves of natural resources.

The social contract could be administered in a variety of ways, including **law**, **custom** and **etiquette**. Violators of the code could receive anything from a dirty look from a maître d' to death by lethal injection. (The mark of a good maître d' was that he could make the two seem equivalent.) On the other hand, those who went out of their way to serve society would often receive a certificate of commendation.

But reinforcement, both positive and negative, was not the only way society enforced its social contract. Which brings us to **war**. War was the ultimate contract enforcer, a way of determining by purely physical means which party was morally correct. Untold hundreds of millions of us died in wartime, approximately half as heroic martyrs and half as dishonorable villains. But they did not die in vain. Through war we arrived at definitive answers to questions at the very heart of our existence, from "Which is the one true religion?" to "Which European power gets to kill the Zulus?" (Answers: Pantheism, Judaism, Roman Paganism, Christianity, Islam, Christianity again, Catholicism, Nazism, then finally Democracy; and the Dutch.)

We begin our examination of society with a look at its most primitive, and thus worst, incarnation.

Nomadic Tribes

IN TERMS OF SOCIAL organization, **tribes** were one step up from a single family—a large group of people living together bound by related bloodlines or a shared appreciation of the music of Jerry Garcia. Many tribes were **nomadic**, meaning they had no fixed physical address and traveled constantly, racking up record numbers of Frequent Walker Miles. These movements were usually in response to changing seasons, their prey's migratory patterns or the orders of the federal government.

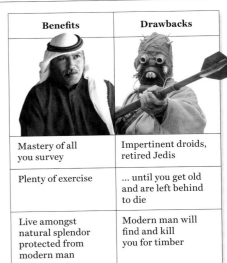

Benefits	Drawbacks
Mastery of all you survey	Impertinent droids, retired Jedis
Plenty of exercise	... until you get old and are left behind to die
Live amongst natural splendor protected from modern man	Modern man will find and kill you for timber

Notable Resident: Chief
Often identifiable by his elaborate head-dress. His responsibilities included planning war parties, signing easily broken treaties and resisting but eventually accepting the white hero of the movie into tribe.

Notable Resident: Gatherer
Main responsibility was collecting wild plants for sustenance. In spare time reared children, wove blankets and baskets, maintained cooking fires, did basically everything except hunting and relaxing.

Typical Domicile: Tent
These dirt-floored havens were as comfortable as they were permanent.

Notable Resident: Hunter
The better he was at putting his spear into things, the more things he got to put his spear into, if you know what we mean.

Transport: The Horse
Known for its prowess as a transport animal and it's "generosity" as a lover on cold Mongolian nights.

Notable Resident: PBS Documentary Crew
Not technically members of the tribe. Just pretend they're not here.

Transport: The Camel
Ideal for desert crossings due to their ability to store water (straw sold separately).

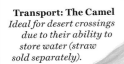

Villages

WITH THE ADVENT of agriculture, nomadic tribes learned the value of sleeping in, and established permanent **villages** for this purpose. The earliest villages were simple collections of huts whose proximity to one another provided safety from predators and the reliable transmission of tribal oral histories, also known as **gossip**. Later, villages grew large enough to accommodate new enterprises such as churches, schools and alcohol-consumption facilities, which often became the center of village life due to the fact that they were the only buildings that didn't remind people of goddamn farming.

Benefits	Drawbacks
Enough boobs to fill a National Geographic Special	Enough elderly scrotum to fill your worst nightmare
Small size meant shared assumptions and values	Trivial disagreements blown up into decades-long feuds
Everyone participates in communal events	Participation may include "being burned to death as a witch"

Notable Resident: Sheriff
Representative of the law, often saddled with comically incompetent deputy.

Notable Resident: Blacksmith
Could beat swords into plowshares; mostly did it the other way round.

Notable Resident: Farmer
Linchpin of the village economy; able to conduct no more than three minutes of conversation, all of it weather-based.

Typical Domicile: Thatched Hut
Though houses of sticks and straw withstood most threats, it was not until the invention of the brick house that we finally defeated the big bad wolf.

Notable Residents: Village Elders (a.k.a. "Town Council")
You want to put in an above-ground pool? You better start greasing these palms.

Transport: Plow and Oxen *Sexy? No. But that didn't stop the kids from borrowing it to cruise "The Strip" on Saturday nights.*

Cities

SUCCESSFUL VILLAGES grew into **cities**, where trade and culture flourished alongside crime, squalor and fecal- and pest-borne diseases. The large population allowed for ever-greater specialization among artisans and craftsmen, until every city had one guy who did nothing but stand around the market playing Peruvian flute all day. It was fucking maddening. Great surges in ideas and technology were counterbalanced by periodic plagues that wiped out two out of every three inhabitants, setting civilization back almost as far as it had come but also making rents considerably more affordable.

Benefits	Drawbacks
If you could make it here, you could make it anywhere	Many did not make it here
Teeming masses from across the globe exchanging cultures, ideas and cuisines	Teeming masses meant no room for a bathtub except the middle of the kitchen
Sex! Drugs! Depravity!	Sex, drugs, depravity.

Transport: Public Transportation
Making your way around a major city was as easy as following a map like this.

Notable Resident: Mayor
Richest man in town and/or whoever was best at persuading you he'd "do something about the immigrants."

Notable Resident: Businessman
Went to work, smoked a cigar, looked at some ticker tape, had sex with his secretary, came home, ate dinner, counted his money, repeated.

Transport: Automobile
*Personal high-speed transporation. Some, like this **taxicab**, came complete with foreign-born drivers who would spout crazy shit until you reached your destination.*

Notable Resident: Gang Member
In case the Zephyrs make the mistake of coming south of Prescott Blvd.

**Typical Domicile:
Apartment Building**
*We paid dearly
for these little slices
of heaven, and we
protected our IKEA
futons and drawers full
of takeout menus with
fortifications worthy of
a medieval armory
(see right).*

Locks
*Although we trusted
our neighbors, we
never, ever wanted to
meet them.*

Air Conditioning
*Temporarily cooled the
indoors for the small
price of permanently
warming the outdoors.*

**Notable Resident:
Intellectual**
*Unfit for physical labor,
he devoted his time to
writing unreadable
articles/unpublishable
novels/letters home
for money.*

**Notable Resident:
Sanitation Worker**
*Whether they were
cleaning our streets or
holding us hostage with
their many strikes, these
mobbed-up rascals were
never boring.*

Transport: SegWay
*You have undoubtedly
found millions of these
wonders littering
our streets. They
revolutionized the way
man both traveled and
fought crime.*

NO STANDING
ANYTIME

Waste Management
of New York
A WMX Technologies Company
718-386-7900

DCA LIC.# 0928527

Nation-States

WHEN CITES, VILLAGES and tribes banded together under one common title—as the individual people had previously banded together to form cities, villages and tribes—then they became mighty **nations**. Or **states**. Or **nation-states**. We used the words kind of interchangeably. Perversely, we were often more attached to our nations than we were to our cities, villages and tribes, even though we tended to have less in common with the other members. That's just the way we rolled.

Benefits	Drawbacks
Disparate population bonded by strong sense of national pride	Disparate population bonded by strong sense of hunger
Security assured by standing army	Congratulations, soldier! Now drop and give me 20.
Welfare state supports vulnerable in society	Who knew the poor could be so expensive?

Notable Resident: General
Leader of a nation's armed forces, who provided strategic advice for a head of state to ignore.

Notable Resident: Olympic Athlete
Inspired a nation by winning gold, before disappointing that nation by testing positive for nandrolone.

Notable Residents: Celebrities
Nationally agreed upon distractions, there to remind us of our physical and professional shortcomings.

Notable Resident: Head of State
The supreme leader; frequently former generals who got tired of having their advice ignored.

Typical Domicile: Army Barracks
Large landmasses required large standing armies to defend them. We warehoused these honored citizens in "camps" and "forts"— which, despite their kid-friendly names, did not teach lanyard-making and were not made of pillows.

Empires

Empire was a term reserved only for our grandest, most expansive nation-states and kosher chickens. An empire spread its influence not only into surrounding countries, but around the globe, establishing **colonies** that enriched the homeland while destroying the natives. Basically, empires were like McDonald's, but less profitable.

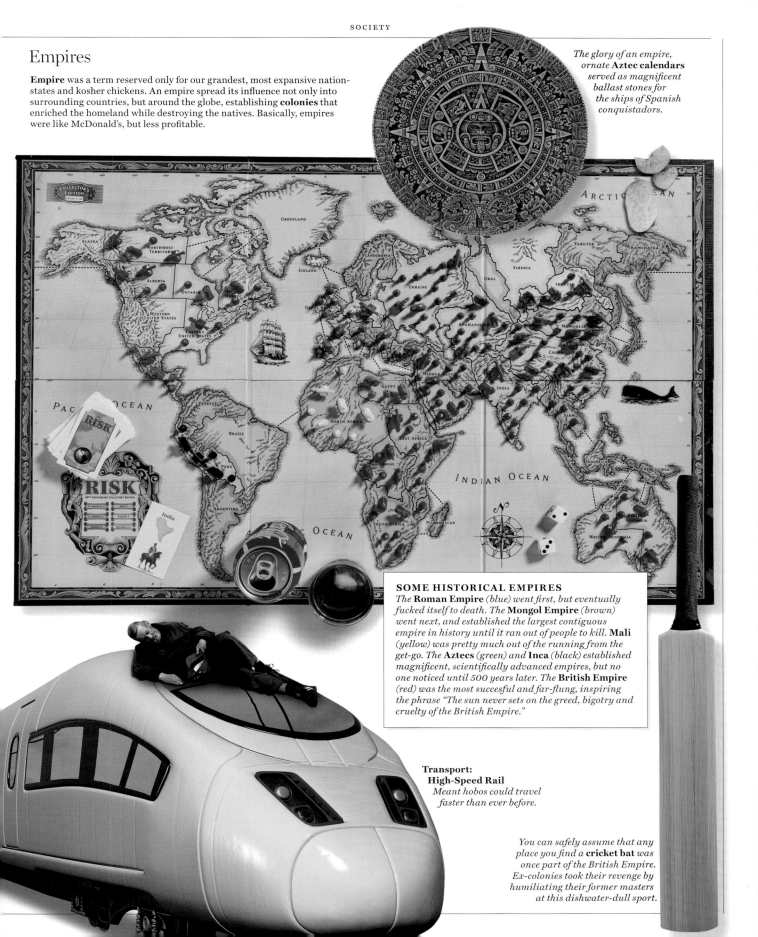

*The glory of an empire, ornate **Aztec calendars** served as magnificent ballast stones for the ships of Spanish conquistadors.*

SOME HISTORICAL EMPIRES

*The **Roman Empire** (blue) went first, but eventually fucked itself to death. The **Mongol Empire** (brown) went next, and established the largest contiguous empire in history until it ran out of people to kill. **Mali** (yellow) was pretty much out of the running from the get-go. The **Aztecs** (green) and **Inca** (black) established magnificent, scientifically advanced empires, but no one noticed until 500 years later. The **British Empire** (red) was the most succesful and far-flung, inspiring the phrase "The sun never sets on the greed, bigotry and cruelty of the British Empire."*

Transport:
High-Speed Rail
Meant hobos could travel faster than ever before.

*You can safely assume that any place you find a **cricket bat** was once part of the British Empire. Ex-colonies took their revenge by humiliating their former masters at this dishwater-dull sport.*

Government

JUST AS WE HAD no one language, we also had no one form of **government**, though many throughout history were advertised as "imperfect, but the best ever devised."

Monarchy

Monarchy spoke to our primal desire for an alpha male who would fight off our enemies, make decisions for us and tear out our throats if challenged. Of course, we did try to dress it up a bit. The Greek thinker Plato envisioned an ideal society ruled by **philosopher-kings**: enlightened guardians who would steer the ship of state with wisdom and justice. This happened exactly zero times. The most common path to the throne was **hereditary succession**, which was frankly a bit of a crapshoot.

Charles II of Spain (1661–1700) was ideally suited to lead due to his pure royal blood: His mother was his first cousin, and his aunt was his grandmother. Unfortunately, sorcerers hexed Charles with sub-moronic intelligence, madness and a tongue so large he couldn't chew his food.

Emperor Hirohito of Japan *(1901–1989) was half-man, half-origami swan.*

Russian Tsars *were incubated and hatched from these ornate, jewel-encrusted eggs.*

Kings, like England's Henry VIII, were known for their lavish daily menus.

Wednesday May the Thirde,
The Year of Our Lorde 1546

BREAKFAST
Small Flagon of Mead
Giant Turkey Leg

LUNCH
Large Flagon of Mead
2 Giant Turkey Legs

DINNER
Choice of Mead or Ale
Giant Turkey Leg Surprise

DESSERT
Giant Turkey Leg Mousse
with Mead Sauce

Thrones

We liked big chairs and we cannot lie. You aliens can't deny that when you sit in a chair made of shiny shiny brass with a cushion for your ass, you get sprung.

Crowns

Monarchs the world over donned elaborate **headgear** to convey strength in both kingdom and neck muscles, which came in handy during the inevitable beheading attempts.

Hongwu Emperor of China (*Ming Dynasty*), 1368. *Royal, elegant, mosquito proof.*

Crown of Denmark, *1595. Adorned with seven points representing the King's principal virtues: Shininess, sparkliness, glitteriness, gaudiness, jewelocity, awesomeness and richitude.*

Thailand's **Great Crown of Victory**, *1782. Later served as a docking station for the Thai Imperial Navy's fleet of mini-zeppelins.*

Heraldry

In pre-literate societies, important families and nations advertised their virtues with **heraldry**—emblems whose imagery expressed carefully crafted messages.

Aquitaine:

"Hi!"

England:

"Hi! Hi! Hi!"

Henry II:

"Hi! (No, not you!)"

Knighthood

A monarchy's rise and fall was best judged by which of its citizens it chose to **ennoble**.

Sir Lancelot Du Lac (c. 900)
Grail-seeker

Sir Francis Bacon (1603)
Philosopher, statesman

Sir Isaac Newton (1705)
Scientist

Sir Edmund Hillary (1953)
Explorer

Sir Elton John (1996)
Pop star

Sir Gordon Ramsay (2006)
Nasty cook

KNIGHTS OF THE BRITISH EMPIRE

Communism

MANY PEOPLE BELIEVED the ideal society should maximize human happiness by treating all people as absolute equals. This system, under which millions were enslaved and murdered, was called **communism**. It was premised on the belief that private property should be abolished and that poverty could be eliminated if everyone worked as well as they could and consumed nothing excessive. This was expressed in the maxim, "From each according to his ability, to each according to his need," which aptly set the stage for a form of government that excelled in producing a bounty of cumbersome maxims.

The Communist Manifesto

In the middle of the 19th century, Karl Marx and Friedrich Engels (pictured right) wrote *The Communist Manifesto*—the theoretical "paper" on which communism looked so good. In it, they spelled out both a descriptive **class-based theory of history**, and a prescriptive theory of political and social equality, which would have a profound influence on stoned college sophomores for centuries to come.

THE COMMUNIST MANIFESTO

Translated from the original German

Have you ever thought about how crazy it is that, like, there's so much stuff? But some people have a lot of stuff, like, way more than they need? And then other people don't even have enough to live with dignity, right? Shit, man. That's not fair! It's no wonder that the guys who don't have anything are totally pissed at the rich guys who are basically, like, hoarding the stuff they need. That's the whole history of the world, you know? Those guys being mad at those other guys. And sometimes they get really mad, and just fucking take what's theirs, you know? That happens over and over again, forever.

But it doesn't belong to them anymore than it belonged to the other guy. It belongs to everyone. We all work hard, and—hey, pass me that shit. Hold up. <Cough> Whoa. What were we talking about? Right, so what if we just, like, admit that it belongs to all of us? And maybe not everyone signs on, so we have to force 'em to admit it to start with, with a strong central government, but they'll come around, because it's awesome. Who wouldn't be into it? So then it's all about, just, y'know, sharing what we've got. Basic pre-school stuff, man—we knew this stuff as kids, we just forgot it. Think about it. It's in, like, our muscle memory. From each according to their ability, and then, you know—fuck that's good shit, did you get this from that new guy? Todd? I heard it's from Vermont, you know, organic and shit. Right, but I was saying, it's just, like, to each according to their needs, 's brilliant. You wanna order a pizza? If I order a pizza, will you have some, though?

67

China

A glorious People's Republic that eventually metastasized into a glorious people-crushing, pollution-spewing megalith that bought the whole world.

Quotations of Chairman Mao, *also known as the* **Little Red Book**, *was filled with the inspirational words of the Great Leader, and also an array of late night booty-call options.*

最高指示

The Soviet Union

One of Earth's best examples of communism in practice, until it ate itself from the inside out after about 70 years.

Unfortunately, the Union of Soviet Socialist Republics used up all its happiness in its posters, leaving none for its citizens.

Currency
For most of its history, the Soviet central banks issued various paper monies. Later, they turned to a toilet paper and Levi's-based economy.

1921–1983

1984–1991

Walls

Necessary to thwart the populace's self-destructive impulse to flee Paradise. From Berlin to Beijing, you couldn't have a communist dictatorship without walls.

Currency
One-billionth of each of these bills belonged to each Chinese citizen. They were warned not to "spend it all in one place," under penalty of death.

Socialism: Communism Lite

Another of Marx's proposals was low-carb communism, also known as **socialism**. Socialism allowed for private property, as well as democratic input into governance, while reserving certain vital enterprises for "the people" as a whole. Pure socialism was not tried on a truly large scale until it was adopted by the United States in late 2008.

Sweden *was the happiest country under socialist rule, largely because whatever form of government they had, their women always looked like this.*

SWEDEN

Fascism

FASCISM WAS GENERALLY defined as "that thing someone else is doing that I disagree with. Not communism. The other one." In practice, fascism was a **totalitarian** system of government whereby citizens lived under a strong central authority that exerted control over nearly all aspects of their lives. Again, not communism. The difference being fascism's penchant for spiffy uniforms, cool logos and a fanatical devotion to the state. With an emphasis on **nationalist pride** and **ancestral bonds**, fascists believed that a nation's strength came from its people, minus the darkies, queers, oldies and 'tards. Citizens who objected were dubbed "intellectuals" and loaded onto the same trains as the 'tards and queers. And those trains, mind you, *did* run on time.

Philosophy

By no means monolithic, fascism encompassed many streams of thought, from "the state is all I will ever care about" to the more nuanced "make it stop, make it stop, dear God … yes, I will tell you the names of the resistance leaders."

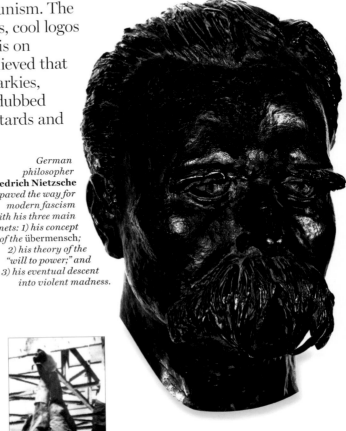

German philosopher **Friedrich Nietzsche** *paved the way for modern fascism with his three main tenets: 1) his concept of the* übermensch; *2) his theory of the "will to power;" and 3) his eventual descent into violent madness.*

Art

Spanish leader **Francisco Franco** proved there was a limit to how far power, a uniform and heroic iconography could go towards making a man sexy.

Although the subject of much heroic portraiture, Italy's **Benito Mussolini** *was much less intimidating in the flesh.*

A fascist without **jackboots** *was just an angry barefoot guy.*

Architecture

Because paramilitary thugs couldn't be everywhere at once, fascist regimes designed **buildings** that would scare the crap out of people whenever they weren't around to do it personally.

Nazis

Look, we really can't go any farther here without explaining these guys. Yes, **Nazis** were fascists, but they were also *the* fascists, the ones who defined the movement forever. Nothing horrified— or amused us—like Nazis. Their defining characteristics were competence, brutality and a fetishization of masculinity that turned all of Germany into one big smelly **homoerotic gym class**.

Nazi leader Adolf Hitler used pseudo-scientific theories of racial superiority to justify killing millions in death camps and destroying most of Europe. He was also a vegetarian. There is apparently no word for "irony" in German.

The swastika was an eight thousand year old symbol of peace and stability that the Nazis ruined for everyone.

The sinister lines of Nazi uniforms revolutionized the way troubled teenagers doodled in the margins of their math notebooks.

As exemplified by this SS emblem, the Nazis were one of the few political movements to admit right off the bat that they were evil.

IN THE RUINS
CONCENTRATION CAMPS

There's a possibility you might find some **barbed-wire compounds** that just radiate death and horror. Okay, yeah, we built them. And then we preserved them. But we only preserved them to remind us how *ashamed* we were of building them! And it's not like we set more than a handful of children's movies in them. Please don't judge us on this one terrible thing we did. We'd rather you judge us on the thousands of slightly less horrible things we did.

Anarchy

FEW POLITICAL IDEAS provoked such wildly divergent opinions as **anarchy**—the state of no government. To anarchy's fans, such as the philosopher Jean Jacques Rousseau and teen skateboarder Matt Gudmundsun, it was a condition of unfettered personal liberty, where individuals could realize their full potential, free from stifling authority and bullshit. To critics, such as Thomas Hobbes and Matt Gudmundsun's hardass father, it was a perilous hellscape where violence ruled, human enterprise was dissipated in **chaos** and furniture was never moved down to the basement despite repeated instructions to move it before you go out skateboarding. Who was right? We never figured it out. Because we never lived in anarchy for any sustained period. Really it was less a system of governance than a transitory state, like orgasm, adolescence or drunkenness.

"I wanna be Anarchy. Oh what a name. And I wanna be anarchist. I get pissed, destroy!"
—*John Lydon (1956–???), British Philosopher*

Mrs. Mikhail Bakunin
Mrs. Mikhail Bakunin - Greenberg
Mrs. Rachel Bakunin Greenberg

The Adventures of Super-Succo and Ultra Vawze

YOU HAD TO BE HERE

The **"Circle-A"** symbolized anarchy.

The **"Circle-K"** symbolized a "wide variety of quality products and services in a fast, friendly and clean environment."

After a tough day sticking it to the man, these young anarchists headed to Binky's parents' lake house for a sick kegger.

LITTLEBOROUGH ANARCHISTS MEETING AGENDA
12/17/10
SAINT SEAMUS SCHOOL ASSEMBLY HALL

7:30 pm	Call to Order -- Chair
7:32 pm	Breaking chairs over Chair's head
7:40 pm	Minutes of last meeting shouted through megaphone
7:55 pm	Smash The State weekly progress update
8:05 pm	Reports from the Dumpster Tipping, Car Burning, Window Breaking, and Utility Pole Toppling committees
9:00 pm	The floor is opened for full-throated general melee of anti-authoritarian rage; procedural questions
	BREAK (please return promptly after five minutes of breaking things)
	Abusive prank calls to local police station
9:30 pm	Discussion of how to spend proceeds from William Powell Cooking Club Bake Sale
10:00 pm	Guest Presentation: "6 Things You Didn't Know Were Flammable"
10:30 pm	Discussion and resolution to adopt new slogan "WE DON'T GIVE A FUCK" to replace "FUCK THE FUCKING COUNTY COMMISSIONER"
11:00 pm	Select two volunteers to convey Chair to ER for gavel removal
11:15 pm	Adjourn. Burn school.

Ink and paper for these flyers was generously stolen by Lillian Pertwee and George Allsop from their patriarchal racist capitalist employer, Kinko's. Thanks, Lil and George!

Groceries
- Milk
- Eggs
- Sugar
- Whatever I can shove down my pants

Anarchy in
the bUKakke
-porn title? Re

Bureaucracy

BUREAUCRACY WAS THE OPPOSITE of anarchy. Whereas anarchy destroyed property, bureaucracy generally destroyed the soul. It wasn't even a real form of government. It was just a parasite that attached itself to whatever form of government was around. And though bureaucracy's goals could be called laudable—the **standardization** of procedure in otherwise large, ungovernable groups—it always wrapped itself in a protective cocoon of inflexibility, paperwork and mean ladies who were too busy with their personal calls to talk to you.

*An **artifact of bureaucracy** was planned for this space and was due to arrive at the printers in time for publication, after final review by the Senior Editorial Council, the Artifact Sub-Protectorate and the Secretariat for Greater Intra-Council Cooperation. If, for some unfathomable reason, no artifact appears, simply bring this copy of* Earth (The Book) *to the pile of ashes at the corner of 52nd Street and 11th Avenue in what was New York City. A life form will evolve to see you shortly.*

Democracy

FIRST PRACTICED BY the ancient Greeks, **democracy** came from their word *demokratos* meaning "a short break from pederasty to deal with this zoning issue." The major strength of democracy was that every citizen had a voice in government. The major weakness of democracy was that every citizen has a voice in government. The risks were high for short-sighted rule by mob whim, inaction caused by deadlocked interest groups, or your favorite TV shows being pre-empted by some boring debate. In exchange for control over their own destinies, democracy demanded one great sacrifice from its practitioners: a lunch-break trip to an elementary school gym once every two to four years. Generally, this was too much to ask. Citizens found the energy to vote only when they believed their wealth, guns or vaguely defined concept of "freedom" were threatened. In fact, a democracy's health could best be measured by the number of people who *didn't* vote, thus signaling they were completely satisfied. Democracy proved to be surprisingly resilient in times of chaos or social change. This helped mask the fact that it didn't really work that well.

In his Republic,
Plato *described the perfect government as an illusory democracy secretly controlled by a handful of elites. He turned out to be right.*

Magna Carta
In 1215 A.D., some English subjects wrote a list of demands on a cocktail napkin and forced the king to sign it. Thus was the long road to modern democracy begun.

The **back of a train**
was the best place to swear fealty to your constituents before skipping town, never to see them again.

LEARNING CURVE
VOTING

500 B.C.
Ostraka—*Greece*
"If you would exile Gorocles, scratch his name on a shard."

1200 A.D.
Ballota—*Italy*
"A single black ball will prevent the election of Pope Gorialanus I."

1500 A.D.
Viva Voce—*England*
"All those in favor of Lord Gorington-Gore's measure, say 'Aye!'"

1988 A.D.
Voting machines—*USA*
"I'm voting for Gore!"

2000 A.D.
Butterfly Ballot—*USA*
"I'm voting for ... Buchanan?"

Elections

The mechanism by which the people ruled was called the **election**. It was a series of discrete events—encompassing **nominations**, **rallies** and **back-room deals**—that completely dominated the news of the day, unless someone famous got married, divorced or died.

IN ASSESSING THE FITNESS OF SENATOR SESTUS, FOR THE OFFICE OF PROCONSUL, THERE ARE NO DOUBT THOSE WHO APPROVE THE CHOICE, BASED ON HIS "HEROIC SERVICE" AS CAPTAIN OF A SWIFT-BIREME IN THE GALLIC WARS; BUT I DECLAIM UNTO THEM ON THIS DAY, THAT HE NEVER SERVED ON A SWIFT-BIREME; AND THAT HE IS NO HERO; AND THAT HE IS A LIAR AND A COWARD. [CROWD MURMURS.] AND I SAY THIS WITH CERTAINTY, FOR I HAVE AN ACQUAINTANCE, WHOSE COUSIN HEARD THESE VERITIES DIRECTLY, FROM A GUY WHO WAS THERE. [CROWD IMPRESSED.] FURTHER, IS IT NOT TROUBLING, THAT NO CERTIFICATE EXISTS, PROVING BEYOND DOUBT, THAT SENATOR SESTUS WAS NATURAL BORN OF ROME, RATHER THAN, SAY, KENYA? [CROWD DEEPLY TROUBLED.] I AM WILLING TO BELIEVE THE SENATOR, WOULD HE JUST PROFFER THE PAPERS IN PLAIN LATIN. [CROWD APPLAUDS.] OH, AND IS IT JUST THIS ORATOR, OR DOES IT SEEM AWFULLY SUSPICIOUS THAT PUBLIUS REFUSES TO DENY SIRING AN ILLEGITIMATE ÆTHIOPIAN BABY? [CROWD SHOUTS IN DISGUST.] I KNOW, RIGHT?

Political oratory could lift us above the mire, and sink us deep beneath it. As the above speech from the Roman Senator **Cicero** *shows, the latter was much more common.*

By dipping their fingers in purple ink, participants in fledgling democracies got to choose both their leaders and which body part would be hacked off by insurgents.

In **peep show booths**, a flimsy partition gave us all the privacy we needed to vent our personal demons.

In **voting booths**, we got a sticker afterwards.

The Campaign

In order to win an election, the white male Ivy League-educated heir to a major fortune (or "**candidate**") had to show how much he had in common with voters.

I have respect and love for this country.

I have empathy for the plight of the working stiff.

I have no chance of winning this election.

Taxation

GOVERNMENT DID MANY THINGS, most of them badly and none of them free. To pay for its works, virtually all governments collected money from their citizens in the form of **taxes**. Typically, people would surrender a percentage of their income or produce and in return would be granted the right to complain about having to surrender a percentage of their income or produce.

WE SAID IT

"In this world nothing is certain but death and taxes. And also the rotation of the earth. And gravity. And using the bathroom. Look, just put down 'death and taxes.'"
—*Benjamin Franklin (1706–1790), American inventor, statesman and kite enthusiast*

Some 5,000 years before this book was written, Sumerian tax collectors kept records on **tablets** *like this. The fact that they were able to carry around tablets like this made them excellent tax collectors.*

An ancient "notebook," the **Inca Qipu** *used knots to keep track of who owed what.*

Later, this young woman used a similar method to calculate how many **Grand Slams** *she would eventually win.*

America, *Earth's most powerful nation, was the result of an argument about taxes, though we later gussied up the story with some bullshit about liberty.*

Most of us knew **Lady Godiva** *was a beautiful woman who rode naked through the town of Coventry, but few remembered that she rode to demand her husband lower the town's taxes.*

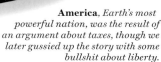

Later **tax protests** *were considerably less glamorous.*

The most substantial taxes were **tariffs** *on imports and exports, in order to both protect local businesses, and punish foreigners for talking funny.*

SPOTLIGHT
SIN TAXES

We frequently placed onerous taxes on things we liked but knew were bad for us, in order to discourage us from buying them. The end result was that our governments were largely funded by people like the man on the right.

Write-Offs

To promote entrepreneurship, governments often waived taxes on **business-related expenses**.

	19	Add lines 10 through: 18		
Casualty and Theft Losses	20	Casualty or theft loss(es). Attach Form 4684. (See page A-		
Job Expenses and Certain Miscellaneous Deductions (See page A-10.)	21	Unreimbursed employee expenses—job travel, union dues, j education, etc. Attach Form 2106 or 2106-EZ if required. (Se page A-10.) ▶		
	22	Tax preparation fees		
	23	Other expenses—investment, safe deposit box, etc. List type and amount ▶ *Non-terrestrial Market Research* *Office Mascot* *Refreshments for Company Picnic*	23	
	24	Add lines 21 through 23	24	
	25	Enter amount from Form 1040, line 38	25	
	26	Multiply line 25 by 2% (.02)	26	
	27	Subtract line 26 from line 24. If line 26 is more than line 24, enter -0-		
Other Miscellaneous Deductions	28	Other—from list on page A-11. List type and amount ▶		
Total Itemized Deductions	29	Is Form 1040, line 38, over $166,800 (over $83,400 if married filing s		
		☐ **No.** Your deduction is not limited. Add the amounts in the far right lines 4 through 28. Also, enter this amount on Form 1040, line 40a.		
		☐ **Yes.** Your deduction may be limited. See page A-11 for the amount to enter		
	30	If you elect to itemize deductions even though they are less than your standard deduction, check here . . . . ▶ ☐		

For Paperwork Reduction Act Notice, see Form 1040 instructions.   Cat. No. 17145C   **Schedule A (Form 1040) 20**

Accountants

One of the perversities of our tax code was that it was so complicated we had to hire other people to calculate our taxes for us. This was to make sure we didn't a) pay too much or b) go to jail. We called these people **accountants**, and we hated them.

Not all accountants looked like this but the vast majority of accountants looked like this.

If our accountant was good, we got a tax **refund check** *from the government. Every year we contemplated using these to pay off our credit card debt, and every year we thought, naaaaaah, and bought a new* **gaming system** *instead.*

United States Treasury
15-01 / 000   S 289,643
AUSTIN, TEXAS
Check No. 2306 2471546
04 09 04 95   SORM FRESNO TAX REFUND
27715465 I30 002128988 12/00
65   $***4020*00
Pay to the order of   HENRY R NORM & LESLIE E PLATON
3667 SILENT WILD RD
HENDERSON NV   89050-1014
VOID AFTER ONE YEAR

Infrastructure

LIVING IN GROUPS ALLOWED US to improve our environment for easier **transportation**, **hygiene** and **comfort**. These projects, from Roman roads to the Channel Tunnel to wireless Internet access, represented staggering human achievements. And yet the only time we thought about bridges was when they collapsed. Sewers? Great—just don't raise my taxes to maintain them. And electric utilities were best known for the three or four times they couldn't prevent a blackout. We took our infrastructure utterly for granted, contemptuous of those who ran it, furious over both its cost and its occasional failure to be perfect. Yeah, we were real charmers.

Roads were the long, thin ribbons of flattened land you're finding all over our planet, which we used for high-speed travel and as depositories for used condoms, milk jugs full of urine and slow-moving raccoons.

Bridges allowed us to cope with bodies of water whose size fell between "jump-acrossable" and "sail-acrossable." They revolutionized agriculture by enabling farmers to at last transport a fox, a chicken and a sack of grain across the river without stopping to solve a goddamn Mensa puzzle.

Railways provided humans with convenient commuter travel, industrial transport and flattened pennies.

Tunnels were giant holes that we drilled into the planet, as a way of bypassing obstacles or—if you were an adherent of Freud—subconsciously doing our moms.

Power plants were large facilities that produced electrical energy to power most of the things in our homes; they were indispensable to any industrialized nation, and it was considered absolutely essential that they be located nowhere near anyone's home.

Airports were large, noisy expanses of asphalt that had been set aside for airplanes to take off and land; they were usually built on the outskirts of major metropolitan areas, and directly beside "gentleman's clubs" called "The Landing Strip."

Wastewater treatment plants were where human feces and poisonous agricultural chemicals were turned into refreshing drinking water.

NAILED IT
THE ZIPPER MERGE

Wherever two lanes of hateful, constipated car-borne bastards had to suddenly merge into a single lane, you'd assume the result would be mass carnage. You'd be wrong. For some reason, humans happily and quite automatically agreed to perform a **zipper merge**, alternating one car at a time from each lane as if an invisible traffic cop was hovering above the scene, waiting to write us a traffic ticket for just enough money to piss us off but not quite enough for us to take a half-day off work to go downtown to fight it.

Sea ports were designed to streamline a sailor's search for prostitutes.

IN THE RUINS
HOOVER DAM

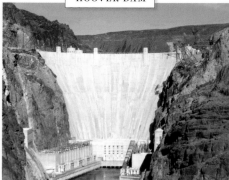

Built as a "screw you" to the beaver community, this engineering marvel consisted of 80% concrete, 15% steel and 5% dead construction workers.

Sewers were underground tunnels designed to speed our urine and feces away from us and deposit them safely in someone else's drinking water. The speed with which we were able to do this was an indication of how advanced our civilization was.

Unfortunately on rare occasions sewers also provided a hiding place for ravenous cannibalistic clowns.

Law and Order

IN THE CRIMINAL JUSTICE SYSTEM, the people were represented by two separate yet equally important groups: the **police**, who investigated crime, and the **district attorneys**, who prosecuted the offenders. These are their stories. *Chung-chung!*

Order

Throughout human history, bands of brave men and women, largely Irish, were tasked with keeping the criminal element at bay.

*The first professional metropolitan police force, London's "**Bobbies**," was founded as a means of providing employment for men with enormous melon-shaped heads.*

*Law was sometimes meted out by **vigilante mobs**, though thankfully many of these **lynchings** were later overturned by DNA evidence.*

*Modern law enforcement would have been impossible without the two totems of police power: the **badge** and the **gun**. The badge was society's permission slip to transgress behavioral norms in pursuit of justice. The gun was the most extreme form of that transgression. Also important: the **mop handle** (not pictured).*

Law Enforcement: Chain of Command

The Commissioner
Between the weasels at the Mayor's Office and the hotheads at the ACLU, he never slept more than three hours a night.

The Captain
Usually black, always angry, he was sick and tired of covering up for his underlings—but a good cop at heart.

The Guy Who's About to Retire
Just one more day, and he'd open that charter fishing business he'd always dreamed of.

The Loose Cannon
Rules? Rules were for people who didn't have death wishes.

Forensic Science

Forensics—the scientific pursuit of justice—was based on the principle that it was impossible to commit a crime without leaving behind copious amounts of semen.

*No two **fingerprints** were alike. The fingerprint to the left belonged to the never-apprehended Zodiac killer, who murdered dozens of Californians in the 1970s, while the one to the right belonged to beloved '70s character actor and California resident, Buddy Ebsen.*

*By examining striations on ammunition, **ballistics** experts could determine if two bullets were fired from the same gun. But it was far from perfect. For instance, the bullet at left was fired by that infamous sexual sadist, the Zodiac killer, while the seemingly identical one at right was fired by beloved Beverly Hillbillies star Buddy Ebsen.*

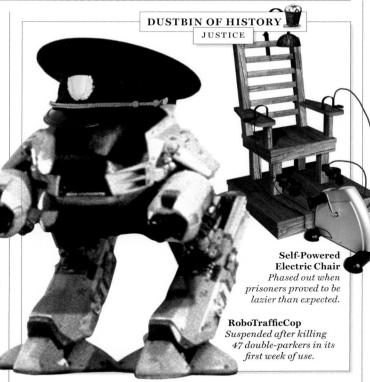

Self-Powered Electric Chair
Phased out when prisoners proved to be lazier than expected.

RoboTrafficCop
Suspended after killing 47 double-parkers in its first week of use.

*Before **Luminol** was invented, we thought hotel rooms were clean.*

The Stocks. *Pretty funny, huh? Now imagine being locked in these for a week, soiling yourself while your neighbors spat in your face. Yeah, keep laughing, big boy.*

Forensic scientists on television were just like real forensic scientists, except they were attractive and respected by their colleagues.

*The philosopher Jeremy Bentham posited that crime would cease to exist if a hypothetical machine, called a "panopticon," allowed all humans to observe one another at all times. In the late 20th century, this machine, now known as a **helicopter**, became a reality, but paradoxically served to amplify, not reduce, bad behavior.*

Law and Order: Law

The codification of the law was a process as old as humanity itself. Though legal codes varied through time and geography, murder was almost universally forbidden, except in 21st-century Baltimore.

Placing your hand on this **magic book** *made it physically impossible to lie.*

Community Chest

GET OUT OF JAIL, FREE

THIS CARD MAY BE KEPT UNTIL NEEDED OR SOLD

© 1935 PARKER BROTHERS, INC.

The actual card used by Orenthal James Simpson on October 3, 1995

*The **gavel**, symbol of a judge's power, was respected by criminals, pimps, parasites, cockroaches, mosquitoes and walnuts alike.*

Trial by Jury

The legal process reached its apex with the formulation of this adversarial system. At its essence, it required five **main players**.

❶ **The Judge**
Presided over trials, decided punishments. The robe was worn in order to "leave something to the imagination."

❷ **The Prosecutor**
Was interested in only two things: justice and keeping her conviction percentage high. Not in that order.

❸ **The Defense Attorney**
One of the 5% of law school graduates who actually used his degree to help people—or to subvert society from within, depending on who you asked.

❹ **The Scumbag**
Knew if she kept her pretty little trap shut, those saps on the jury would let her off.

❺ **The Jury**
Twelve angry people, each with assigned roles: #8, the lone dissenter; #10, the racist; #3, the lonely retiree who never, ever wants the trial to end.

1
The Judge

2
The Prosecutor

4
The Scumbag

3
The Defense Attorney

5
The Jury

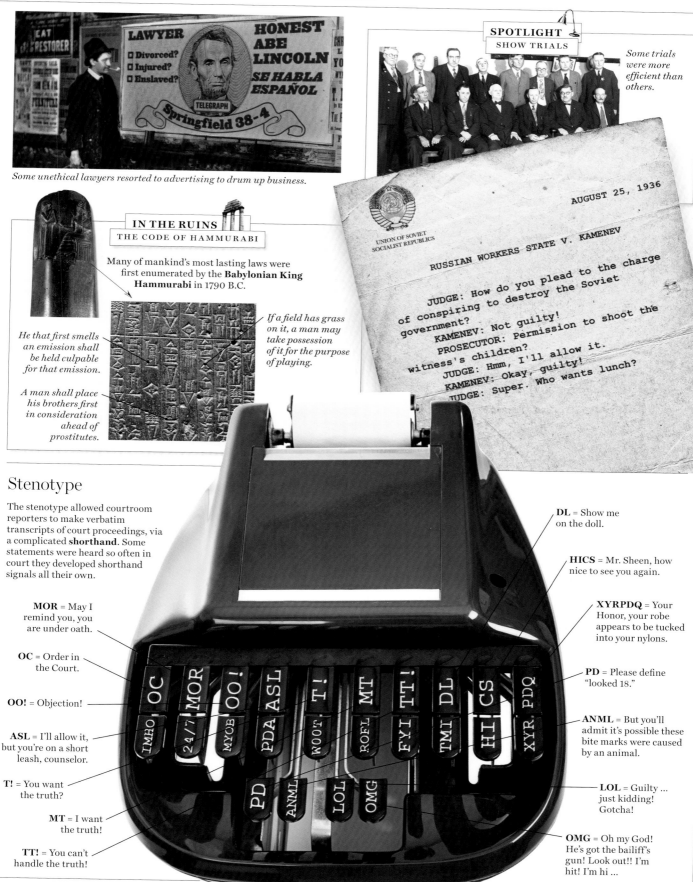

Some unethical lawyers resorted to advertising to drum up business.

SPOTLIGHT
SHOW TRIALS

Some trials were more efficient than others.

AUGUST 25, 1936

UNION OF SOVIET
SOCIALIST REPUBLICS

RUSSIAN WORKERS STATE V. KAMENEV

JUDGE: How do you plead to the charge of conspiring to destroy the Soviet government?
KAMENEV: Not guilty!
PROSECUTOR: Permission to shoot the witness's children?
JUDGE: Hmm, I'll allow it.
KAMENEV: Okay, guilty!
JUDGE: Super. Who wants lunch?

IN THE RUINS
THE CODE OF HAMMURABI

Many of mankind's most lasting laws were first enumerated by the **Babylonian King Hammurabi** in 1790 B.C.

He that first smells an emission shall be held culpable for that emission.

If a field has grass on it, a man may take possession of it for the purpose of playing.

A man shall place his brothers first in consideration ahead of prostitutes.

Stenotype

The stenotype allowed courtroom reporters to make verbatim transcripts of court proceedings, via a complicated **shorthand**. Some statements were heard so often in court they developed shorthand signals all their own.

MOR = May I remind you, you are under oath.

OC = Order in the Court.

OO! = Objection!

ASL = I'll allow it, but you're on a short leash, counselor.

T! = You want the truth?

MT = I want the truth!

TT! = You can't handle the truth!

DL = Show me on the doll.

HICS = Mr. Sheen, how nice to see you again.

XYRPDQ = Your Honor, your robe appears to be tucked into your nylons.

PD = Please define "looked 18."

ANML = But you'll admit it's possible these bite marks were caused by an animal.

LOL = Guilty ... just kidding! Gotcha!

OMG = Oh my God! He's got the bailiff's gun! Look out!! I'm hit! I'm hi ...

Incarceration

ONE OF OUR CORE BELIEFS was that criminals could be **rehabilitated** by locking them up with other criminals in dehumanizing conditions. In retrospect, we believed a lot of crazy shit.

If criminals put as much effort into life outside prison as they did to making weapons inside prison, they would have never ended up in prison.

In Mexican prisons, guards had to be constantly on the lookout in case any of the prisoners had an escape flan.

Prison tattoos identified the bearer's crime and gang affiliation.

After a tough day working on the chain gang, there was nothing better than a cold, refreshing shower.

Rita Hayworth Poster
This was a way of covering up an escape hole. So keep walking, screw.

Jailer's Keys
Designed to open all the locks in a particular prison. Often kept either loosely hanging from the jailer's belt or on a hook just barely out of reach of the prisoner.

LIVE FREE OR DIE
DEEZNUTZ
6   New HAMPSHIRE   2010

One of the worst prison jobs was making vanity license plates for the insufferable douchebags on the outside.

Prisoners subjected to 18th century Europe's Iron Maiden treatment had a 0% recidivism rate.

YOU HAD TO BE HERE

Bunkbeds—every little boy's dream.

Bunkbeds—every grown man's nightmare.

Customs/Manners

NOT EVERY LAW was written down. **Customs** and **manners** were informal but powerful checks on human behavior. **Etiquette** varied between socioeconomic classes, leading to countless fancy parties being spoiled by uncouth boors who, for instance, complained that the steak still had marks where the jockey whipped it. Manners also changed over time, leading some older people to complain about "kids these days," when they spotted younger humans mixing racially.

Etiquette books taught us the proper way to dress, talk, eat and dance according to whichever cloistered judgmental spinster wrote the book.

Polite Forms of Greeting

Western

Eastern

Middle Eastern

Midwestern

*Basic **toilet etiquette** was fairly standard throughout the world.*

Acceptable   Disrespectful   Totally uncool

In cases where cultures diverged, it was usual to follow the customs of the one with more oil.

Thank You Notes

Upon receiving a gift, the recipient immediately wrote a note expressing gratitude or else risked being forever branded as "rude," and thus unworthy of future gifts.

A thank you note from Egypt, circa 1200 B.C. Roughly translated: "Dear Grandma. Thank you for the loincloth. It almost fits. The kids at school hardly make fun of me at all. Love, Ani. P.S. May the jackal-headed god Anubis find your soul to be of satisfactory weight."

Altruism

AS SOCIAL BEINGS, we were often moved to perform acts that benefited other people without any reward for ourselves. More precisely, we universally believed that we *should* behave this way. This selfless regard for our fellow man was called **altruism**, and it allowed us to build great societies and made us easy marks for con men. Altruism manifested itself in the form of **charity**, which meant giving away something that had very little value for us but a great deal of value for the recipient. Professional charity was called **philanthropy**, which meant giving away something that had a great deal of value in exchange for positive corporate branding and tax write-offs.

What We Donated

Organs
Donated under three circumstances: posthumously; as a gesture of selflessness towards one's fellow man; or against one's will in a bathtub full of ice.

Cars
Usually donated after they were no longer safe to drive. Good enough for poor people, though.

Clothing
Usually donated after it was no longer wearable. Good enough for poor people, though.

Blood
Civic-minded high school students took part in "blood drives," which totally enhanced the shots of Everclear they did later in the school parking lot.

SPOTLIGHT
THE GREAT MID-ATLANTIC TOTE BAG PATCH

Our habit of giving away ecologically friendly canvas tote bags with even the smallest charitable donation eventually came back to bite us in the ass.

Money
We resisted giving cash outright, since most poor people would just spend it on drugs. Because that's what we would have done if we were them.

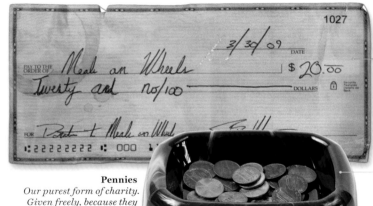

Pennies
Our purest form of charity. Given freely, because they were worthless.

take a penny
leave a penny

Canned goods
These were found in the back of the pantry, behind the unopened tub of SlimFast. And if they were a little old, well ... there was no expiration date on love.

Celebrity Telethons *were televised talent shows of famous people displaying skills for which they were not famous, like answering phones. Viewers made donations in an effort to get the celebrities to stop embarrassing themselves and return TV to its regular programming.*

Rewards of Philanthropy

IN MEMORY OF CAROLYN SCHWARTZ

$500–$2,000
Name on a brick

Vartan Tonuji Scholarship Winners

$10K–$4M
Name on a scholarship

HAITI's ORPHANS NEED YOUR HELP

HAITI's ORPHANS NEED YOUR HELP

$5M–$100M
Name on a major cultural landmark

CARNEGIE HALL · CARNEGIE HALL

Every few years a **natural disaster** *would focus our charitable urges on a group of victims whose plight had suddenly become interesting.*

JANUARY 2009

JANUARY 2010

$7,837 raised.

$45,690,000 raised.

$500M and up
Name totally cleansed of shameful associations with corporate rapacity, union busting, child labor, murder, etc.

Volunteering

We volunteered for two major reasons: to stay out of jail, and to get into college.

What wouldst make thou an excellente addition to Ye College of Scholars? Keep answers to five hundreds of words or less.

Last Summer's vacation I chose to volunteer among Ye Heathen Indians, for no other reason than the goodnesse of mine own hearte. The Savages knew not how to thanke me when I passed out woolen blankets to protect them from ye Winter's chill. Also I am on ye Chesse Team.

College of William and Mary application essay, 1687

THE ROCKEFELLER FOUNDATION

War

ONCE HUMANS ORGANIZED into a society, we immediately noticed that other humans had organized into completely different societies, and we were compelled to attack them. Violent conflict between societies was called **war**, and was one of the few universal constants of human existence. We waged war to acquire land or possessions from others, to retaliate for their attempts to acquire land or possessions from us, or because it was Tuesday. Most world religions denounced war as a barbaric waste of human life. We treasured the teachings of these religions so dearly that we frequently had to wage war in order to impose them on other people.

"War. Huh. Good God, y'all. What is it good for? Absolutely nothing. Except ending slavery. And stopping Hitler."
—*Edwin Starr (1942–2003), American philosopharr*

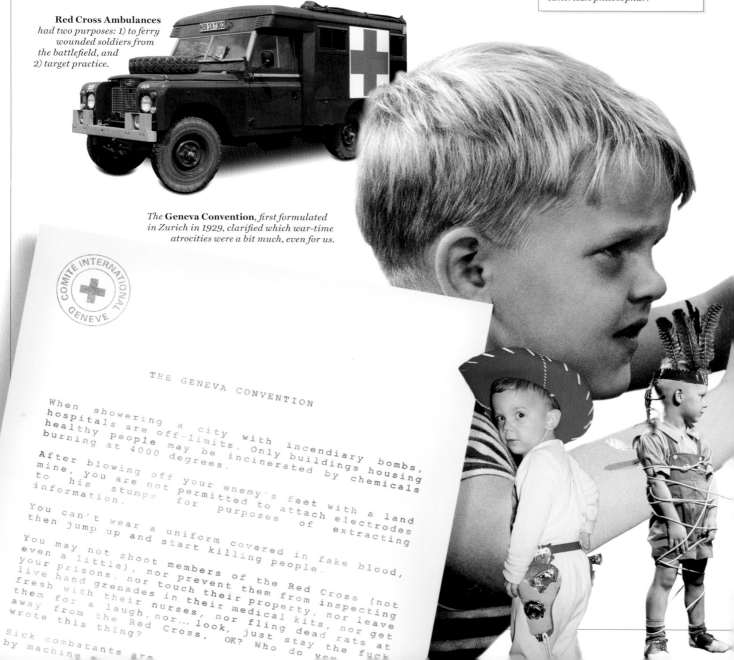

Red Cross Ambulances *had two purposes: 1) to ferry wounded soldiers from the battlefield, and 2) target practice.*

The **Geneva Convention**, *first formulated in Zurich in 1929, clarified which war-time atrocities were a bit much, even for us.*

COMITÉ INTERNATIONAL GENEVE

```
            THE GENEVA CONVENTION

       When showering a city with incendiary bombs,
    hospitals are off-limits. Only buildings housing
    healthy people may be incinerated by chemicals
    burning at 4000 degrees.
       After blowing off your enemy's feet with a land
    mine, you are not permitted to attach electrodes
    to his stumps for purposes of extracting
    information.
       You can't wear a uniform covered in fake blood,
    then jump up and start killing people.
       You may not shoot members of the Red Cross (not
    even a little), nor prevent them from inspecting
    your prisons, nor touch their property, nor leave
    live hand grenades in their medical kits, nor get
    fresh with their nurses, nor fling dead rats at
    them for a laugh, nor... look, just stay the fuck
    away from the Red Cross, OK? Who do you
    wrote this thing?
    Sick combatants are
    by machine
```

IN THE RUINS
LANDMINES

Some hundreds of thousands of these explosive "No Trespassing" signs still dot the landscape. A few of them are probably still active. And we kind of forgot where we put most of them. Long story short: Steer clear of Asia.

*When one people **conquered** another, the same acts were often viewed in starkly different terms.*

Conquerer to Conquered Glossary

CONQUERER	CONQUERED
	Invasion
Landfall	The World
The New World	Invader
Explorer	Invader with cattle
Settler	Restrictive clothing
Civilization	"I'm turned on by how your eyes are shaped."
Exotic	
Diamonds	Blood diamonds
Ethnic cleansing	Time to move
Manifest Destiny	"Actually, we want the whole thing."
Emancipation	Slight downgrading of oppression
Religion	The great cultural scourge our ancestors warned about but believed would come in the form of a dragon or something
World music	Our fucking music!
Reparations	Blood money
Casinos	Our revenge

280

*We warned our children about the horrors of war through the use of intricately crafted **visual aides**.*

669

SPOTLIGHT
A NEW KIND OF WAR

War on Poverty

War on Terror

The atomic bomb (see chapter 8, "Science") did have one downside: It really took the zing out of war. Once we could kill millions of people in an instant, the whole "fighting another country's army to see whose was best" thing began to seem somewhat quaint. But, human ingenuity being what it was, we proceeded to innovate our way out of the problem by developing a new kind of war: **war against abstract concepts and inanimate objects**. We initiated a series of conflicts against poverty, drugs, and terror. Through trial-and-error, we began to learn a lot about these new wars: How they were fought (through rhetoric and legislation), where the fields of battle were located (cable news shows) and how to tell when they were over (when the political party that had declared them was voted out of office).

*The **War on Drugs** created images so surreal they made taking drugs unnecessary.*

117

Mesopotamia—
Birthplace of
Civilization

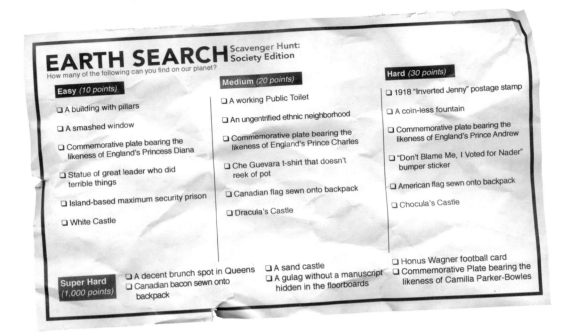

EARTH SEARCH
Scavenger Hunt: Society Edition

How many of the following can you find on our planet?

Easy *(10 points)*
- ☐ A building with pillars
- ☐ A smashed window
- ☐ Commemorative plate bearing the likeness of England's Princess Diana
- ☐ Statue of great leader who did terrible things
- ☐ Island-based maximum security prison
- ☐ White Castle

Medium *(20 points)*
- ☐ A working Public Toilet
- ☐ An ungentrified ethnic neighborhood
- ☐ Commemorative plate bearing the likeness of England's Prince Charles
- ☐ Che Guevara t-shirt that doesn't reek of pot
- ☐ Canadian flag sewn onto backpack
- ☐ Dracula's Castle

Hard *(30 points)*
- ☐ 1918 "Inverted Jenny" postage stamp
- ☐ A coin-less fountain
- ☐ Commemorative plate bearing the likeness of England's Prince Andrew
- ☐ "Don't Blame Me, I Voted for Nader" bumper sticker
- ☐ American flag sewn onto backpack
- ☐ Chocula's Castle

Super Hard *(1,000 points)*
- ☐ A decent brunch spot in Queens
- ☐ Canadian bacon sewn onto backpack
- ☐ A sand castle
- ☐ A gulag without a manuscript hidden in the floorboards
- ☐ Honus Wagner football card
- ☐ Commemorative Plate bearing the likeness of Camilla Parker-Bowles

FAQs
(Future Alien Questions)

Q. How did the police know if criminals were lying?
A. They used a device known as a **lie detector**, which involved measuring the suspect's heart rate while they punched him until he confessed.

These didn't really work.

Q. How was anyone supposed to remember all your ridiculously arbitrary rules of etiquette?
A. The shameful memory of being ostracized from polite society was usually enough to remind people which fork to use when eating shrimp.

Q. Why did humans spend so much time worrying what others thought about them?
A. Why? Does it make us look needy? Because we didn't really care what anyone else thought. Did that sound cool? God, we hope so.

Q. Was communism ever successful?
A. "Successful" is a relative term. If your needs were met by bread and toilet paper, then yes. As long as you weren't in a hurry.

Q. Tribes, villages, towns, cities— which was the best place to live?
A. Each living arrangement had its charms, so it would be reductive to single out one type of locale as "better" or "worse" than the other, or to suggest, for instance, that the "real" citizens of a given country lived only in small towns. But as a general rule, the best place to live—whether within a tiny hamlet or a giant metropolis—was in a rich person's house.

Q. How did countries strike the balance between governmental control and personal liberty?
A. Each country would, over time, reach its own equilibrium point, after which, even the most minute adjustments to the status quo would be greeted with competing cries of "Fascism!" and "Socialism!"

Q. What was the best system of government?
A. While it had its flaws, democracy was the finest and most just system of government, provided that the party one supported was in power.

(If the party one opposed was in power, however, democracy was a horrible mistake, forcing citizens to live by the hideous whims of the tyrannical, brainwashed, sub-moronic majority.)

Q. It seems like, under your legal systems, it was possible that sometimes the guilty would go free, or the innocent would be convicted of crimes they didn't commit.
A. Yep. What's your question?

THE DEFENDANT IS:
- ☐ **Innocent**
- ☐ **Guilty**
- ☑ 2 cute to execute

Q. Was it worse for an innocent man to be sent to prison or a guilty man to go free?
A. Well, if the man was innocent anyway, it's not like he was going to do any harm in prison.

Q. If ridding the earth of war and strife was a goal, why wasn't the entire globe under a single government?
A. Good question, fascist.

"Welcome to the
Commerce Chapter!
I used to be a dentist."

Commerce

FIRSTLY, LET US *congratulate you on reaching this chapter. We know you've got a lot of page choices and we appreciate your business. Here at "The Chapter on Commerce" we pride ourselves on delivering the kind of state-of-the-art, ready-to-read, sentence-based wordperience that other chapters talk about but rarely provide. We hope you enjoy your time here. This is Lou. He'll be happy to take you through the rest of the chapter and answer any questions you might have. Thanks again, and if you need anything, don't feel shy. Lou here is the best. Lou?*

Thanks, Bill. Hey, nice to meet you. First time in "ChapCom"? You're gonna love it. Did you just open to this chapter, or have you been going in order? By the way, those are some clear, piercing eyes you've got there. Nice readers. They new? They look like they can really pick reflected light off an object and convert it to electrical impulses that pass along the optic nerve to be reconverted by the brain into the original image ... Anyhow.

Where would you like to begin? Now, I could sit here and pretend, like some chapters have, that we can fully and accurately represent the entire history of man's **commercial endeavors** over the next thirty or so pages. But—and believe me, I could lose my job for saying this—we can't. And if anyone tells you they can, they're a liar and you're a fool for believing it. As a matter of fact if you're that kind of reader, you know what? This chapter's not for you. Why don't you head on over to Culture or Science with the other balloonheads who wouldn't know an honest paragraph if it indented up their vertical margins.

Hi, I'm Lou. Nice to meet you.

I knew you'd stay. You know how I knew? Because *I know*. I've been doing this a long time, my friend. Before your eyes hit the caption on the chapter heading I said to myself, "This ain't no tourist looking to pass some time on a bowel break. I got me a reader." Hell, I spotted you before you had finished the FAQ section of the Society chapter.

So what'll it be? A straightforward overview of **supply and demand**'s effect on the basic exchange of **goods and services**? A subtle whitewashing of exploitation and slavery *vis-à-vis* the success of colonial economies and the devastating human toll? **Keynes vs. Smith**, a helpful comparative?

You know what? Forget that stuff for now. You strike me as more of an evolution-over-time type. Yeah. Well, you're in the right chapter. We've got an **advertising timeline** that blows away any other attempt to chart the growth of a single industry across the x-axis that I've ever seen—and I used to work in timelines. True story! Before I came to Commerce I worked for a company, their entire business was "circas." Timelines, obituaries, any instance where you sort of knew about when something happened. Point is, blows away anything those guys ever put together.

I see you're checking out the introductory chapter image. I swear to god sometimes at night I think the old guy's eyes follow me wherever I go. Gives me the heebie ... what's that? No, no absolutely. Feel free to just browse around. Sure, sure. If you need anything, I'll be here in the opening essay. It was nice meeting you. ...

(Asshole.)

Trade

ONE DID NOT always possess everything that one needed to survive and prosper. And just taking these things from other people led to fights, feuds and socially awkward genocides. So eventually we worked out ways of exchanging goods and services called **trading** that left both parties, if not quite happy, then at least less homicidal.

History of Trading

At first, only expensive luxury items (such as **silk**, **spices** and **slaves**) were cost-effective to trade across long distances. Over time, improved modes of transportation (such as **carts**, **boats** and **slaves**) eased travel, enabling us to profitably trade goods of much shoddier quality.

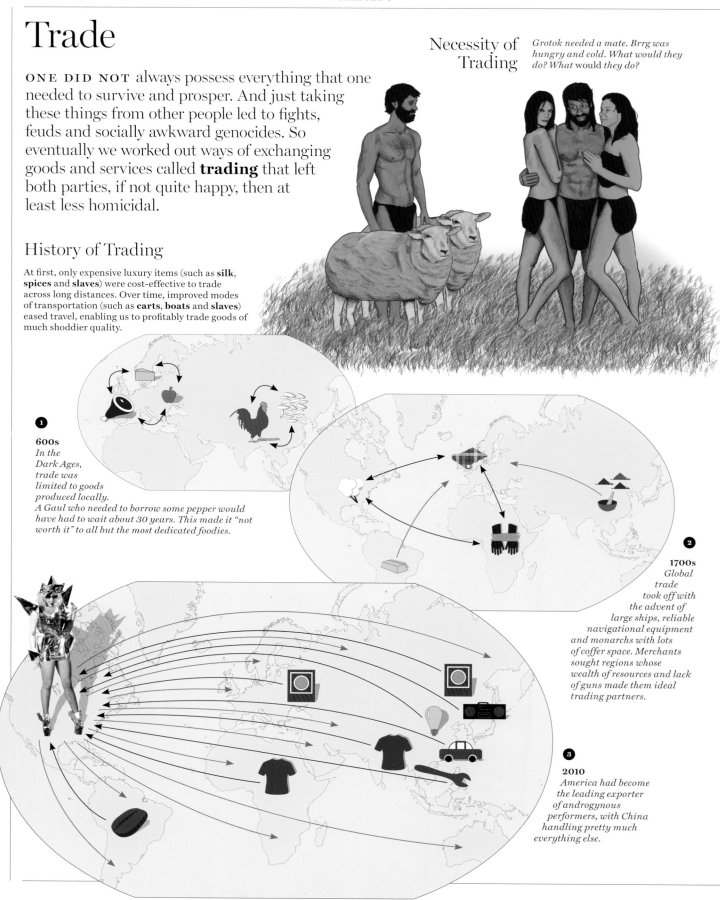

Necessity of Trading

Grotok needed a mate. Brrg was hungry and cold. What would they do? What would they do?

❶ 600s
In the Dark Ages, trade was limited to goods produced locally.
A Gaul who needed to borrow some pepper would have had to wait about 30 years. This made it "not worth it" to all but the most dedicated foodies.

❷ 1700s
Global trade took off with the advent of large ships, reliable navigational equipment and monarchs with lots of coffer space. Merchants sought regions whose wealth of resources and lack of guns made them ideal trading partners.

❸ 2010
America had become the leading exporter of androgynous performers, with China handling pretty much everything else.

The Basics

The essence of commerce could be understood through a few **key concepts**.

Supply and Demand

The market's iron guiding principle was the law of **supply and demand**, which stated that an item's value derived purely from its scarcity and how much people wanted it. Irrelevant factors included the item's utility, quality, storage requirements, what your wife will say and whether there was any good reason at all to spend $3100 on the only "authenticated" pair of ears Lenny Nimoy wore while filming *Star Trek VI*.

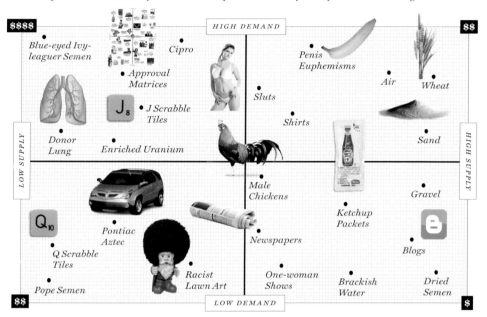

$$$$

HIGH DEMAND

$$

Blue-eyed Ivy-leaguer Semen

Cipro

Penis Euphemisms

Approval Matrices

Air

Wheat

Sluts

J Scrabble Tiles

Shirts

Sand

Donor Lung

Enriched Uranium

LOW SUPPLY

HIGH SUPPLY

Male Chickens

Gravel

Pontiac Aztec

Ketchup Packets

Newspapers

Blogs

Q Scrabble Tiles

Racist Lawn Art

One-woman Shows

Brackish Water

Dried Semen

Pope Semen

$$

LOW DEMAND

$

Buy Low, Sell High

There was no commercial principle more elementary than that it was good to sell a thing for more money than you bought it for. Doing so produced a **profit**, and meant you were really smart. Failure to do so produced a **loss**, and meant your broker was an idiot.

The alternative to "buy low, sell high" was often "jump high, land low."

Location Location Location

When choosing where to live or do business, one thing mattered so much that everyone always said it three times. Of course, the description of a property mattered as well. Early agents found buyers responded better to "near fresh water source" than "malarial swamp-adjacent."

Dubai Airport Boutique: $350

Kalamazoo Wal-Mart: $16.99

Back of a guy named Lenny's truck: $4 or two for $7

The value of merchandise like this purse depended on where it was sold.

"It's Not Personal. It's Just Business."

We considered actions taken in a commercial context to be morally distinct from other actions. Social norms such as compassion and integrity—otherwise highly valued—simply did not apply to trade.

Accepted Business Practice	Unacceptable Real-Life Practice
"Strategic default"	Being a deadbeat
Changing one's name to disassociate oneself from one's past (Philip Morris → Altria)	Changing one's name to disassociate oneself from one's past (convicted child molester Dave Radczik → "Bill Johnson")
Short-selling stock	Selling someone else's stuff to buy it back cheaper before they notice it's gone
Burying extra fees in small print	Whispering STD notification while sex partner is asleep
Merger followed by massive layoffs	Marriage followed by putting new stepkids up for adoption
Hostile takeover	Busting in neighbor's door and forcing him to sell you his house for less than it's worth

Anybody who said something was "just business" had just fucked or was about to fuck you over.

Economics

ECONOMICS AROSE as a way to explain the behaviors of markets. It became known as "the dismal science" because it couldn't compete with the pure *joie de vivre* of particle physics or metallurgy. By the early 21st century, we'd gotten so good at economics that advanced nations only suffered major financial collapses twice every decade or so.

Market Principles

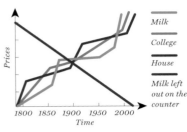

For no real reason, almost everything got more expensive.

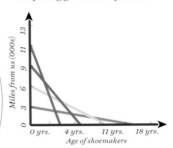

The farther they were from us, the younger the people making our shoes could acceptably be.

Our Four Most Important Economic Thinkers

The Middleman

Nearly all transactions involved one or more intermediaries who would facilitate deals for a cut of the final price. The chief duty of these **middlemen** was to ensure buyers and sellers could never simply talk to each other directly like human beings.

This drawing cost $500: a $400 illustrator's fee, plus $100 to get some guy to hand the illustrator $400.

ADAM SMITH
(1723–1790)

For most of history we naively believed it was sometimes good to put our fellow man's well-being ahead of our own. **Adam Smith** called bull∫hit on that, showing that pursuing self-interest (**free-market capitalism**) was itself the highest form of altruism. Smith believed markets were guided by an "invisible hand" that scuttled around under people's beds waiting to rationally allocate resources. Governments should avoid trying to control this creepy hand, Smith said, as doing so would only make it mad.

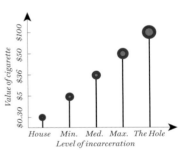

JOHN MAYNARD KEYNES
(1883–1946)

John Maynard Keynes countered Smith, asserting that governments could correct a free market's occasionally errant course by manipulating levels of public spending and interest rates, much as one might steer a Ferrari by alternately yanking and pushing two levers in the trunk. Keynesianism is credited with ending the Great Depression, but in later decades faced opposition from the sorts of people whom the Great Depression didn't hurt anyway.

KARL MARX
(1818–1883)

In *Das Kapital* (German for "The Kapital"), **Karl Marx** theorized that when a small group of property owners exploited a much larger number of workers, the workers would inevitably revolt, seize control of the means of production and build a proletarian **communist** paradise. This bold prediction remained on the verge of coming true for 140 years.

Regardless of circumstances, prices obeyed the law of supply and demand.

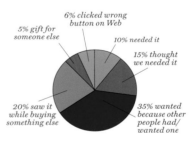

Reasons We Bought Things

CHARLES PONZI
(1882–1949)

Like his contemporary Albert Einstein, **Charles Ponzi** unlocked an explosive equation: *belief = wealth.* If enough investors believed a **scheme** would make money, it would. The trick was perpetually finding enough new investors to pay off the old ones, a figure Ponzi estimated at $6(\infty)$. While Ponzi schemes inevitably failed, his revered principles were central to such successful 21st-century markets as real estate, tech stocks and everything else.

The Black Market

Some goods and services were difficult or impossible to obtain due to scarcity, taxes and tariffs, and/or the ethical strictures of our respective societies. (One man's loyal companion was another's indentured servant.) Naturally these unavailable or banned items were highly sought after. It was precisely because endangered white tiger brains wouldn't chill and serve themselves that illicit **black markets** sprung up to deliver the most difficult and/or odious products. Black markets are of course not to be confused with **markets for black people**, which we also had.

April in Macau

Tanner wasn't good for much more than a few laughs at cocktail hour. So when I saw that flame in his eye and a damp cigarette on his lip, I only expected a story from the Jockey Club. "What now?" I wheezed. "Did Weng whip another man's horse behind the tote board?" But Tanner hadn't come from the track. He'd come from a the Great People's Prison – and not empty handed, either.
Full-functioning Human Liver
$25,000 (surgery not included)

Fat of the Land

I'm the sort who'll send my plate back to the kitchen if the rosemary sprig looks soft. So it might surprise you to hear about the best meal I ever ate. It was midnight about 90 miles upriver from Kinshasa. We'd had a long day, Yuri and I, on account of his De Havilland losing power at 4000 feet. The crash wasn't bad. But the walk out, dear God... Luckily, a local widow's stove was still hot.
Bush Meat (genuine primate)
$0.12/lb.

Room Service

Bangkok was made for men like my friend Matti. He's poor but loves to show off. He'd return with a flock of dancing girls and lead them up to his room, making sure we all saw them from the lobby bar. Two minutes later he'd come back stag and order a beer. "Matti," we'd say, "Go upstairs! Are you mad?" He'd just sip the foam off his Singha, and announce: "I'm paying them to leave me alone."
Teen Prostitute
500 baht ($15) and up

Pistol Whipped

Bill Webster was the best prefect I ever saw. He called himself *Tah-Nahk*, "Ghost Lord." Scared the yellow piss out of the peasants. But when the time came for him to go, he had other plans. Not a problem. I knew a man in Cairo who knew a man in Russia. Next thing, a company of "patriots" were peppering the mansion with automatic fire as old Webster ran for the river. Did I mention he anchored the relay team at Eton?
AK-47 Assault Rifles (case of 1 dozen)
Price: Ask your server

Here's Your Proof

More than anything, I remember the sunsets. That crepuscular glow of another Paris evening gleamed through my curator friend Marie-Josee's 7th Arrondissement *pied a terre* window: the perfect time, she said, for a well-aged single-malt. And the Scotch was all the smoother for not having any government tariff aftertaste. Of course that wasn't the only surprise Marie-Jo had planned that night...
Unstamped beverage alcohol
40% off wholesale

THE MACGLHENRRH
Single Malt
SCOTCH WHISKEY

Carried Aloft

When he wasn't smuggling unmentionable substances up from the south, Badrang made the best kites in Feyzabad. I promise I was only interested in the latter. Unfortunately, so were the local Taliban. In the end it didn't matter to a man like Bedrang. He just called the Canadian captain up the road and that night the Taliban's house disappeared in a blast felt halfway to the olive groves. "Like a hot wind in June," he told me over a typically potent cup of tea. "My son could have flown his kite in it."
Kite
50 Pakistani rupees

Money

YOU WANT TO know us? *Really* know us? Then study this page. *This* is what we fought, killed and died for. Sometimes, we even worked for it. It was **money**. To the untrained eye it just looks like odd bits of paper and metal, but it made the world go around. We parted it from fools, even though it burned holes in our pockets and couldn't buy us happiness or love. It was the root of all evil, but we took it and ran: smart, seed, serious, easy, earned, funny, found, front, good after bad, mad, cash, old, new, blood, honest, even, real and hush. We weren't made of it, but we followed it. Why? Because it took money to make money and it sure didn't grow on trees … Anyway, you guys can have it if you want.

YOU HAD TO BE HERE

In 1913, this Liberty Head nickel was worth $0.05.

In 2010, it was worth $5,000,000.

Coins

These metal tokens represented smaller units of currency. Early coins were made of actual precious metals, which were later deemed "too valuable" to be money. Coins also played a key role in deciding issues like who got to sit in the front seat and who got to kick off in overtime.

U.S. coins provided a convenient way to compare the sizes of former presidents.

Dictators often adorned currency with their own name and face, to solidify their claim to power.

Not all coins were round. These ancient Chinese coins commemorated the space visitors who inseminated the monkeys to create the human race.

2000 A.D. saw an important victory for civil rights whereby Native Americans would finally be recognized for their full dollar value.

The Euro was a transnational currency meant to test how small a nation could be and still drag an entire prosperous continent into economic collapse.

A single €2 coin could buy a small cheese sandwich, or two weird tiny sodas, or if you went farther east a three-piece suit and a retired circus bear.

This Roman brothel coin was exchangeable for one fellatium.

Paper

Lightweight, foldable, easy to print in massive quantities, filthy, flammable: three of these traits made paper the medium of choice for higher-value currency. Here is a typical specimen.

This **cryptic freemasonish symbol** was meant to spur conspiracy theories about who really ran the government.

*It just didn't feel like money without someone's **portrait** on it. Often it was a figure of national pride who had positively contributed to the country's history. More often, it was the Queen of England.*

*The name of the **issuing country** was a handy reminder of where it was OK to pass this off as money.*

*The **denomination** was spelled out and repeated at least ten times for the benefit of foreigners and morons.*

*Money was full of **random little shit**.*

*Some currencies had their own one-character **symbol**. Others included €, ¥, and ♀, a currency whose value peaked in 1999.*

*This space was filled with celebrated local **architecture**, fauna or event of historical importance. Sometimes all three.*

***Serial numbers** came in handy in the event of a money recall.*

Eagle Eye Challenge: Can you spot the five **Easter eggs**?

Other Currencies

*Yap Islanders used these **enormous stone disks** to gain entry to the world's largest subway.*

While not legal tender, this $100 bill was still widely used by hats, racecars, thimbles and Scottish terriers to buy property, pay taxes and post bail from the jail in which they were sometimes arbitrarily incarcerated.

I, Jasper McGinty owe Orville Jones 10 dollars

***IOUs** were valid only between two individuals: 1) the party who owed the money, or "debtor," and 2) the sucker.*

Gift cards were worth a designated sum at a specific store. They were purchased as gifts by someone who felt it was too impersonal to give cash to someone they knew only well enough to guess what general category of goods might please them.

*Not all money was man made. Widely used in ancient China, Africa and North America, **cowry shells** were the world's second most popular form of vagina-shaped currency.*

SPOTLIGHT
THE GOLD STANDARD

You already read about our love of gold in Chapter One. But did you know we adored it so much that we used it as the very basis of our concept of value? For a long time, most paper money was "backed" by an agreed-upon amount of actual shiny gold, which for some reason made people feel better. But as our economies grew, gold's chief attribute—its scarcity—became inconvenient. Earth obviously had a finite amount of gold, yet modern capitalism was based on the idea that we were all going to end up rich. So we ditched gold, and kept the paper. It's not like we were ever going to run out of trees! Right?

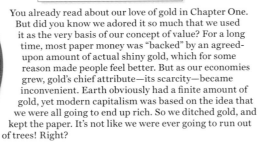

Uh ... happy birthday? We've been really busy.

Work

FOR SOCIETY TO flourish, it would take **work**. So what was work? Tasks we performed for compensation in the service of an employer, be it an individual or corporate entity. And yes, it was as exciting as it sounds. We didn't want to work. In fact, that's about as good a definition of "work" as you could have—"that which we didn't want to do, but had to, if we didn't want to eat dirt." Of course, some workers attacked their jobs with passion and creativity. These people were known as **brown-nosing jagoffs**.

Growing Things

The practice of cultivating crops, or **agriculture**, enabled man to feed thousands of people living in a relatively small area, meaning that finally we could put away the tents and bow and arrows and start shoveling acres of manure. Millennia later, mechanized farm equipment, manmade fertilizers and genetic engineering allowed us to end the scourge of human hunger once and for all. Just kidding! Towards the end we inevitably experienced a trend back toward the "organic" farming of yesteryear, but this proved to be little more than the pipe dreams of wealthy elitists whose children were for some reason plagued by countless undocumented food allergies.

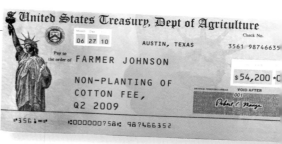

There were two ways to make a living from farming: 1) growing food and then consuming or selling it; or, 2) not growing anything and getting paid anyway.

We put a lot of work into devising better ways to not work.

"This is hard."

"This is still pretty hard."

"Not bad. Though I have a nagging feeling this may be corroding my soul."

"There we go."

QUICK QUIZ

Scientists introduced genes from an arctic flounder into tomatoes in order to make them frost-resistant but otherwise indistinguishable from regular tomatoes. Can you tell which of the above tomatoes was genetically modified?

Typical Worker
There was a quiet dignity to coaxing life and sustenance from the earth, though it was sometimes hard to notice over the irremovable stench of shit.

Typical Fear
Rain: not enough; too much; right amount but wrong kind of; crop surplus resulting from perfect amount of.

Typical Joy
That day the rooster died and you got to sleep until 5 A.M.

Typical Tool
Used for digging earth to plant seeds, uproot weeds, bury relatives dead from harsh winter.

Making Things

All the things you're finding that aren't plants, rocks or other animals—we made those! From aluminum foil to Zithromax, diapers to dioxin—our clever brains and agile hands conspired to **manufacture** things to make our lives more bearable. Early man lovingly hand-crafted these items with care, skill and soul. Luckily, mass production came along to end all that.

Typical Worker
The most important skill for an Industrial Age laborer was to be utterly replaceable.

Typical Tool
Life was so much easier when the small mechanical parts you were told to assemble would come directly to you, hour after hour, day after day, year after year …

*At our civilization's height, factories employed both millions of semi-skilled workers and industrial **robots**, performing a single repetitive task for thousands of hours a year. Note that in our fiction, it was the robots who rose up against us.*

Typical Joy
Beer. Wait, not "joy." Anesthestic.

Typical Fear *Thumb loss (fingers expendable).*

*Henry Ford revolutionized manufacturing by using the **assembly line** to mass-produce Model T cars affordable to workers of average means. As Ford famously said, "Any color, so long as it is seafoam green. Also, if it can be helped I'd rather not sell to Jews."*

IN THE RUINS
SHIPPING CONTAINERS

Hey. Lou here. I see you're looking at the **shipping containers**. They made globalizing our economy so easy it was stupid. They were all eight feet wide, eight feet high and twenty feet long. Why that size? Wrong question. It was the fact they were all the same size that mattered. Our ships, cranes and trucks were all built to haul these boxes and nothing else. The upshot was, we could move cargo from Hong Kong to Long Beach at $1.50 a cubic foot. (Asshole.)

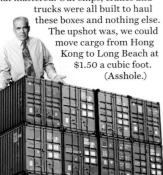

Doing Things

If you were not making or growing things, you were part of our other vast work sector: the **service industries**. There were financial services, food services, customer, administration, medical and tech services. There were services that placed individuals into other service jobs, and services to complain about the lack of service you had been receiving from the aforementioned service services. You would think any such well-serviced society would be happy and satisfied. Well, you never spent three hours being passed back and forth between an automated response menu and a persnickety 22-year-old Calcuttan named "Chuck." Just tell me how to activate my goddamn cellphone, Chuck, and NO! NO, DON'T SEND ME BACK TO THE MACHINE LADY ... AAAAAAAAAGGHHHHHHHHH!!!

Other Service Jobs

Fast Food Worker
A large number of humans were forced to "wear the paper hat," a reference to the uniform that was part of the humiliation process central to producing crisp yet yielding fries.
Came home smelling of:
Grease, cleaning supplies, self-doubt.

Service Industries

Typical Worker
This is Barb. She's the best. If you need to know where anything is, just ask her. Or call or IM her, or just email or send a text. Barb's great. Oh, but don't fuck with her yogurt in the shared fridge or she will *cut* you.

Hospital Orderly
Some of us grew up to be doctors. Others grew up to be the people who changed the soiled bedding before the doctor came in.
Came home smelling of:
Hospital food with a soupçon of diarrhea.

Typical Tools
Technology enabled global communication and trips to the snack machine without ever leaving a sitting position.

Cable Installer
These renegades of the service sector played loose with the very idea of "service." You'll be home between 10 and 2? How about 6:20, *hombre?* Because that's when he's showing up.
Came home smelling of:
Your couch.

Typical Joy
Wearing slightly more comfortable pants on Fridays.

Typical Fear
Loss of comfortable pants privileges.

WHEN DID WE WORK?

We started out working seven days per week with no days off, gradually got one day, then two and finally in 21st century Western Europe, six and a half days off plus vacations.

The Value Chain

Our products began as raw materials, to which we humans **added value** with labor and ingenuity.

STEP ONE: *Extraction*
It all began when a **miner**, 12-year-old Saa Bairoh, found the rough stone in the Sierra Leone mine where he worked at gunpoint. As a reward, Saa received an extra huff of solvent that night.
Stone's value: $470
Miner's pay: $1.12/day

STEP TWO: *Transportation*
Next, a **smuggler** employed his knowledge of local warlords and the human digestive tract to carry the rough stone from countryside to capital.
Stone's value: $1,220
Smuggler's pay: $200

STEP THREE:
Negotiation
A **middleman** played prospective buyers off each other, raising the stone's price. He took a modest percentage for his service.
Stone's value: $3,900
Middleman's pay:
$950

STEP FOUR:
Processing
An Antwerp **diamond cutter** shaped the stone so as to maximize its capacity to engender envy.
Stone's value: $10,700
Cutter's pay: €11,000/month

STEP FIVE: *Distribution*
If we knew how this happened or the names of the **parties involved**, we'd be in another line of business.
Stone's value: Unknown; **Distributor's pay:** Ha!

STEP SIX: *Retail*
A **retailer** showed the diamond—now set in an elegant platinum ring—to young men who could not afford it. One of them would buy it anyway.
Stone's value: $17,100
Retailer's pay: $230,000/year

STEP SEVEN: *Flaunting*
The ring's **recipient** never left home without it, sending a gleaming "fuck you" to her closest friends.
Stone's value: $17,100
Recipient's pay:
Amex #3727 224534 24385

131

Buying and Selling

ALL OF EARTH'S organisms were consumers in that to survive they required and obtained inputs from the outside world. But, where a plant needed nothing but sunlight, water and CO_2, man required Dairy Queen Blizzards, rhinestone BlackBerry covers and time-share condos in Cabo. Somehow, the species that stood atop the evolutionary ladder defined itself less by sophistication of thought and action than by stuff—specifically, the relentless pursuit of more, and whether you knew someone who could get it for you wholesale.

WE SAID IT

"There's a sucker born every minute. Get that down to 50 seconds by next month or you're fired."
—P.T. Barnum (1810–1891), American entertainment executive

We commemorated our every transaction with a receipt full of important information.

Walmart
Save money. Live better.

```
      WE SELL FOR LESS
          ALWAYS
1 LOAF  OF BREAD
                        2.95 N
         SUBTOTAL   2.95
            TOTAL   2.95
        CASH TEND   2.95
       CHANGE DUE   0.00

# ITEMS SOLD 1
```

50¢ OFF OF 10,000 COUNT Q-TIPS!

APRIL IS DIAPER MONTH! TAKE 6.4% OFF ALREADY LOW PAMPERS PRICES!

NOW IN STOCK! HARRY POTTER AND THE ENDLESS ADVENTURE: SPECIAL EDITION DIRECTOR'S CUT BLU-RAY DVD LIMITED EDITION SET ONLY $44.99. BUY TWO, GET THIRD FOR HALF PRICE!

WALMART SUPPORTS OUR TROOPS

32 OZ. LOW-SALT DIET WHITE CHEDDAR HABANERO RANCH CHEEZ-ITS ONLY $7.99 THROUGH EASTER!

SAVE THIS RECEIPT! SEE IF YOU'VE WON THE WALMART RECEIPT OF THE WEEK SWEEPSTAKES! RANDOM DRAWING FOR UP TO $100 IN PRIZES. CLAIM YOUR PRIZE BY CALLING 1-900-WALMART ON SUNDAY BETWEEN 2 & 4 PM CST. CALL COSTS $2.99/MINUTE.

TREAT YOURSELF! BUY MORE CANDY!

WALMART ALLOWS RETURNS AND EXCHANGES WITHIN 4 DAYS OF PURCHASE WITH RECEIPT FOR STORE CREDIT OF 65% ORIGINAL RETAIL VALUE.

APPLY NOW FOR THE VISA WALCARD! $50,000 CREDIT LIMIT! NO BACKGROUND CHECK! POWER OF ATTORNEY!

VISIT WALMART.COM FOR AMAZING DEALS

IN THE RUINS
SHOPPING AIDS

You'll find these everywhere. I guess we should have said "paper."

THANK YOU *Have A Nice Day*

Popular conveyances among people with either lots of money to spend, or no home.

THE MATTRESS SHACK
New & Pre-owned

HOLOCAUST REMEMBRANCE DAY SALES EVENT

Elie says: "You'll never forget...the savings!"

We could turn any national observance into a commercial opportunity.

Evolution of Shopping

Over time the locus of our shopping moved from our homes, to the streets, to stores and eventually—in what was widely hailed as a paradigm-shifting breakthrough—back into our homes.

Could sell you anything you wanted, provided it was made of old rags and if he had any left by the time he got to your street.

Merchant paid 20 silver pieces for this rug, but due to personal rapport, let you have it for 10. (Actual value: 2.)

Perfect if you wanted to buy a TV, a gun, a 3-pack of diaper-rash cream and some cotton/poly sweatpants.

Perfect if you wanted to buy a TV, a gun, diaper cream and sweatpants, and didn't want to be wearing pants while doing it.

Perfect if you wanted to buy those things, and—what? They're at the front door? Thanks, BrainWave.com!

WAL★MART *We Sell For Less*
Pharmacy Photo Tire & Lube Express

amazon.com

BrainWave.com

Bargaining and Haggling

While basic supply and demand were always central in determining an item's value, we often arrived at its actual selling price via **haggling**—back-and-forth negotiation between buyer and seller. In the end, one could assume final price was fair if, and only if, both parties walked away unhappy.

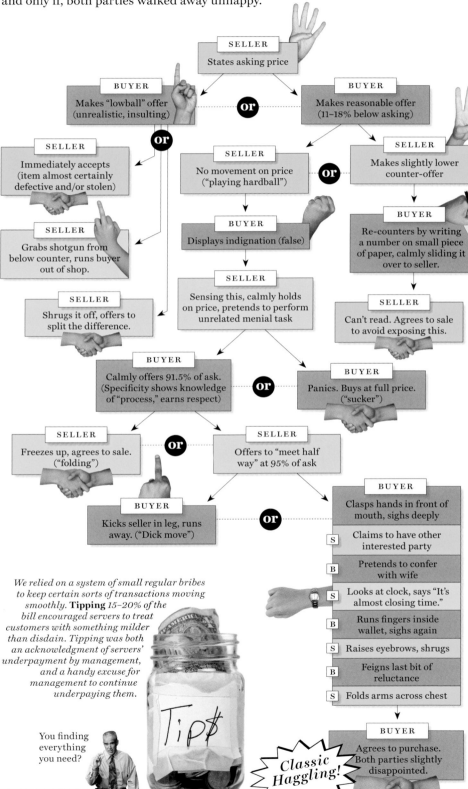

SELLER — States asking price

BUYER — Makes "lowball" offer (unrealistic, insulting)

or

BUYER — Makes reasonable offer (11–18% below asking)

SELLER — Immediately accepts (item almost certainly defective and/or stolen)

SELLER — No movement on price ("playing hardball")

or

SELLER — Makes slightly lower counter-offer

SELLER — Grabs shotgun from below counter, runs buyer out of shop.

BUYER — Displays indignation (false)

BUYER — Re-counters by writing a number on small piece of paper, calmly sliding it over to seller.

SELLER — Shrugs it off, offers to split the difference.

SELLER — Sensing this, calmly holds on price, pretends to perform unrelated menial task

SELLER — Can't read. Agrees to sale to avoid exposing this.

BUYER — Calmly offers 91.5% of ask. (Specificity shows knowledge of "process," earns respect)

or

BUYER — Panics. Buys at full price. ("sucker")

SELLER — Freezes up, agrees to sale. ("folding")

or

SELLER — Offers to "meet half way" at 95% of ask

BUYER — Kicks seller in leg, runs away. ("Dick move")

or

BUYER
- S — Clasps hands in front of mouth, sighs deeply
- S — Claims to have other interested party
- B — Pretends to confer with wife
- S — Looks at clock, says "It's almost closing time."
- B — Runs fingers inside wallet, sighs again
- S — Raises eyebrows, shrugs
- B — Feigns last bit of reluctance
- S — Folds arms across chest

BUYER — Agrees to purchase. Both parties slightly disappointed.

Classic Haggling!

We relied on a system of small regular bribes to keep certain sorts of transactions moving smoothly. **Tipping** *15–20% of the bill encouraged servers to treat customers with something milder than disdain. Tipping was both an acknowledgment of servers' underpayment by management, and a handy excuse for management to continue underpaying them.*

You finding everything you need?

Advertising

EVEN SOPHISTICATED CONSUMERS like humans weren't always sure which product they had to have. **Advertising** answered that question, informing potential customers which goods would, if bypassed, render one too boring, stupid, hairy or generally unfuckable to go on living. As people acclimated to any given sales technique, advertisers grew both more and less subtle, finding deft ways of incorporating their messages into our daily lives. We went from being exposed to one or two ads a day (1900) to 5,000 a day (2010). It wasn't easy for the human brain to process this quantity of information, but we found space for it in the cranial regions formerly occupied by our capacity for introspection, wonder and joy.

Advertising Techniques

Branding

A **brand** was more than just a name or logo. Through advertising a brand could become part of a narrative, into which a consumer was invited to insert himself. The less distinctive the product, the more need for branding. For example: All the vodkas shown below tasted exactly alike. To help consumers know which to choose, ads identified their respective 40% grain alcohol solution as appropriate for specific **target audiences**.

Anthropo-morphism

Our tremendous narcissism led us to find any product 65% more appealing if it exhibited human traits. Thus, advertising was a fantasyland of dancing, talking and implicitly suicidal food.

If it was cute enough, humans would even buy fake meat from a severed hand.

Target:
Brash fitness models

Target:
Graphic-design enthusiasts

Target:
Art-world sophisticates

Target:
Robot fetishists

A collar that lays flat
That's the Hanes® Comfort Promise.
Hanes

Celebrity Endorsements

Corporations could often get us to transfer our feelings of goodwill for a celebrity to a product they were paid to endorse. This technique never backfired.

Element of Surprise

The ad on the left grabbed a consumer's attention by calling the VW bug a "lemon." This technique was highly effective although—as the ad on the right shows—it required careful deployment.

Appeals to Authority

We responded especially well to any product valuation enumerated out of a group of five or ten unnamed medical professionals.

Crisco
9 OUT OF 10 DOCTORS SAY: "IT'S DIGESTIBLE!"

Crest Most Dentists Recommend

9 out of 10 Doctors Prefer

Chesterfields and Bareback Sex with Atlantic City Street Hustlers

Subliminal

Subliminal advertising aroused our innermost desires without us even realizing it. This advertisement implicitly associated cigarettes with our desire—possibly never acknowledged even to ourselves—for a thick, hard cock.

Hail Mary

If an advertiser was truly stuck, he could fall back on a desperate gambit: offering a quality product at an affordable price. But this was strictly a last-ditch measure.

Target: Rohypnol distributors

LUXURY REBORN

Granny Smith Apples
$1.29/lb.
this week at Food Lion

MTA New York City Bus 8816

Advertising Timeline

1932 This spot for Scot Towels was a legend in ad circles for leading to the eventual arrest, conviction and execution of Julius and Ethel Rosenberg.

1901 The blockbuster launch of Uneeda Biscuits definitively proves the value of a good brand name, bringing riches to founder Francis K. Uneeda, and bankrupting his chief competitor, James J. Uvomita.

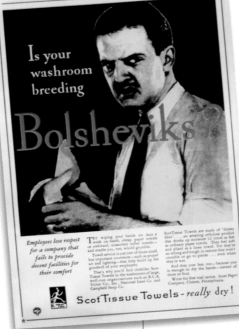

Is your washroom breeding Bolsheviks?

Employees lose respect for a company that fails to provide decent facilities for their comfort

Scot Tissue Towels – really dry!

1950s This hit TV campaign prominently featured the only parts of the human body that cigarettes didn't ruin.

1963 PepsiCo touches off the "cola wars." By the time they end, millions of lives are lost to adult-onset diabetes.

2560 B.C. Although it's often considered a strictly modern phenomenon, advertising dates to earliest civilization.

Lest you forget, We say it yet
Uneeda Biscuit 5¢
NATIONAL BISCUIT COMPANY

2000 B.C. | **1900** | **1910** | **1920** | **1930** | **1940** | **1950** | **1960**

1828 First known "product placement"—surreptitious insertion of products into works of art, in the hopes of subliminally influencing people.

1922 Using only sound, radio advertisers find a unique way to drive their message into the listener's subconscious.

Faust
Fear not that I will break this covenant: My sole desire in life, is what I've promised!

Mephistopheles
Just scratch your name there, in a drop of blood. Blood it must be — blood has peculiar virtues. Though not as many virtues as Koenig & Bauer's miraculous new AutoSchreiber III printing press. Available now! Koenig & Bauer — they put the customer uber alles.

1914 Political propaganda: Lord Kitchener's iconic advertisement recruiting soldiers to fight in the Great War. The sales pitch, a huge success, results in the deaths of 9.7 million.

Lexington Hotel
Radio Advertisement
Final Script, 7 October

GILBERT: "Hey Edward, did you hear about The Lexington Hotel?"

EDWARD: "The Lexington Hotel? Why, Gilbert, do you mean Manhattan's finest Irishman-free establishment?"

GILBERT: "The same. It's as affordable as it is Irishman-free."

EDWARD: "The Lexington! It has everything you want in a hotel!"

GILBERT: "And no filthy Irishmen."

1950s–1960s Market-research firms enabled campaigns aimed specifically at narrow constituencies.

1704 The first newspaper personal ad appears.

NEWS-LETTER.
by Authority.

7. to **Monday** April 24. 1704.

MISSED CONNECTIONE:
Thou: Grey Breeches 'neath a dun-hued Tunic I: Blue Waiftcoat o'er mofsy-green Troufers Thou wert faftening thine Horfe in the Towne Square when we briefly clept gazes, Wouldft thou care to partake in a Heated Beverage of fome fort? Contactft thou me at Pofte Office Boxe feven.

"YOUR COUNTRY NEEDS **YOU**"

Women

EEK! A MOUSE!

Racists

Fair-skinned pedophiles

TAN, don't burn USE **COPPERTONE**

She want to thank you

THREE TIMES A DAY!

An everlasting gift! New In-Sink-Erator Saturn Garbage Disposer

1969 Loosening sexual mores allowed advertisers to incorporate sex into their campaigns, as in this ad, which exploited the well-known connection between garbage disposals and intercourse.

2010 Advertising reaches near-total cultural dominance, as nearly every flat surface is covered with some type of commercial message.

The Hong Kong Chamber of Commerce ascertained how much neon would induce seizures, and backed it off a quarter-step.

1-800-999-9999

My Little V8 Baking Mixer

15 Payments of $24.95

1985 The U.S. lifts regulations limiting the length of commercials. Eventually, whole channels were devoted solely to men in button down shirts selling us gadgets we never used.

1995 Janis Joplin's sardonic song "Mercedes Benz" is used unsardonically in an ad for Mercedes-Benz, marking the moment when commerce and culture stopped fighting and started making sweet, sweet love.

| 1970 | 1980 | 1990 | 2000 | 2010 |

1967 Wells, Rich, Greene becomes the first major ad agency to be run by a woman. The development is considered overdue by firms that had realized men could sometimes be tone-deaf in marketing to women.

1984 Apple's iconic "1984" ad brought TV advertising to the next level, creating a mini-movie about freeing computer users from the Orwellian tyranny of having two mouse buttons.

Early 2000s Our relationship to commercial products entered a new phase, wherein we believed we were expressing our individuality by paying to adorn ourselves with advertisements for goods that other people profited from.

Juicy

1987 The "This is your brain on drugs" ad campaign proves a massive success, with egg sales skyrocketing 47%.

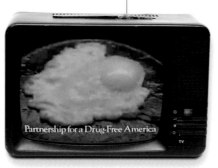

Partnership for a Drug-Free America

1999 The Internet boom opens a new realm of advertising.

Hit the monkey! Get a FREE* PS3*!

Nobody knew what this ad was for, but it was incredibly irritating.

Tampax will help you deal with... *You know...* That thing that happens once a month. Please don't make us say it.

TAMPAX

Corporations

WHILE INDIVIDUALS COULD provide relatively simple goods and services, more complex ones required a coordinated group effort. The name for such a group was a **corporation**—an independent legal entity built by and composed of humans that was granted some of the intrinsic rights of humans without having to be weighed down by their responsibilities or sense of morality. Of course any corporation that did behave immorally would be immediately disciplined by market forces. In the event such a firm chose to continue down a less than righteous path, they would be shunned and cast out of the family of man. (Those last two sentences were brought to you by and cannot be reproduced without the express written consent of the Sarcasm™ Company. The Sarcasm™ Company—doing their "sincere best" since 1936. ◆

Person vs. Corporation

	Person	**Corporation**
Size	1 person	7,000 persons
Motivations	Hunger, sex, complex notion of success and fulfillment	Money
Rights under the law	Those of a citizen	Those of a citizen, except where inconvenient
Legal restrictions	Obey laws or do jail time	Obey laws or whatever

Much of our most prominent architecture reflected corporations' great wit and soul.

Corporate Identity

The choice of a proper **brand logo** was as crucial to a corporation as a nation's flag or a religion's gold-thing-you-wear-on-a-chain. It had to be visually appealing, but it did not have to have anything to do with what your company did.

Gerber

What you'd expect them to sell: White babies
What they sold: Baby food

What you'd expect them to sell: Gay apples
What they sold: Computers

at&t

What you'd expect them to sell: Hands-free egg slicers
What they sold: Sub-par cell-phone service

What you'd expect them to sell: Eagle traps
What they sold: Urine-flavored beer

Budweiser

QUAKER

What you'd expect them to sell: Egalitarian pacifism
What they sold: Oatmeal

What you'd expect them to sell: Three-field crop rotation
What they sold: Your own money back to you

Bank of America

Former Detroit Lions running back Barry Sanders: *CEO really wanted to party with him. Chair of Audit Committee.*

Rewarding Success

Business deals could be complex, and we were very proud of them when finished.

Board of Directors

Most corporate executives' power was held firmly in check by a **board of directors**, a group of outsiders whose approval was required for all major decisions, and who were paid the equivalent of a middle manager's annual salary for showing up four times a year, unless they couldn't make it, in which case, two or three times a year. It was a sign of how exceptionally well CEOs ran our corporations that their boards approved roughly 99 percent of everything they ever proposed.

Corporate Communication

For years, **corporatese**—the specialized dialect spoken by highly-paid executives to obscure their jobs' relative simplicity—was incomprehensible to linguists and laymen alike. That changed with the 2003 discovery of the **Rosetta Memo** behind a filing cabinet in an Atlanta office park.

...that some team members are experiencing a non-satisfactory level of disconnect vis-à-vis our interpersonnel messaging. To ensure we're all on the same page with our ducks in a row, we're opening the kimono to initiate a global refresh on F2F and e-mmunication standards. Therefore, FYI/FFR: Interface, dialogue, touch base, face-to-face, connect and advise indicate interpersonal communication. Execute, implement, leverage, facilitate, synergize, deliver and exploit pertain to the performance of work. Robust, value-rich, seamless, best-of-breed and user-centric denote meritorious quality. Further: to enhiden our task-simplicity quotient (the revealing of which could result in significant new awareness of human-capital redundancy, and attendant downsizing), all comm's should going forward be both redundant and repetitive, with the occasional wordvention utilized in place of vocables of greater brevity, clarity, and brevarity. Augment with occasional impenetrable acronyms (OIAs). These syntactical enhancements add perceived value to each employee's personal brand. Exemplifications are underposted: 4) "I want to circle back and interface about how to rightsize our headcount while still keeping workers incentivized." 2) "Due to unforeseen life events, I'll be offline tomorrow, so can we push our interlock until post-all-hands?" 3) "At the end of the day, net-net, if we have a joint brown-bag to come to agreeance on how to grow mindshare among targeted thought leaders by implementing best practices across the board, we can marketeer our way toward synergizing a frictionless sales environment."

Hey dumbshits: 90% of the stuff we say basically means either "talk," "make," or "good." But nobody pays fat salaries for 'talking about making good things.' So to keep our scam going, only use ungainly words, and always three times as many of them as a normal person. Examples: 1) "Let's discuss how we can fire people without making the ones we keep cry." 2) "My uncle died; can we meet later?" 3) "Lunch?"

Chairman: *In charge of overseeing the corporation's top executives, especially its CEO. Who, coincidentally, happened to be the board chairman. This never struck anyone as odd.*

Two women: *Because having none looked sexist and one looked token-y. One of the two was either black or ... what's the other thing? Asian.*

Partner in law firm: *As head of Regulatory Compliance Committee, specialties included Cayman tax code, Cambodian child-labor law, and the ability to say exactly where international waters began.*

Head of some sort of charity: *Nothing controversial—maybe involving, like, feeding hungry kids. Is there a charity called Feed The Hungry Kids? That would be perfect.*

Founder's least embarrassing grandson: *If no grandsons were unembarrassing, founder's most presentable great-nephew.*

Speakerphone: *Could be used to "conference in" board members who had more important things to do than take part in a kabuki ritual of corporate governance.*

Exotic wood conference table: *Acquired at cost equal to salary of one janitor. Fit into budget by firing one guess who.*

Mediocre Danish.

Former cabinet member: *Lunched in government capitals to pave path for company's actions. Knew the relevant legal loopholes because he wrote them.*

Satan: *Now it can be told.*

Money We Didn't Have

WITH THE INVENTION of money, several new problems emerged. Those who had more money than they needed required a place to keep it. Those who needed more money than they had required a place to borrow some. And those who loved money so much they didn't know what to do with themselves required a place to work. With characteristic enterprise, we created one solution to all these problems.

Banks

Banks were excellent places to store one's savings because, as they said, they could "put your money to work."

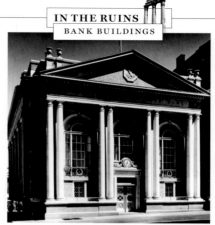

Banks were built as virtual fortresses so customers would believe their money was safe while somehow overlooking the buildings' obviously excessive cost of construction and the one and only place those funds could have come from. Note that in contrast to actual fortresses, banks were generally protected only by a solitary, tired middle-aged man.

❶ *After customers **deposited** their money, it could be locked in a big vault for safekeeping.*

❷ *More commonly the bank **loaned** your money to someone who needed it to buy a house, start a business or pay off another loan.*

❸ *To meet expenses (i.e. pay bonuses), banks could also take small **fees**, though not nearly as small as the fine print explaining that they could do so.*

❻ *Part of your money could go to burnishing your bank's **image**—for instance, by sponsoring professional sports. Because overpriced beer and nightmarish parking were positive associations compared to "bank."*

❺ *Of course, there was always a chance someone would come and just **take** your money.*

❹ *Your money might get **invested** in sound business opportunities your bank deemed worthy of money that wasn't theirs.*

❼ *In the end you could **withdraw** your funds, minus one last ATM fee to cover expenses. It's not like banks were made of money.*

Whether joining the fight against feline lymphoma or celebrating a Publishers Clearinghouse winner, nothing said "big event" like a **giant novelty check**. Though unwieldy, novelty checks became much easier to deposit with the advent of **giant ATMs**.

Some people would try anything to keep their money away from the Jews.

Credit

When physically carrying money—or even having any—became too much hassle, we invented **credit cards**. These enabled us to buy things with a bank's money by pledging to repay the bank later under terms spelled out in a **monthly statement**.

CUSTOMER SERVICE: 1 800-UMB-BANK (24 HOURS 7 DAYS A WEEK)

UMB
UNITED MUTUAL BANK   **VISA® CARD**

Account Number: 5871684613856248

Summary of Payment Due:

MINIMUM PAYMENT DUE	
PAYMENT DUE	$20
NEW BALANCE	4/12/10
REVOLVING CREDIT LIMIT	$9842.31
CASH ADVANCES	$36,000
FREQUENT FLYER MILES	$200
FINANCE CHARGE	12,088
	$229.59 – BALANCE x 27.99%APR

Warning: If we do not receive your minimum payment by this date, you may incur a $39 late fee, your APR may rise and you may be sodomized without lube by our CEO or his designees.

Activity Section:

Date	Merchant	Amount
3/07/10	NETFLIX	
3/09/10	GAS PLUS MINI MART	
3/11/10	WHISPERS GENTLEMEN'S CLUB	19.99
3/12/10	ROSEBUD'S FLOWER SHOP	45.79
3/13/10	MANOLO BLAHNIK	1,250.00
3/14/10	TIFFANY & CO.	135.00
3/15/10	HOLIDAY INN EXPRESS	853.46
3/16/10	BENDER & ROSENFELD DIVORCE ATTORNEYS	2,783.59
3/16/10	APPLEBEES 1212 FRONTAGE RD.	79.31
3/16/10	APPLEBEES 1212 FRONTAGE RD.	750.00
3/16/10	APPLEBEES 1212 FRONTAGE RD.	13.09
3/17/10	HOLIDAY INN EXPRESS	17.97
3/17/10	GAS PLUS MINI MART	16.43
3/17/10	APPLEBEES 1212 FRONTAGE RD.	79.31
3/17/10	APPLEBEES 1212 FRONTAGE RD.	44.03
3/17/10	APPLEBEES 1212 FRONTAGE RD	13.09
3/18/10	TINSELTOWN CINEMA	17.97
3/18/10	HOLIDAY INN EXPRESS	16.43
3/18/10	APPLEBEES 1212 FRONTAGE RD.	9.00
3/18/10	APPLEBEES 1212 FRONTAGE RD.	79.31
3/19/10	APPLEBEES 1212 FRONTAGE RD.	13.09
	HOLIDAY INN EXPRESS	17.97
	WHISPERS GENTLEMEN'S CLUB	16.43
		79.31
		985.00
	Total Charges	7686 23

First-Class Mail

0-25-483

Cash Advances *Blackjack tables didn't take credit cards.*

Frequent Flyer Miles *For every $1 we charged, we would be given a "point" worth about ¼ ¢ toward an airline ticket. To get one $300 ticket, we had to charge about $10,000, paying 14% interest, or up to $1400 a year. Which we did. Because, hey— free ticket.*

Account Number *Unique, 16-digit code to keep our accounts secure.*

Phone Number *To call after someone stole your account number.*

Minimum Payment Due *Lenders wanted borrowers to pay them back—just not too soon.*

New Balance *The only number on this page we couldn't blame on anyone else.*

Revolving Credit Limit *The bank's estimate of the most we could repay. Always much higher than the most we would repay.*

Finance Charge *In the Middle Ages, this rate of interest would have been cause for death-by-burning for usury.*

Due Date *Late penalties could be onerous.*

Types of Credit Cards

Credit cards were a sacred financial trust between a faceless corporation and anyone who had survived to their 18th birthday. Specialized cards were designed to appeal to as many such people as possible.

"You're a person of notable quality, unlike the scum stuck with green cards."

"You're not just a 'cardholder'; you're an exclusive club's 'member.'"

"So you finally figured out: Any asshole off the street can get a gold card."

AMERICAN EXPRESS   3717 1   RALPH FIENNES   MEMBER SINCE

"Z. Jay-Z."

Popular "affiliation" cards advertised the bearer's loyalty to a sports team, college or race.

4147 0   3456 7890
4147
JOHN Q. NAMSHAVER   01/14
VISA

BLANCHE   4556 0494 5595 3496   VISA   VALID THRU 01-14

Eventually a single card could simultaneously display everything you had any interest in whatsoever.

Twelve of these could be traded for a head of lettuce.

BANK OF ZIMBABWE REWARDS CARD
4916 9029   HARPO YERFNIW   07/14
VISA

Investing

PEOPLE LUCKY ENOUGH to have more money than they needed for survival were faced with the decision of how to handle the surplus. Many used this extra money to buy assets in the hope their value would rise over time. Such **investments** could be low-risk (bank or mattress deposits) or high-risk (loaning one's brother-in-law $1000 to market the Bowflex rip-off he designed one night in his basement). The skilled investor had to balance the potential **reward** of great profits and short-lived joy against the **risk** of loss and permanent sadness. This is why the very best investors were unfeeling sociopaths.

If you find this machine and it still makes noises, do the opposite of whatever it tells you.

IN THE RUINS
WALL STREET

Wall Street—the southern tip of the island of Manhattan—was the world's white-hot financial center for the entire 20th century and nearly eight years of the 21st. This famed bronze bull reflected both a hard-charging, fast-growing stock market, and Wall Street traders' approximate ball size.

The Stock Market

Public companies' values were constantly changing, based on rigorous macro- and micro-economic data, plus rumors, gossip and whether it was a summer Friday and traders wanted to beat the traffic out to Quogue. Though many so-called "analysts" pretended to understand these fluctuations, these same people's predictions often proved less accurate than those of a monkey throwing darts at the *Wall Street Journal*, or in later years, at *WSJ.com*.

Newspapers *printed current stock prices so readers could look impressive while riding trains.*

Some people made a living peddling made-up **financial instruments** *so complex and abstruse that they themselves had no idea what they were or how they worked. They were the most successful people in the history of our species.*

| GPS 18.99 ▲ 0.19 | DEI 140.60 ▲ 8.38 | CIRL 3.22 ▼ 1.07 | HSY 66.82 ▲ 1.18 | SPX 66.82 ▲ 1.18 |

The Gap Stores up on report that US men even doughier, flatter-assed than previously thought.

Dutch East India Company sent word it discovered amidst the savages vast reserves of saffron, rarest of spices.

Polio cure leads **Consolidated Iron Lung** to record loss.

Hershey gains after traders smelled someone baking cookies on exchange floor.

S&P 500 Index up 1% when Goldman trader's 22 oz. diving watch fell on the "Buy" button.

Manias, Booms and Busts

Though our modern economy was completely terrific, it did tend to destroy itself every 10 to 15 years. This was because our instinctive **greed** drove us regularly insane. The thing we went insane about varied: technology stocks in the 1990s, tulip bulbs in 17th-century Holland.[1] These patently irrational obsessions went in cycles everyone knew about and almost everyone ignored anyway. The pattern: As more people invested in Thing X, its price rose, drawing more people to invest in Thing X. The **cycle** escalated until something happened to remind everyone that their investment thesis in no way mirrored reality. The bubbles burst, clearing the way for us to make the same mistake, but different, a little later.

1 Choose a Commodity
- Real estate
- Stocks and/ or bonds
- Tulip bulbs

2 Choose a Reason Why This Time It's Different
- "Interest rates will never be this low again!"
- "This is a once-in-a-millennium paradigm shift!"
- "Tulips smell good and they're pretty!"

3 Choose a Guru
- Shouty person on television
- Ayn Rand
- Your florist

4 Hang On to That Commodity Until …
- You've surpassed even the highest price you ever imagined you'd definitely sell it for
- Everyone's out of money
- You develop a tulip allergy

5 Choose a Bursting Event
- Sudden discovery of lots more of the commodity
- Sudden mass realization that the commodity is just an abstract concept with no intrinsic value
- Realization that peonies are just as nice, and 98% cheaper

6 Choose a Scapegoat
- The government for failing to protect you
- The guru from step 3
- De bloem markt man Jan vanTerBeek

7 Vow to …
- Put your money in something safe, like [choose other commodity from Step 1]

It was important to start financial education early.

Goofus and Goldman

GOOFUS thinks his car is well-made, so buys 100 shares of stock in the company that makes it.

GOLDMAN knows the car company's pension obligations are unsustainable, so buys put options on its bonds, triggering a credit downgrade and bankruptcy.

Highlights For High Net Worth Children 39

1. Seriously. In 1637, the Dutch wrecked their whole country by going banana-shit crazy for tulips. At the peak, a single bulb was worth the annual wages of 16 skilled workers. Though to be fair, those workers merely made barrels and horseshoes, and it was a very pretty tulip.

C 9.14 ▲ 8.12   **MON** 12.11 ▼ 8.12   **SWHC** 9.11 ▲ 2.10   **CON** 4.55 ▼ 7.45   **TOJ** 17.50 ▲ 1.00

Citigroup surged on news it was bankrupt, insuring another government bailout.

West Coast Zombie plague traced to **Monsanto** lab accident.

Smith & Wesson Holding Co. up on news of black man being elected US President.

Cedent Corp. shareholders sell after realizing they have no idea what Cedent Corp. does.

Tropicana Orange Juice rises after Dept. of Agriculture says orange crop unaffected by frost this year, causing massive selloff by Duke Brothers LLC.

CHAPTER SEVEN

That's it? You're going to Chapter 7? That's that God shit. You'll be back, my friend. You'll be back.

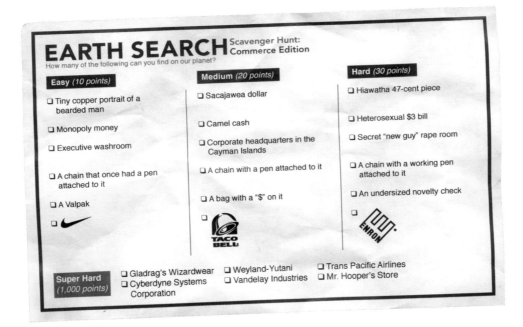

EARTH SEARCH Scavenger Hunt: Commerce Edition
How many of the following can you find on our planet?

Easy (10 points)
- ☐ Tiny copper portrait of a bearded man
- ☐ Monopoly money
- ☐ Executive washroom
- ☐ A chain that once had a pen attached to it
- ☐ A Valpak
- ☐ ✔ (Nike swoosh)

Medium (20 points)
- ☐ Sacajawea dollar
- ☐ Camel cash
- ☐ Corporate headquarters in the Cayman Islands
- ☐ A chain with a pen attached to it
- ☐ A bag with a "$" on it
- ☐ (Taco Bell logo)

Hard (30 points)
- ☐ Hiawatha 47-cent piece
- ☐ Heterosexual $3 bill
- ☐ Secret "new guy" rape room
- ☐ A chain with a working pen attached to it
- ☐ An undersized novelty check
- ☐ (Enron logo)

Super Hard (1,000 points)
- ☐ Gladrag's Wizardwear
- ☐ Cyberdyne Systems Corporation
- ☐ Weyland-Yutani
- ☐ Vandelay Industries
- ☐ Trans Pacific Airlines
- ☐ Mr. Hooper's Store

FAQs
(Future Alien Questions)

Q. Johnny has $89.00 and Billy has $2.05. How much more does Johnny have than Billy?
A. We considered comparisons of net worth tacky. Anyway, it almost sounds as if you are trying to incite class warfare.

Q. What was the most effective form of advertising?
A. Forcing someone to buy your product at gunpoint equaled guaranteed sales. Unfortunately, as of this writing it had been outlawed in every country except Brazil and Ireland.

Q. The Acme company appears to have made low-quality products. How did they stay in business?
A. Free shipping to remote desert locations.

Q. Could money buy happiness?
A. No. But it could buy a 60" 1080p LCD with NFL Weekend Pass, which was indistinguishable from happiness.

Q. Which service jobs particularly lent themselves to spur-of-the-moment sexual liaisons?
A. Great question. Pizza deliverymen were notorious for ravaging their female clients, as were sweaty gardeners, dampened pool boys and the occasional pantsless window washer. But when it came to neck-deepness in wealthy middle-aged nook-nook, you had to go with "country club tennis pro." They couldn't even get the job without references from at least five clients they were already banging behind their husbands' backs.

Q. Imagine: Fresh fruit juice in your own home, for a fraction of what you'd spend at the health food store. How much would you pay for that?
A: $39.99?

A $75 value!

Q. What if I told you you could also make zesty salsa?
A. $49.99?

Q. And perfect guacamole?
A. Uh …

Q. And clean-up is a breeze?
A. Why don't you give us all the information first, and then let us guess.

Q. You had the word "Trump" on many of your buildings. What did that word mean?
A. A Trump was a demon who sometimes appeared to us in quasi-human form in order to fire us from a job we never wanted in the first place.

Q. It appears many "industrialized" countries had very few actual factories. Why?
A. We realized most products could be made more cheaply elsewhere.

Q. So then what did people in industrialized countries do?
A. We ran the companies that made the things—you know, brand strategy, marketing, supply-chain management. That sort of thing.

Q. So you just told other people what to make? And then took the profits?
A. That's a 10-4.

Q. What was to keep other countries from figuring out they could pretty much do all of this themselves?
A. We tried not to think about that.

Q. One last question: Where do you get off wasting the time of a dedicated salesman who was only trying to provide the service you …
A. Let it go, Lou.

**Michelangelo's depiction of
Adam collecting donations for
Eden's building fund.**

Religion

As the smartest and most evolved creatures on earth, humans had it pretty good—our position atop the food chain kept us fat and happy, mineral resources abounded and public restrooms dotted the landscape. But being human did carry with it one terrible burden: Awareness. This awareness led us to some difficult realizations that never seemed to occur to dolphins or collies ... realizations like, "We die." (Dolphins and collies were two of our most communicative animal brethren and would often warn us of trouble, whether it be down at the mill or out past the old shipwreck on Breakers' Point)

Humans seemed to be the only creature that realized that life did not last forever, that everyone, every living thing, even famous celebrities like television and film star George Clooney—eventually died. The thought that we would one day cease to exist—all our passions and hatred subsumed by nothingness—was, as the noted philosopher Soren Kierkegaard once said, "a total mindfuck."

The knowledge of our eventual demise presented two options: A) find comfort in life as a transitory and purposeless sideshow; or B) find comfort in death as a doorway to a far richer and fulfilling state of being.

We went with B. And we called it **religion**. Religion usually centered on an omnipotent being or beings, known as **God**, **gods**, or—for reasons too tedious to get into here—**G-d**. These beings were responsible for all the mysteries of life, and loyal service to them assured an eternal life in their protection and glory. Life suddenly had meaning. We weren't a chance collection of organisms careening aimlessly through the universe. We were created for a purpose: to show our appreciation for being created. The earth, the heavens, night, rain—God created them all so that we would have a nice place to worship, exalt, praise, honor and

His affable brand of raffish charm could not stave off his date with oblivion.

generally kiss the ass of the One who made it all possible. Narcissistic? Not if you can back it up. And religion proved not only an existential salve but a practical one.

Religious doctrine provided very specific step by step instruction on every aspect of life, from dress to morality to diet. Should I eat this pork chop? (No.) Cover my head? (Sure.) Can I have an oyster? (For crying out loud, just order the chicken. Provided it's been killed with one cut to the throat. One.) I am mad at my neighbor. May I poke out his eye? (Only if he poked out yours.) Religion rendered the world simple, and appealed to peasant and aristocrat alike. Peasants took comfort that their suffering in this world was merely a golden ladder to eternal justice and plenty. Aristocrats took comfort that the peasants who believed that were less likely to foment bloodshed against aristocrats. So for a while there, the whole "God" thing was really working well for us.

But there was one problem. We agreed religious dogma was the inerrant word of God, we just couldn't agree on *which* god, or even agree to disagree on which god. So minor disagreements on diet and wardrobe became centuries long battles to the death. It turned out that killing a person was hard, but killing an infidel was easy ... even rewarding. And an infidel was simply someone who maybe disagreed that Jesus was the actual son of God, or that one must pray five times daily, or that anyone could eat matzah for eight straight days without becoming irregular. Thus, religion helped overcome man's catastrophic tendency toward neighborliness and smoothed the way for millennia of wars—allowing millions of people to discover, first-hand, whether or not their religion was right about the whole "post-death non-oblivion" thing.

To sum up: Religion provided great comfort to a world torn apart ... by religion.

Polytheism

POLYTHEISM HAD MUCH to offer early civilizations: Exciting characters, lots of holidays and plenty of good old-fashioned animal sacrifice. It also explained the origins of man and the various mysteries of life with rivetingly implausible stories. The gods that made up a particular polytheistic religion were referred to as a **pantheon**. The stories of a particular pantheon together created a **mythology**, the name we gave to every collection of crazy nonsense stories besides our own.

Roman Messenger God
You'd run fast too if you didn't have any clothes on.

Mesoamerican Creator God
Created world with blood from penis, so ... you're welcome.

QUETZALCOATL

ISIS

MERCURY

KU-KA-ILI-MOKU

Egyptian Fertility Goddess
Hot, but crazy! Tap at your own risk.

Hawaiian God of War
Ruled over the entire known universe, all eight islands of it.

Ancient Egyptians believed the sun god Ra masturbated the world into existence. Since he was the only thing in the universe, this raised the question of what he could possibly have been fantasizing about.

A hieroglyph on the tomb of Ramses II relates the story of Ra. Can you identify the moment when he created the Earth?

Native American Fertility God
Though he couldn't stop the genocide of his people, he did sell a lot of T-shirts.

Hindu God of Wisdom
Notable because—let's face facts— he had an elephant's head.

KOKOPELLI

GANESH

Norse Creator God
His chief priest, Hagar the Horrible, slaughtered whole villages in his name.

ODIN

Hinduism

The longest-surviving (and therefore most theologically accurate) of the polytheisms was Hinduism. It had hundreds of divine beings but centered on three: **Brahma** (The Cute One), **Vishnu** (The Smart One) and **Shiva** (The Destroyer).

Enlightened One · Untouchable · Brahma Bull · Sir Ben Kingsley · Slumdog Millionaire · Customer Service · Very Touchable · Dung Beetle · Cable News Doctor · Kipling Character

*Hindus believed in **karma**, the idea that "what comes around, goes around." This often played out in the form of **reincarnation**. For example, an untouchable who lived a virtuous life would be rewarded by coming back as a "semi"-touchable. Or, even better, a dung beetle.*

YOU HAD TO BE HERE

*The red dot on this woman's forehead meant she was retaining her **kundalini** energy.*

*The red dot on this man's forehead meant the **CIA** no longer required his services.*

Monotheism

AS THE MILLENNIA flew by and man grew ever more sophisticated, the idea that the world was controlled by a cast of invisible emotionally unstable supernatural beings grew laughable. Instead, the world was actually controlled by *one* all powerful invisible emotionally unstable supernatural being, known hereafter as **God**. God loved man. All that He asked in return was that man acknowledge His singularity and return His love. The lure of monotheism over polytheism was clear: Exalt this all-powerful being in whose image you were created, or sit around and wait for the god of thunder to get bored, disguise himself as a bull and come fuck you in the ass for no good reason.

Judaism

The oldest of the monotheistic religions, **Judaism** is based on the ancient covenant between God and a Middle Eastern shepherd named **Abraham**. To test Abraham's faith, God commanded him to slit the throat of his son Isaac. Abraham, clearly a real team player, agreed, but at the last second God had him sacrifice a ram instead. To commemorate this event all Jewish males have their **foreskins** cut off at a catered brunch on their eighth day of life. Abraham's devotion earned the Jews the title of "God's Chosen People," and nothing bad ever happened to them again.

A FLOCK DIVIDED

JEWS

Primary religious divisions:
Reform, Conservative, Orthodox

Areas of disagreement:
- *How Jewish was "too Jewish"?*
- *Kosher socks: a bit much?*
- *Women: unclean or rabbinical candidates?*

10 And Abraham stretched forth his hand, and took the knife to slay his son. 11 And yea, did he hear tittering from on high; for the LORD was richly amused; 12 And He came down in a cloud of thunder, saying, "Oh! Thou shouldst see the look on thy face!"; 13 And Abraham threw down his knife in great confusion, saying, "Wouldst thou truly hath had me extinguish my beloved son?" And he wept with anguish; 14 And the LORD said, "Surely thou art awestruck, in the fullness of thy punking." 15 But Abraham would not be consoled.

When reading from their Torah, Jews used metal pointers, or **yads***, to protect the sacred writings from human touch and also to help them pretend their hands had been replaced by those of a tiny robot.*

The Jewish **Torah** *(German for "kindling") was read aloud over a year's time in a language most Jews didn't understand.*

CENTRAL FIGURE

*Although **Moses**, author of the Jewish Torah, lived some 3,000 years ago, we had a good idea of what he looked like.*

*In keeping with Biblical law, Jews affixed **mezzuzahs** to their doorposts so the Chinese delivery boys knew where to go.*

*Many Jews kept a **Go Kit** under their beds, because, well ... it couldn't hurt.*

*The **bar Mitzvah**, the ritual passage to Jewish adulthood often came with a "theme" that called into question how complete the passage was.*

TODAY I TRANSFORM INTO A MAN

*Jewish boys and men wore **yarmulkes** to symbolize their subordination to their mothers.*

Monotheism:
Christianity

The second oldest monotheistic religion, **Christianity** is based on the Old Testament belief that the God of Abraham prophesied a **messiah**. Christians believe that this messiah was **Jesus of Nazareth**. A carpenter by trade, Jesus spread wisdom and compassion throughout the land, which, back then, was the kind of thing that could get a fella killed. Jesus was nailed to a wooden cross, then **rose from the dead** three days later. It is this part of the story, the rising from the dead part, that gave his teachings what we called "legs." Jews agreed that Jesus lived, but disputed that he was the messiah. Of course, we all know how much they liked to argue.

670

10 And Jesus said "Behold, I give unto you power to tread on serpents and scorpions, and over all the power of the enemy: and nothing shall by any means hurt you."
20 And Simon Peter was sore curious, and cried "Lord! Does that mean we should pick up poisonous snakes in church, and shake them around?"
21 So Jesus said, "Sure, go ahead," and his sarcasm was palpable. But when Jesus saw the disciples were writing his words down, he said, "Wait—don't do that!"
22 But Simon Peter said "Too late" and the youngest disciple was already running around wreathed in cobras crying:
23 "Look at me! I'm Holy!"
24 And though Jesus swore up and down he was joking, the disciples would hear him not. Jesus mourned in spirit, but after a while even he had to see the humor in the situation.
25 And, after they had buried the youngest disciple, Jesus and his followers met a chick named Martha, who w

LUKE 10:19

WE SAID IT

"Anyone who dares to lay hands on the highest image of the Lord commits sacrilege against the benevolent creator of this miracle and contributes to the expulsion from paradise."
—Adolf Hitler (1889–1945), German theologian

The questionable workmanship of the **Holy Spice Rack** suggested that Jesus's first miracle was getting hired as a carpenter.

Christianity was split in two when, in 1517, a dissident priest named Martin Luther nailed his "95 Theses," a list of complaints about Catholic practice, to the door of a German church. Within hours, William Donahue of the Catholic League had issued a press release calling for an apology and a boycott.

People often wore religious **symbols** *around their necks. This could send mixed messages.*

Luther schlägt seine Thesen an der Schloßkirche zu Wittenberg an. (Text S. 210)
Nach einer Originalzeichnung von G. Spangenberg.

A FLOCK DIVIDED
CHRISTIANS
Primary religious divisions:
Catholic, Protestant
Areas of disagreement:
• *Papal infallibility*
• *Wine: magic or just delicious?*
• *Were Irish people human?*

CENTRAL FIGURE

Although Jesus Christ, whose teachings were collected in the Gospels, died 2,000 years ago, we had a good idea of what he looked like.

IN THE RUINS
ICONS

You'll frequently find statuary depicting Christianity's Holy Family stored in the ruins of our garages.

When properly assembled, they should look like this.

Not this.

*Many believed the **Shroud of Turin** to be the burial cloth of Jesus Christ. It exhibited two miraculous properties: 1) a perfect imprint of Christ's body, and 2) the supernatural power to mislead carbon-dating tests into showing it dated from the 13th century.*

*The **Vatican** was the global headquarters of the Catholic Church, which was constructed as a monument to Jesus Christ's love of gold and other shiny things.*

Monotheism:

Islam

Islam is the youngest of the Abrahamic religions and no discussion of its tenets can start without first stating its **peaceful** nature. It cannot be stressed enough how **peaceful** this religion was. If you are looking for a belief system that can be twisted to support a violent extremist ideology you have come to the wrong place. Islam was a **beautiful harmless happy daffodil** that blossomed in the desert. It was based on devotion to Allah, who revealed his words to the prophet Mohammed. These teachings form the basis of the **Koran**, the sacred text of this beautiful and again **very peaceful** religion. (Psst! Meet me in the image credits. ...*)

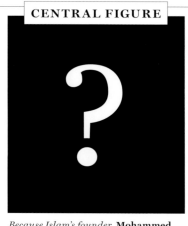

CENTRAL FIGURE

*Because Islam's founder, **Mohammed**, lived 1,400 years ago, we had no idea of what he looked like.*

*Koranic injunctions against creating accurate representations of the physical world led to some fascinating family pictures. Above, the **Ramadan card** for the Nawad Family, 1843. From left: Karim Nawad, wife Aishah, daughters Mahfiyah and Mahfuza (not pictured: Karim Nawad, Junior).*

*The **takiyah** was a traditional cap worn by Muslim men to emulate the Prophet, and ensure special treatment at airports.*

*Some Muslim sects wore **bow ties** to honor their founder, The Right Honorable Popcorn Magnate Orville Redenbacher.*

*Muslims thought the **prayer mat** was a near-essential component for their required five daily prayers. Non-Muslims thought maybe they could fly.*

*Islam's **political power** skyrocketed after a practicing secret Muslim was elected President of the United States.*

A FLOCK DIVIDED

MUSLIMS

Primary religious divisions:
Shi'a, Sunni
Areas of disagreement:
• *Who should succeed Mohammed?*
• *America: Great Satan or just Average Satan?*
• *Apostrophes*

QIBLA
DIRECTION FINDER
الكعبة المشرفة
كاشف الاتجاهات

The Muslim requirement to pray five times daily while facing Mecca caused a lot of fights between couples when the husband invariably refused to ask for directions.

The **Hajj**, *Muslims' pilgrimage to the Holy City of Mecca, drew two million people annually, in a mass demonstration of religious pacifism.*

The **burqa** *protected its wearer from the sun, and also from being stoned to death.*

THINGS WE LIKED
INERRANT TEXTS

Our faiths were bolstered by inerrant, infallible, divinely revealed **holy books** that were perfect down to the last "jot and tittle." And if new scholarship proved that the universe *wasn't* actually created in seven days … well, screw you, too. We believed, and that was enough.

THE NEW TESTAMENT

Venerated By: Christians; presidential candidates
Who "Wrote" It: Jesus's disciples
Who Actually Wrote It: Some guys who knew some other guys who said they knew Jesus
Main Themes: God loves you, so believe in Him or go to hell.
Questionable Claim: The meek shall inherit the Earth.
Okay to Burn?: No

THE OLD TESTAMENT

Venerated By: Jews; Christians who didn't like homosexuals
Who "Wrote" It: God, Moses, various Prophets
Who Actually Wrote It: Babylonians who loved genealogy but hated shellfish
Main Themes: There is only one God, and He's pissed.
Questionable Claim: Pick any page and you'll find three.
Okay to Burn?: No

THE KORAN

Venerated By: Muslims; American prison inmates
Who "Wrote" It: Allah, via the angel Jibril, via Mohammed
Who Actually Wrote It: We're not gonna touch this one.
Main Themes: Holiness of the Koran, correctness of the Koran, infallibility of the Koran, handsomeness of the Koran's typeface, excellence of the Koran's binding, etc.
Questionable Claim: Heaven is a cathouse full of virgins.
Okay to Burn?: It's not even okay to *ask*.

THE 2010 WORLD ALMANAC

Venerated By: People who still hadn't discovered the Internet
Who "Wrote" It: A staff of Ph.D.s in New York City
Who Actually Wrote It: An intern with last year's almanac and access to Wikipedia
Main Themes: Humanity's compulsive need to catalogue
Questionable Claim: Somebody somewhere cares when Vivian Vance was born.
Okay to Burn?: Knock yourself out.

Jerusalem: City of Peace

ALTHOUGH ANY PLACE could theoretically be holy (The Nation of Islam was founded in *Detroit*), some locations tended to accrue the miraculous more than others. Of all earthly locations, the ancient city of **Jerusalem** was hands-down the place where more important religious events happened to more important religions. Truly, it was the Mecca of cities.

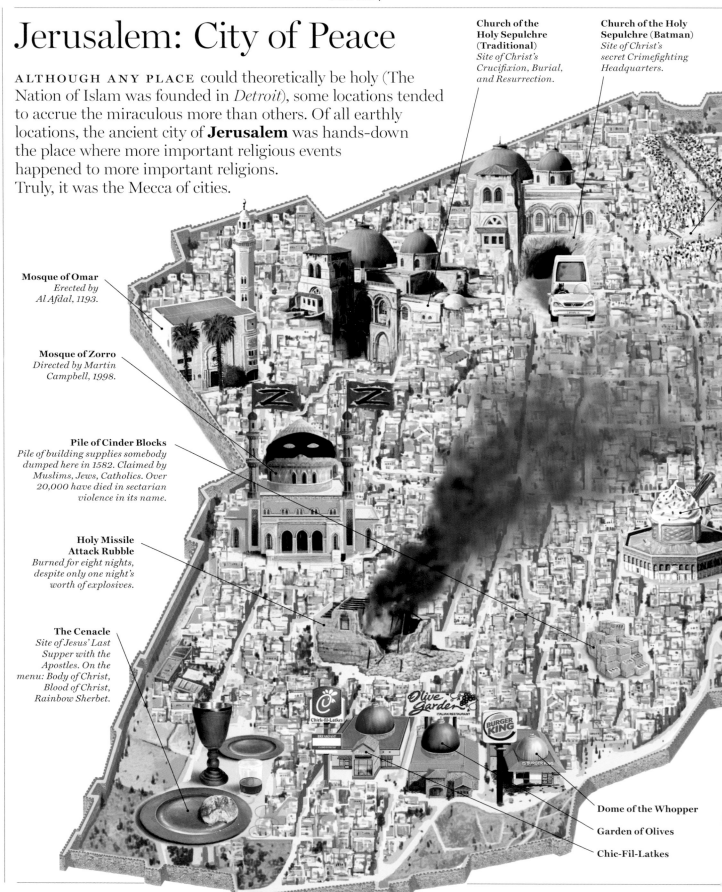

Church of the Holy Sepulchre (Traditional)
Site of Christ's Crucifixion, Burial, and Resurrection.

Church of the Holy Sepulchre (Batman)
Site of Christ's secret Crimefighting Headquarters.

Mosque of Omar
Erected by Al Afdal, 1193.

Mosque of Zorro
Directed by Martin Campbell, 1998.

Pile of Cinder Blocks
Pile of building supplies somebody dumped here in 1582. Claimed by Muslims, Jews, Catholics. Over 20,000 have died in sectarian violence in its name.

Holy Missile Attack Rubble
Burned for eight nights, despite only one night's worth of explosives.

The Cenacle
Site of Jesus' Last Supper with the Apostles. On the menu: Body of Christ, Blood of Christ, Rainbow Sherbet.

Dome of the Whopper

Garden of Olives

Chic-Fil-Latkes

Via Dolorosa
The path Christ took to his execution. Lazier Messiahs generally took the Shortcut Dolorosa.

Bethesda Pool
Where Jesus cured a paralyzed man by throwing him in the water and shouting "Swim!"

Bethesda Wading Pool
Where Baby Jesus learned to crawl on water.

Dome of the Rock
Holy to Muslims, Jews and Christians, marks the spot where the Patriarch Abraham nearly sacrificed his son Isaac at God's command.

Ice Cream Parlor of the Rock
Site where Abraham took Isaac to apologize.

The Southern Wall
Not as holy, but much better parking.

Western Wall
The last remnant of Judaism's Holy Temple, which in its original form had a second wall.

Al Aqsa Mosque
In Islam, the site where the Prophet Mohammed ascended to Heaven on his Night Journey. In Judaism, a violation of local zoning ordinances.

The Temple Mount

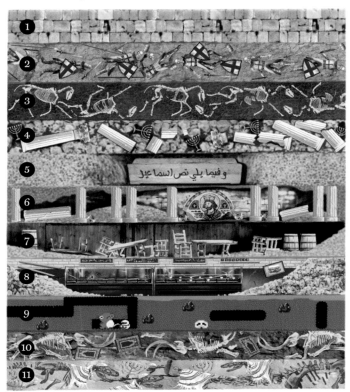

The Temple Mount served as home to the Al Aqsa Mosque since 685 A.D. Jews, however, claimed the land rightfully belonged to them, since the Mosque was built on the ruins of their Holy Temple. A cross-section of the Mount reveals the tangled evidence over who had "dibs."

1. **Al Aqsa Mosque** *(Muslim)*

2. **Crusader Burial Ground** *(Christian)*

3. **King Herod's Stables** *(Roman)*

4. **Second Temple** *(Jewish)*

5. **Tomb of Ishmael** *(Muslim)*

6. **Solomon's Temple** *(Jewish)*

7. **Habib's Hummus Hut** *(Muslim)*

8. **Katz's Deli** *(Jewish)*

9. **Dig Dug** *(Namco)*

10. **Woolly Mammoth Mosque** *(Muslim)*

11. **Dinosaur Temple** *(Jewish)*

Other

SOME RELIGIONS DIDN'T fit neatly into the "mono" or "poly" model of theism. Many of these religions felt instead that the highest form of religious expression was **perfection of the self**. One of these religions thought the self was covered with the souls of invisible people who got blown up in a volcano. This is usually when the Buddha would yawn and remark on how late it was getting.

Taoism

Taoism was a loosely organized set of religious beliefs originating among Chinese peasants that taught the best way to find inner peace was *wu wei*— literally, "action without action." In practice, this meant moving as little as possible, which proved a popular choice amongst people subsisting on 600 calories a day anyway.

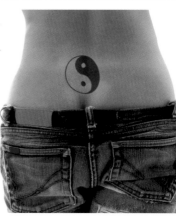

Taoism's **Yin Yang** *was by far our most lower-back tattoo-able symbol of the interrelated qualities of seemingly opposing forces.*

Buddhism

Buddhism was founded by **Siddhartha Gautama**, an Indian prince who traveled around teaching that to end human suffering one must end craving through silent **meditation**. As you can imagine, he did a lot of shushing.

As of 2010 the spiritual leader of Tibetan Buddhism was the **Dalai Lama**, *a 500-year-old violent subversive who was bent on destroying China's harmony and refused to stay dead.*

Not all uses of the Buddha's image were officially sanctioned.

Scientology

Like many religions, The **Church of Scientology** was incorporated in New Jersey in 1953. Its highest-level practitioners learned that Earth's problems began when Xenu, evil ruler of the Galactic Confederacy, brought billions of humans to earth 75 million years ago and killed them with hydrogen bombs. This information was kept hidden from non-Scientologists, as learning it before years of costly preparation could induce involuntary physical responses, including but not limited to laughter, eye-rolling and exclamations of "Are you serious?!"

Scientologists embraced the gaudiness of older religions, while rejecting the beauty.

The point of entry for many converts to Scientology was the **Free Personality Test**.

Free SCIENTOLOGY PERSONALITY TEST

1 Are you happy?

2 Are you satisfied with how much money you make?

3 How much money do you make?
$ ☐☐☐☐☐☐☐☐☐☐☐☐☐ / _____

4 Where do you keep it?

5 Do you know any celebrities?

6 Do you know any gay celebrities?

7 Quick – what's your pin number?
☐☐☐☐

Through judicious use of the **E-Meter**, *Scientology auditors were able to remove countless Thetans ("dollars") from followers.*

Church of Jesus Christ of Latter Day Saints

The LDS, or **Mormonism**, was founded in 19th century upstate New York by a gentleman named Joe Smith. No lie ... Joe Smith. Smith and his followers were eventually chased to Utah, where he set up a polygamist utopia. Smith never actually thought of himself as a polygamist, preferring to think of himself as "in love with being in love."

The Book of Mormon, *First Draft, 1827. Editor's notes in red.*

DULL *consider:*   2nd Nephi, Chapter 34

NEPHI 2: The ReNefining

1. Verily, verily I say unto you that ye shall spread the word of the gospel from home to home in a manner bothersome to the residents of those homes.   NOT

2. Wherefore it shall come to pass that "one wife is not cutting it ← therefore it shall be that marriage not be restrictive to man, and his seed shall see the bosom of many wives at the same time and that the wives shall accept it with-out question and even team up every once in a while.

Better angel name?
Samantha? Anything.

3. Behold and bear witness that the prophet upon being shown to the golden plates by the angel Moroni didst interpret their etchings by aid of Doctor Fielding's Interpro-Spectacles.

Seer Stone

4. And thus a special garment shall be worn between the body and clothing as a symbolic reminder of the sacred covenants, and such garment be viewed as a symbolic source of protection from the evils of the world.

Latter Day Saints? What does that even mean ??

OVERALL: Tone is kind of fruity. Fewer "therefores," MORE ACTION.!

A little on the nose.

∈ Joseph, right?

Product placement deal fell through. :(

Could this be misconstrued as some kind of magic underwear? Potentially Embarrassing...

Joseph wants to keep this in.

STET.

Management

ALTHOUGH GOD'S WORDS were literal truth, understanding what He actually meant was too important and complicated to be left in the hands of worshipers. Luckily, each religion had God's **emissaries** on Earth to make sure people weren't screwing things up or taking God out of context. These people were typically supported financially by the community and were held in high esteem, except for Reform rabbis, who were kind of a joke.

Buddhist Monks *were identifiable by their orange vestments and poverty ...*

... attributes which frequently got them confused with **Home Depot** *employees.*

God spoke directly to many **evangelical preachers***, but He wouldn't loan them money. That's where humanity came in.*

The **Popemobile** *was the personal transport of the head of the Catholic Church. It was actually just a Mercedes customized by the design geniuses of MTV's Pope My Ride.*

The **Oracle at Delphi** *was definitely one of the top reasons to visit Delphi.*

Priestly vestment designs varied. **Eastern Orthodox priests** *wore richly patterned silk robes, while* **Lutherans** *favored wall hangings made by third-graders out of glitter, felt and macaroni.*

The idea that **shamans** *spent all their time exorcising tribal demons was a misconception. In truth, the job was mostly about fundraising and organizing ice-cream socials for troubled youth.*

Organization

Every religion had its own unique system for channeling God's authority, from highest to lowest.

Christianity

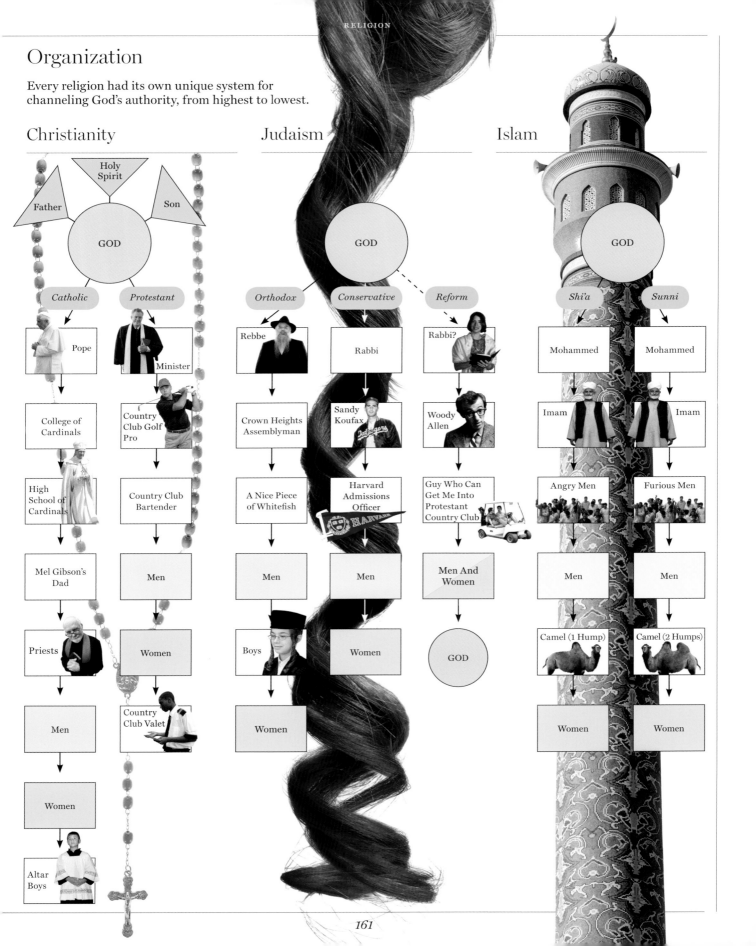

Holy Spirit

Father

Son

GOD

Catholic

Pope

College of Cardinals

High School of Cardinals

Mel Gibson's Dad

Priests

Men

Women

Altar Boys

Protestant

Minister

Country Club Golf Pro

Country Club Bartender

Men

Women

Country Club Valet

Judaism

GOD

Orthodox

Rebbe

Crown Heights Assemblyman

A Nice Piece of Whitefish

Men

Boys

Women

Conservative

Rabbi

Sandy Koufax

Harvard Admissions Officer

Men

Women

Reform

Rabbi?

Woody Allen

Guy Who Can Get Me Into Protestant Country Club

Men And Women

GOD

Islam

GOD

Shi'a

Mohammed

Imam

Angry Men

Men

Camel (1 Hump)

Women

Sunni

Mohammed

Imam

Furious Men

Men

Camel (2 Humps)

Women

Prayer

DIVINE BEINGS HAD thousands of ways of communicating with us: A lightning bolt, a rainbow or a cameo appearance on a piece of toast. But our only way of communicating with them was through **prayer**, which we used sparingly, only in cases when we wanted something. That something could be anything from forgiveness, health (for ourselves or others), wealth (for ourselves), vengeance (for others) and the strength to survive the latest ordeal He had perpetrated. Prayers were often organized as part of the routine of daily life, but they could also be uttered spontaneously, as in the event of catastrophic engine failure. Were our prayers answered? Always, although the answer was often "No." But that was all right, because the act of prayer was cathartic in itself. It was like talking to your old grandfather: You knew he couldn't hear you, and you couldn't forget the horrible things he'd done to you, but you loved him, and it still felt good to say this stuff out loud.

Protestantism

Typical Prayer: *"Thank you for making the restrictions on TARP money non-binding."*

Judaism

Typical Prayer: *"Please protect me from violent pogroms/ offensive stereotypes/ negative reviews of my new Broadway show or novel/negligence lawsuits from my podiatry practice."*

Catholicism

Typical Prayer: *"Please don't-a-let them take-a my Johnny away. He's a-such-a good-a boy. He would no-a steal-a car like-a they say! Not-a my Johnny!"*

Islam

Typical Prayer: *"Please let me see a lawyer. I don't know why I'm here."*

IN THE RUINS
STONEHENGE

The **Celtic Pagans** who assembled these monoliths were truly masters of stone-cutting. Unfortunately, they were not masters of written language, so we had no idea what this is. Do you? Is it a Druid Temple? Is it some kind of space port for aliens like you? A calendar? A pet cemetery? Not knowing what this was, along with not knowing the identity of the Zodiac Killer, were the two great frustrations of Western civilization.

Scientology

Typical Prayer: *"Please, Ron, I really need this part, and also if you could help me be a little less gay, that would be great."*

Wicca

Typical Prayer: *"Goddess, please use your eternal powerness to make those bitches on the pep squad stop picking on me."*

Buddhism

Typical Prayer: *"   "*

Reform Judaism

Typical Prayer: *"If I leave now I can make it home in time for 'Friday Night Lights.'"*

Rites and Rituals

WE DEVISED CEREMONIES to help us through birth, death and every moment in-between, often with the aid of ritual objects to help us focus our minds.

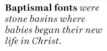

*The **foreskin** was a Jewish boy's receipt for entering into a covenant with God.*

*The **dirty mattress** was used throughout the world by cult leaders, who impregnated their child brides in a holy ceremony known as "Statutory Rape."*

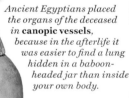

*The **Okipa Ceremony** of North America's Mandan people, in which men were hung from hooks piercing their chests, celebrated the fact that the Mandans were fucking hardcore.*

*In the annual **Ashura** rite, Iraqi Shiite Muslim men cut their scalps with machetes to commemorate the martyrdom of Imam Hussein. There was no faking this one. You either hit your scalp repeatedly with a machete until you bled profusely, or you didn't.*

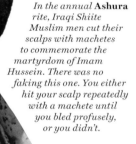

*Ancient Egyptians placed the organs of the deceased in **canopic vessels**, because in the afterlife it was easier to find a lung hidden in a baboon-headed jar than inside your own body.*

Relics

RELICS WERE SOUVENIRS of holy people and events, scattered around the world so that all believers could come close to something that had come close to holiness. Some relics, like the head of Christian martyr **John the Baptist**, were so revered that multiple locations claimed to own the *real* one. But as John himself liked to remind the ladies, "There's plenty of me to go around."

Head
Amiens Cathedral, Amiens, France

Head
Residenz Museum, Munich, Germany

Head
Church of San Silvestro in Capite, Rome, Italy

Sternum
Lucky Sternum Hotel and Casino, Macau, China

Left Humerus
Friars Club, New York, NY

Saint John the Baptist, beheaded 36 A.D.

Right Index Finger
Nelson-Atkins Museum, Kansas City, MO

Right Arm
Topkapi Palace, Istanbul, Turkey

Ribcage
Hard Rock Cafe, Memphis, Tennessee

Pelvis
Bill Gates' sock drawer, Medina, WA

Intestines, rectum
Hot Dog stand on the corner of 52nd & 11th, New York, NY

Right Leg
Skull and Bones Tomb, New Haven, CT

Right kneecap
Stapled inside one lucky copy of Earth (The Book)

Left Hand
Sort-of-Holy Cathedral of John the Baptist's Hand (The One He Didn't Use to Baptize Our Savior) Johannesburg, South Africa

Feet
Basilica of the Holy Shoe Tree, Rome, Italy

Taboos

RELIGIONS OFTEN FORBADE us to engage in certain practices as a sign of submission. These **prohibitions** frequently involved foods, and what they prohibited said a lot about the religions that prohibited them.

Jew (Orthodox)

What He's Eating: The meat, but only if slaughtered according to prescribed religious ritual. No pork. No shellfish. Coffee okay; Sanka preferred.

"A little cake might be nice."

Jew (Reform)

What She's Eating: Everything but the challah.

"I'm back on Atkins!"

Christian (Protestant)

What She's Eating: If it can be served on white bread with mayonnaise, it's allowed.

"No centerpiece? What are we, animals?"

Muslim

What He's Eating: The meat, but only if slaughtered according to prescribed religious ritual—but different ritual than Jewish ritual. No alcohol, no pork, no sex before a fight.

"Float like a butterfly, sting like a bee, taste like chicken."

Hindu

What He's Eating: Just the rice—until Hindu scientists create a cow without a soul.

"You just had to order the burger, didn't you?"

Scientologist

What She's Eating: Everything, unless undergoing periodic detoxification. Then, nothing but megadoses of Niacin, astronaut ice cream and ThetanChow™.

"Let's take Travolta's chopper to the Celebrity Centre for dessert."

WINE LOBSTER RICE MILK

NAILED IT
STAINED GLASS

Stained glass did more than just colorfully fill out a window that didn't open. The dazzling play of sunlight in its thousands of polychrome fragments was beautiful enough to move even those of us who thought the events depicted were literally unbelievable. A bitch to clean, though.

Sin and Penitence

MANY RELIGIONS SHARED the concept of **sin**—a thought or act (usually involving orifices) that violated God's moral code. Some of it was **original sin**, but mostly it was plagiarized. Sinners faced punishments ranging from an eternity of damnation to a few minutes in a dark booth next to an old man with wafer-breath. Mankind was, in the phrase of one famous group of theologians, "naughty by nature"; but through the process of **penitence**, sinners could wipe the slate clean ... until a few hours later, when temptation once again led them to befoul that slate with profanity and/or semen.

The Seven Deadly Sins

Although these sins were technically only "fatal" to our souls, they could still kill our bodies if left unchecked.

Greed *"Although I am already the world's richest man, I simply cannot live without that giant diamond that that mother bear is using as a pillow for her cubs."*

Lust *"I'm so horny I'm gonna fuck that shark!"*

Sloth *"Zzzzzz ... Head going below bath water ... I'm sure rubber duckie will save me ... Zzzzzzzzzzz ..."*

Gluttony *"I'll have one Meat Lovers Pizza, one Taco Lovers Steak and one Pizza Lovers Taco."*

Pride *"After this battle, the name 'Custer' will be synonymous with tactical genius!"*

Envy *"Marcy got an iPod when she broke her arm. Let's see what I get when I get hit by this car."*

Anger *"Demoted back to letter carrier? DEMOTED BACK TO LETTER CARRIER?!?"*

Religious Prohibition

Religious prohibitions didn't just have spiritual benefits. The Mormon refusal to consume caffeine or alcohol made them an unusually healthy population. Strictly vegetarian Hindus felt no pangs of guilt when watching slaughterhouse videos. And the 19th century Shaker sect in America, which banned sex altogether, were able to channel their energies into some of the most beautiful furniture ever carved (see below).

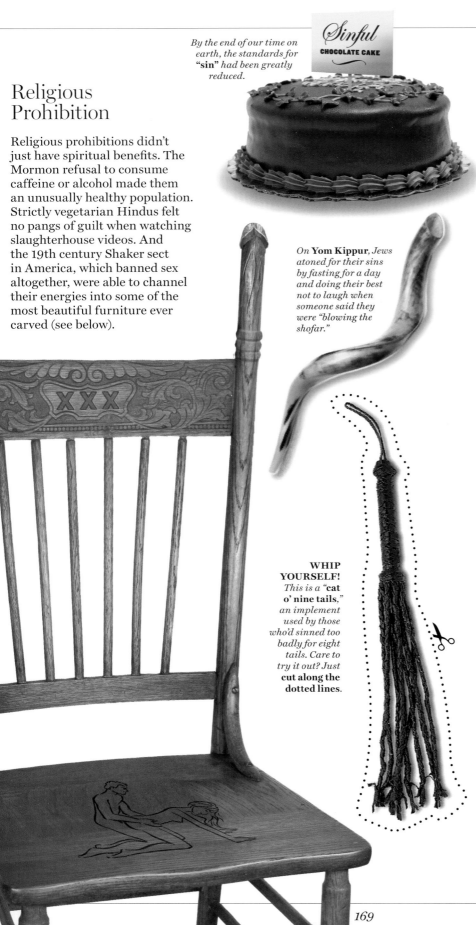

By the end of our time on earth, the standards for "sin" had been greatly reduced.

Sinful CHOCOLATE CAKE

On Yom Kippur, Jews atoned for their sins by fasting for a day and doing their best not to laugh when someone said they were "blowing the shofar."

WHIP YOURSELF! *This is a "cat o' nine tails," an implement used by those who'd sinned too badly for eight tails. Care to try it out? Just* **cut along the dotted lines.**

Confessionals

The first step in **repentance** was confessing our sins to God, which we did freely because he already knew about them anyway. Some religions required this message to go through a middleman, who could better make your case for you because he wasn't as hateful in God's eyes. Imagine if you found out that the guy you were confessing your sins to was actually into way more twisted shit than you were. That would have been weird, huh?

Confessionals were a private moment between person and confessor. The stenographer was there for insurance purposes.

CONFESSIONAL TRANSCRIPT

Date: 02/08/1973
Time: 16.22 EST

Penitent: Forgive me father for I have sinned. It has been six years since my last confession.
Priest: Go ahead my child.
Penitent: I took the Lord's name in vain.
Priest: An all too common sin, I'm afraid.
Penitent: Normally I wouldn't, but it was just after I hit someone with my car.
Priest: I see. Was this person you hit injured?
Penitent: I don't know. I drove away without stopping to check.
Priest: You didn't stop?
Penitent: Yeah, is that sin?
Priest: Yes, that's a terrible sin.
Penitent: Does it make it worse if it's a cop?
Priest: Wait — you hit a cop?!
Penitent: I can't be sure. I was going really fast when I hit him. Is speeding a sin?
Priest: Speeding's kind of beside the point, here...
Penitent: Well, that's a relief.
Priest: Did you call the hospital at least?
Penitent: I haven't really had time. It happened, like, three minutes ago.
Priest: Three minutes?! You just ran over a cop and the first thing you did is go to confession?!
Penitent: Why? Is going to confession a sin?
Priest: No, of course not, but —
Penitent: Hey! I guess I'm not as bad as I thought!
Priest: OK, I'm not sure you want to be telling me this. You need to go to the police. Immediately.
Penitent: No way. They'd put me in jail. But you've just gotta take it, right?
Priest: Yes, I am bound to silence, but surely —
Penitent: Besides, even if the cop lived, they'd probably want to put me in jail for stealing the world's largest diamond. Which is what I was driving away from when I hit the cop.
Priest: [silence]
Penitent: Father? Are you there?
Priest: You stole the world's largest diamond?
Penitent: Is that a sin?
Priest: Yes! Yes! That's a sin!
Penitent: Well, if it makes you feel any better, I didn't kill anyone to get it.
Priest: I guess that's something...
Penitent: I need to confess another thing. I also lied father.
Priest: That's kind of inconsequential at this —
Penitent: It was when I told you I didn't kill anyone to get that diamond. Man, it feels good to get that off my chest.
Priest: Jesus Christ...
(Transcript ends)

Holidays

ALTHOUGH WE TRIED to practice our religions every day, sometimes we were given special days off school and work called **religious holidays**. These days were fully utilized to further our respective relationships with the Lord and were in no way an excuse for a three day weekend to Hedonism Jamaica.

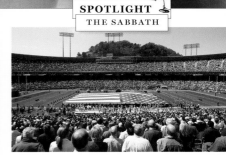
DECEMBER

SEAN – WEST METRO

Sunday	Monday	Tuesday	Wednesday	Thursday	Friday	Saturday
		1 **Doubtmas** (Agnostic) — Modern Medicine Unawareness Month (Christian Science)	2 Hanukkah (Judaism)	3 **Chanukah** (Judaism) — Ghost Dance of the Loose Slots (Cherokee)	4 Channukkah (Juudaism) — **Cthluhu's Birthday** (Cthluhuism)	5 **Hânâkâ** (Japanese Judaism) — Day That Is Not a Day Day (Zen Buddhism)
6 Ha'a'nu-u-ka'a (Polynesian Judaism)	7 Chakakhan (Disco Judaism) — **Muslim New Year** (Unitarianism)	8 **Charmonukkah** (Blues Judaism) — Flagellebration (Shi'ite)	9 Guernica (Abstract Judaism) — **Dick Van Patten's Birthday** (Van Pattenism)	10 **Feast of St. Boyardee** (Catholicism) — Bring-Your-Daughter-to-Life Day (Voodoo)	11 Great Shame Ritual (Shinto) — **Summer Solstice Festival** (Polish Catholic)	12 Sattavayanashivarti-lakshmittarjunijinalan-jiyanatti Eve (Hindu)
13 Sattavayanashivarti lakshmittarjunijinalan-jiyanatti (Hindu)	14 Mission Impossible IV Premiere (Scientology)	15 Flogstravaganza (Sunni)	16 **Poonteenth** (Druid, Unitarianism) — Ba'high Holy Day (Ba'hai)	17 **Moderate Meal of Filial Prostration** (Confucianism) — Fuckfest (Reformed Amish)	18 Ceremony of a Thousand Dishonors (Shinto) — **Opposite Day** (Gnosticism)	19 Lesbian Harvest of Menstrual Patchouli (Wiccan)
20 Somet'ing (Rastafarianism) — **Winter Solstice** (Druidism)	21 **Feast of Starvation** (Zen Buddhism)	22 Accidentally Trodden Ant Memorial Day (Jainism)	23 **Airport Security Personnel Awareness Day** (Sikhism)	24 Yom Chinatown Eve (Judaism)	25 **Christmas** (Christianity, Reformed Judaism) — Life Day (Wookieism)	26 **Kwanzaa** (unobserved, Unitarianism)

Religious Villains

WHILE WE WERE all sinners, a few really stood out from the pack.

Galileo Galilei objectively observed the universe through a telescope. For shame! For shame, blasphemer!

Judas Iscariot *betrayed Jesus with a kiss, and even though Jesus knew he was going to do it—in fact, needed him to do it in order to fulfill His Divine Destiny—Judas was damned for all eternity, anyway. Nice.*

Salman Rushdie *wrote* The Satanic Verses, *a book that angered many Muslims. His follow-up only made matters worse.*

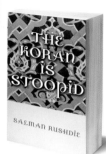

The Devil

The major monotheisms all posited an evil adversary to God. And though we called him by many names—Satan, Lucifer, Rob Schneider, Mephistopheles— we all agreed, he was a real turd. Luckily he could be defeated, either in high-stakes fiddle contests or in a court of law (see *Satan et al. v. Webster*).

Deals With the Devil

Satan was said to offer worldly power and knowledge in exchange for one's immortal soul. Was a **lifetime of power** a fair trade for an **eternity of torment**? Elizabeth Bathory, Paul Harvey and Timmy Milliken thought so.

Souls sold for, respectively: Eternal youth, Fame, Date to the junior prom

*Although the Devil represented everything we feared, we also really, really wanted to **do** him.*

This **sandwich spread** *forced those who ate it to turn their backs on all that was holy.*

John Milton's **Paradise Lost** *depicted Satan as a Fallen Angel, doomed to spend all eternity reading John Milton's* Paradise Lost.

Heaven

GIVEN HOW EASY and fun earthly sinning could be, you'd think that our vision of "heaven" would have to dazzle us. However, the furthest our collective imaginations got was that heaven was white, well-maintained and looked like the clean room in a hospital burn ward. Best we could tell, Heaven was a place where you and everyone you'd ever known did happy things to harp music—something you never would have been caught dead listening to when you were alive.

Hell

HELL WAS A fiery stygian pit of endless suffering, punctuated by noxious odors, bubbling semen and unrelenting Muzak. You earned this fate by either A) being bad; B) being good, but worshiping the wrong God; or C) being good, worshiping the right God but neglecting some other fundamental sacrament you didn't even know existed like you're not supposed to get married on a Tuesday.

Grandparents' Sex Farm

Regular Strippers

Dept of motor vehicles

Hugh Grant Film festival

Arby's ROAST BEEF Sandwich IS DELICIOUS!

Tunnel of Hate

Herpes

Enjoy again and again and again

We were willing to die for our gods, but all things being equal, we preferred killing for them. **The Crusades** were a series of a dozen or so military campaigns, fought over two centuries, between Yahweh and Allah. The battles occurred roughly 1,000 years ago. Unfortunately, as so often happened in Godfights, grudges were held.

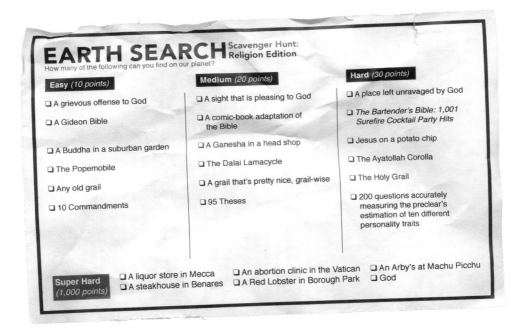

EARTH SEARCH
Scavenger Hunt: Religion Edition
How many of the following can you find on our planet?

Easy (10 points)
- ❑ A grievous offense to God
- ❑ A Gideon Bible
- ❑ A Buddha in a suburban garden
- ❑ The Popemobile
- ❑ Any old grail
- ❑ 10 Commandments

Medium (20 points)
- ❑ A sight that is pleasing to God
- ❑ A comic-book adaptation of the Bible
- ❑ A Ganesha in a head shop
- ❑ The Dalai Lamacycle
- ❑ A grail that's pretty nice, grail-wise
- ❑ 95 Theses

Hard (30 points)
- ❑ A place left unravaged by God
- ❑ *The Bartender's Bible: 1,001 Surefire Cocktail Party Hits*
- ❑ Jesus on a potato chip
- ❑ The Ayatollah Corolla
- ❑ The Holy Grail
- ❑ 200 questions accurately measuring the preclear's estimation of ten different personality traits

Super Hard (1,000 points)
- ❑ A liquor store in Mecca
- ❑ A steakhouse in Benares
- ❑ An abortion clinic in the Vatican
- ❑ A Red Lobster in Borough Park
- ❑ An Arby's at Machu Picchu
- ❑ God

FAQs
(Future Alien Questions)

Q. Wasn't the vast number of religions, each claiming to be the one "true" one, a tipoff that the phenomenon of religion was more a collective neurosis than a metaphysical observation?
A. No.

Q. Was there really a "doggie heaven"?
A. No. There was, however, a doggie hell.

Q. Jews, Christians and Muslims all had a holy book—what about Hindus?
A. Hindus had many sacred scriptures. The most important was the Kama Sutra, which taught enlightenment through yogic techniques like the Reverse Cowboy and the Calcutta Steamer.

You'll find the Kama Sutra in the back of most Hindu supply stores, behind the curtain.

Q. We were surprised you devoted so much time to Judaism, since it made up only one-fifth of one percent of the world's people.
A. What do you mean?

Q. It just seemed disproportionate.
A. Oh. Well. Sorry you had a problem with the pages about the Jews.

Q. We didn't have a problem with them.
A. Really? Because it sounds like you had a problem with them.

Q. No no no. In fact some of our favorite pages in the chapter were Jewish.
A. Good. Good for you.

Q. Can we move on?
A. Do what you like.

Q. Was Buddha really fat or really skinny? There seems to be evidence for both.
A. He started out thin. Then once he achieved enlightenment he kind of let himself go.

Through meditation, the Buddha achieved enheavyment.

Q. Why did bad things happen to good people?
A. We did not know. But we did know it was presumptuous for human beings to attempt to comprehend providence, or the mysterious motivations behind every aspect of the divine plan.

Q. Why did bad things happen to bad people?
A. Divine justice.

Q. You say the Pope was the head of the Catholic Church, yet we're finding many records of people inquiring whether he was even Catholic.
A. "Is the Pope Catholic?" was actually a sarcastic way of letting someone know the answer to the question they just asked is "Yes."

Q. Got it. One last question. Was religion, as Marx alleged, "the opiate of the masses"?
A. Is the Pope Catholic?

HUMAN BRAIN →

METAMORPHIC, BASALT WITH GRANITE FLAKES ↓

FRONTAL LOBE →

SUBLIMATION OF PATERNAL GUILT VIS-A-VIS OEDIPAL COMPLEX ↓

$$L = C1 \times \frac{P \times V^2 \times A}{2}$$

FEMUR ↓

TOTAL WEIGHT: 342.7 Kg →

PITUITARY GLAND

Science attempted to explain the mysteries of life, often by destroying the beauty of it.

Science

As we saw in the last chapter, the fear of death and the terrifying uncertainty of existence prompted early man to seek comfort, or at least assurance, in the supernatural. "Who created us?" "How does the sun travel through the sky?" "Why does it burn when I urinate?" For millennia, the respective answers to those questions were "Invisible Cloud Men," "star-boats" and "you must have angered the Invisible Cloud Men."

But eventually the nerds of our higher intelligence grew tired of being bullied by the Theta Chis of faith, and decided to fight back. Rationality bulked itself up through a rigorous training regimen of experimentation, observation and critical thinking known as **science**. Emboldened, it began offering its own explanations for things. We were created not by Invisible Cloud Men, but through an intricate evolutionary process. The sun's "travels" were actually a perpetual reflection of our own planet's movements. And it burned when you peed because you have dick anthrax, and we both know why that is.

For most of history, science maintained a cordial relationship with religion. Early science was to a large extent astronomy, and there was seemingly nothing in the skies that contradicted religion's idea of a Higher Power. And then came the **telescope**. Magnification began to reveal uncomfortable truths about the universe and our place in it. Through scientific study, men like Galileo began offering a view of the universe quite incompatible with religious teaching. The question then became: Who was right—God or Galileo? For fairness' sake, the Pope got to judge.

The next 500 years saw great geniuses making discoveries and insights that immeasurably deepened our understanding of the universe: The speeds of light and sound; the theories of evolution and relativity; the laws of gravity, thermodynamics and attraction.* But as wondrous as these findings were, science—pure science—tended to have difficulty

The Weber Summit S-670 Propane Gas Grill with Snap-Jet™ Burner Ignition System offered 769 square inches of total cooking area for the true "B-B-Q-noisseur."

expanding beyond its core fan base of 18-to-65-year-old balding bespectacled males.

Luckily, pure science had a friend and patron in its wealthier and better-looking cousin, **technology**. Technology was the branch of human knowledge by which the theoretical became the practical, and the practical became the obsolete. It proved the ideal conduit for human ingenuity, really kicking in with the dawn of the Industrial Revolution, which was different from a "real" revolution in that it killed millions more people. Whereas religion promised eternal life immediately upon death, technology promised an eternally better life immediately upon obtaining, for example, the **Weber Summit S-670 Propane Gas Grill with Snap-Jet™ Burner Ignition System**.

By 2010, science had positioned itself as religion's arch-nemesis. Yet the superficial difference in their methodologies masked a deeper kinship. Like religion, science placed its faith in cosmic forces that were invisible and sounded crazy. Filled with a sense of larger purpose, its high priests often considered themselves above morality and ethics. Its institutions were corporate and bureaucratic, and largely dependent on tax exemptions. More importantly, from the semi-automatic rifle to prosthetic limbs, from the deep-sea oil-drilling rig to the "containment dome," science proved every bit the equal of religion in its ability to almost solve the problems it caused.

Religion, at least, didn't suffer from arrogance. Science's case is more tragic: Conceived as a means of controlling the universe, it wound up getting away from us. Our capacity to achieve scientific breakthroughs was exceeded only by our lack of understanding of post-breakthrough realities. The more we played God, the more we began realizing we had perhaps been too critical of Him. In the end, God was more than happy to stand aside and let us use the toys we'd built, to hasten, if not downright cause, our ultimate demise.

Well played, Invisible Cloud Man. Well played.

Such as: IQ/(bench press) x (guitar skills) = y, where y = years of virginity

The Scientific Method

PIONEERED BY ANCIENT Greeks, developed by medieval Muslims, systematized in the Renaissance, perfected in the Enlightenment and patented by the Dupont Corporation, **the scientific method** improved on man's previous tradition: making shit up. The scientific method added the crucial step of **experimentation**, using real-world data to test a **hypothesis** that, if proven, would be accepted by scientists as a **theory**, which could then be used to get a **grant**, or in some cases, **tenure**.

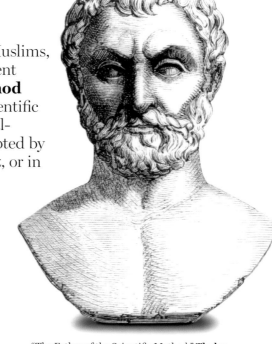

"The Father of the Scientific Method," **Thales of Miletus** refused to accept supernatural explanations for natural phenomena, right up until the day an angry witch turned him to stone.

NAILED IT
VACCINES

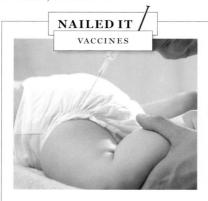

We used to die of diseases spread by microorganisms jealous of our size and good looks. But all that changed with the development of the lifesaving injections known as **vaccines**. Their secret ingredient? A little bit of the deadly microbe itself. Yes, it turned out the same "hair of the dog" approach that cured hangovers also worked on polio and rubella. Vaccines saved countless lives ... although try explaining that to a sobbing two-year-old being pierced by a syringe.

The Scientific Method in Action

❶ Identify a problem.
In 1854, hundreds of people in London's Soho district suddenly came down with cholera. At first, this was considered a slight improvement on their usual state of dysentery.

❷ Research the problem.
Dr. John Snow, *fresh off the discovery of his eponymous form of precipitation, arrives on the scene to gather information. As his notebooks reveal, his suspicions quickly focus on a public well known as "the Broad Street pump."*

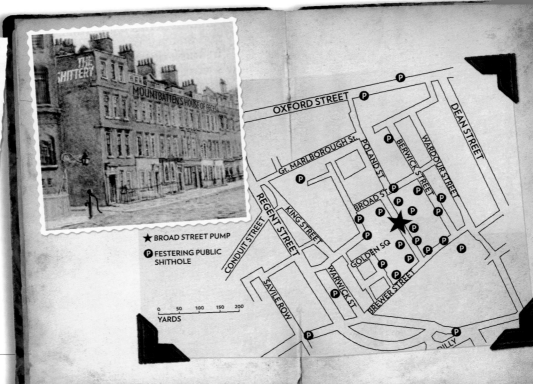

✱ The London *Times*, September 3, 1854 ✱
CHOLERA EPIDEMIC.
127 DEAD IN THREE DAYS
SURVIVORS FLEE SOHO.
SOHO LOFTS NOW AVAILABLE!
VICTIMS SUFFER EXTREME INTESTINAL DISTRESS.
RESIDENT: "WHILST CLIMBING UP A LADDER... I HEARD SOMETHING SPLATTER! DIARRHOEA! DIARRHOEA!

★ BROAD STREET PUMP
🅿 FESTERING PUBLIC SHITHOLE

YARDS

Accidental Discovery

The scientific method was our preferred means of discovery, but breakthroughs could also be the result of sudden **epiphanies** or **accidents**. In the first case, one's mind entered a relaxed state such that the thoughts that had been coalescing in the subconscious burst to the surface in an exquisite moment of inspiration. In the second instance, one's bumbling incompetence was freakishly rewarded, infuriating the conscientious co-workers who'd been busting their asses the whole time.

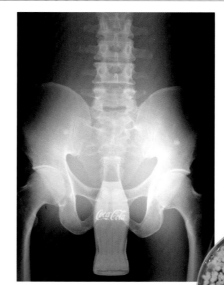

X-rays (Wilhelm Röntgen, 1895)
While performing an experiment on cathode rays, Röntgen noticed a glow in his laboratory. He suddenly realized the rays were penetrating solids. The discovery literally changed the way we looked at our bodies, giving us a miraculous glimpse at the wonders that could be shoved within.

Water Displacement (Archimedes, c. 450 B.C.)
Many of our greatest "Eureka!" moments took place in the bathtub, from Archimedes' discovery of water displacement, to Moronikes' finding that you can't make toast and bathe simultaneously.

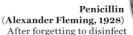

Penicillin (Alexander Fleming, 1928)
After forgetting to disinfect bacteria cultures before leaving on vacation, Fleming found a halo of bacteria around a blue-green mold. It turned out to be the surprise miracle cue for gonorrhea, syphilis and just about anything else bad that could happen to your genitals.

③ Formulate a hypothesis.
As he later recounted, Snow then turned the evidence into a revolutionary new theory.

④ Test the hypothesis.
Snow set out to verify his idea experimentally, pioneering two fields: Epidemiology, and college-student income-earning.

⑤ Analyze the results; draw a conclusion.

On The Possible Health Detriments of Consuming Massive Amounts of Human Excrement
DR. JOHN SNOW

"Having thus gathered the data, I could not help but wonder, whether the epidemic was not in some way related to the fact, that every one of its sufferers had drunk water absolutely teeming with human shit."
—Dr. John Snow

ATTENTION OXFORD STUDENTS.

30
VOLUNTEERS WANTED QUICKLY FOR STUDY.

10
TO DRINK FROM BROAD STREET PUMP;

10
TO DRINK FROM UNCONTAMINED PUMP; AND

10
TO EAT NAUGHT BUT SHIT.
LAST GROUP EARNS 3 PENCE EXTRA.

Dr. John Snow; 45 *Dr. John Snow; 45* *Dr. John Snow; 45* *Dr. John Snow; 45* *Dr. John Snow; 45 Pu* *Dr. John Snow; 45 Pu* *Dr. John Snow; 45 Pu*

"Turned out I was right. It was the shit."

SO ABOUT THE

CHOLERA

THE **SOUTHWARK WATERWORKS COMPANY,**
WITHOUT ADMITTING ANY PRIOR ACTIONABLE WRONGDOING

NOW ADVISES THE

INHABITANTS OF THE SOHO DISTRICT

NOT TO DRINK ANY WATER *which has* **PREVIOUSLY BEEN SHAT IN.**

WE ALSO ANNOUNCE, WITH REGRET, THE DISCONTINUATION OF OUR POPULAR LINE OF BOTTLED REFRESHMENTS,

CESSPIT Spritzers *and* **NIGHTSOIL Nectars.**

Bigger

"**BIGGER IS BETTER.**" A tiny three-word expression that completely belied itself. But it reflected a larger truth: We liked things truly large. In fact **bigness** as an end in itself was a goal in fields as diverse as engineering, architecture, transportation, gastronomy, weaponry and shoulder-padology. Why? Because it spoke to our soaring ambition to make an enduring mark on the planet. Surely it was this noble impulse—and nothing else—that explains all the tall, rock-hard human erections you've discovered thrusting themselves into Earth's virginal skies.

Singapore Triple-Stacker Moonscraper (2010–) (239,592 miles) *Was meant to be thirteen stories higher, but the damn moon got in the way.*

Have you met the Giant Assholes next door?

Timeline
TALLEST BUILDINGS

Great Pyramid at Giza (2750 B.C.E.–1311 A.D.) (481 feet) *For nearly 4,000 years, this unfinished cube was the highest structure in the world.*

Notre Dame Cathedral (1876–1880) (495 feet) *Built to get closer to God, whose condo was just visible from the spire.*

Washington Monument (1884–1889) (555 feet) *Built to honor American basketball star Kermit Washington, who was tall.*

Eiffel Tower (1889–1930) (986 feet) *The French never stopped considering this the world's tallest building.*

Dubai Burj Khalifa (2007–2010) (2,717 feet) *Contained world's highest swimming pool (76th floor), mosque (158th floor), and Successories® poster (162nd floor).*

Smaller

IT WAS A SAD but universal fact of human life that any technology—no matter how incredible—eventually came to be seen as cumbersome. For instance, the first cordless telephone inspired awe. One year later, using the very same phone could only be seen as an ironic tribute to a time when we were forced to lug around comically giant cordless phones. Nearly every technological advancement in human history was quickly followed by the phrase, "That's great, but how am I going to get it on the plane?"

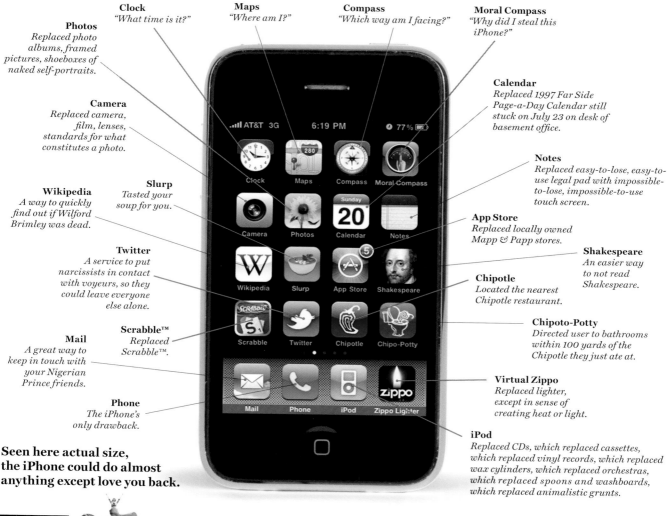

Photos
Replaced photo albums, framed pictures, shoeboxes of naked self-portraits.

Clock
"What time is it?"

Maps
"Where am I?"

Compass
"Which way am I facing?"

Moral Compass
"Why did I steal this iPhone?"

Camera
Replaced camera, film, lenses, standards for what constitutes a photo.

Calendar
Replaced 1997 Far Side Page-a-Day Calendar still stuck on July 23 on desk of basement office.

Notes
Replaced easy-to-lose, easy-to-use legal pad with impossible-to-lose, impossible-to-use touch screen.

Wikipedia
A way to quickly find out if Wilford Brimley was dead.

Slurp
Tasted your soup for you.

App Store
Replaced locally owned Mapp & Papp stores.

Shakespeare
An easier way to not read Shakespeare.

Twitter
A service to put narcissists in contact with voyeurs, so they could leave everyone else alone.

Chipotle
Located the nearest Chipotle restaurant.

Chipoto-Potty
Directed user to bathrooms within 100 yards of the Chipotle they just ate at.

Scrabble™
Replaced Scrabble™.

Mail
A great way to keep in touch with your Nigerian Prince friends.

Virtual Zippo
Replaced lighter, except in sense of creating heat or light.

Phone
The iPhone's only drawback.

iPod
Replaced CDs, which replaced cassettes, which replaced vinyl records, which replaced wax cylinders, which replaced orchestras, which replaced spoons and washboards, which replaced animalistic grunts.

Seen here actual size, the iPhone could do almost anything except love you back.

Timeline
CAMERA

Mammoth
So big, families took vacations to it.

Box
Slightly smaller, but still required a tripod, or three steady Chinamen.

Portable
Let turn-of-the-century journalists capture "breaking news" that they could develop, deliver and publish in less than a month.

Compact
Transformed any douchebag with 300 bucks into Ansel Adams.

Teddy Bear containing tiny spy camera
Finally, people could find out if the babysitter was drinking their rum.

Faster

FASTER WAS SMALLER'S more demanding technology twin. In less than 100 years the travel time from New York City to San Francisco was cut from six months by horse and foot to just six hours by plane. You'd think we would be endlessly grateful for the advancement. Yet God forbid the flight got delayed 40 minutes by fog. "Do you people have any idea how to run an airline? No, I will NOT lower my voice! I AM A DECENT AND UPSTANDING CITIZEN DRIVEN TO SKULLFUCKING THE GATE ATTENDANT FOR CONTINENTAL AIRLINES BECAUSE I MAY OR MAY NOT MISS MY COUSIN'S REHEARSAL DINNER IN MONTECITO!!!" The only thing that increased more rapidly than the **speed** of new technology was the speed with which we became irritated at its now relative slowness. Eventually, we developed the capacity to be instantaneously disappointed. This was the final triumph of **faster**.

YOU HAD TO BE HERE

This man felt the need for speed.

Lt. Pete "Maverick" Mitchell (1964–), Fighter pilot/Danger Zone resident

This man also felt the need for speed.

Street Tweaker (name unknown), Fresno, CA

SPOTLIGHT
THE WHEEL

The invention of the wheel revolutionized man's ability to be mobile. Years later, we used it to solve word problems for moderate amounts of money.

MAN'S GR A T S T INV NTION

Timeline
FASTER

Walking
Brought one child, one basket of berries and two blankets in a 400-mile circle in one year.

Donkey
Transported ten bushels of wheat to the town on the other side of the mountain range in two weeks.

Truck
Shipped 1,000 lbs. of oranges from Florida to the Waldorf-Astoria in four days.

Plane
Delivered 700 packages from Hong Kong to Rome in twelve hours.

Rocket Donkey
Transported ten bushels of wheat into the side of a mountain in thirty seconds ... one way.

Convenience

If necessity was the mother of invention, then laziness was its drunken stepfather. Man created many contraptions to **free up as much of his time as possible**. This helped us achieve our life's greatest goal: doing nothing.

Invention: *Zipper*
What it was for:
Fastening
What it spared us:
Embarrassment; genital drafts
Freed us to: *Spend more time enjoying urinating next to strangers*

Invention: *Bar code*
What it was for: *Inventory management*
What it spared us: *Having to yell for price checks*
Freed us to: *Get high before going to work as cashier at Safeway*

9 780446 579223

Invention: *Washer-dryer*
What it was for: *Washing; drying*
What it eased: *See above*
Freed us to: *Iron and fold; prepare meal for husband*

IN THE RUINS
VELCRO SHOES

Velcro shoes saved us up to fifteen seconds by allowing us not to have to tie shoelaces. This helped guarantee we were never late for our shuffleboard games.

IN THE RUINS
RACETRACKS

These were outdoor arenas where we would sit on benches for entire steamy afternoons watching cars drive around an oval very, very fast. One's affection or lack thereof for this activity was an indicator of whether or not your ancestors owned slaves.

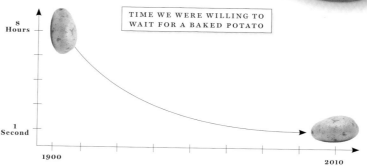

TIME WE WERE WILLING TO WAIT FOR A BAKED POTATO

8 Hours

1 Second

1900

2010

Chart courtesy The Idaho Institute of Tuber Sciences, in conjunction with "Tater Thoughts," UNISPUD, Dr. Franklin "Spuds" MacKenzie, M.D., and Omega—official timekeepers of the Olympic Games and time-related potato studies. Special thanks to the National Institute for Potato Enjoyment and Preparation, the General Electric Foundation for the Study of Culinary Microwave Technology, and the United States Department of Defense. Additional funding provided by the Sour Cream Council, the Bacon Bits Growers of America, and the John D. and Catherine T. MacArthur Foundation.

The Periodic Table of the Synthetic

We assume you're already familiar with all the naturally occurring elements, from #1, hydrogen (which we used to make bombs), to #92, uranium (likewise). But we weren't satisfied with the universe's tawdry selection of atoms. Using all our powers of ingenuity and copyright protection, we mixed and cooked these building blocks to produce wondrous **new substances** that could be eaten, worn, built with or stuffed in our breasts. God may have created life, but Spandex? That was all us.

R Rayon 1892 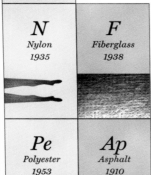								
N Nylon 1935	**F** Fiberglass 1938							
Pe Polyester 1953	**Ap** Asphalt 1910							

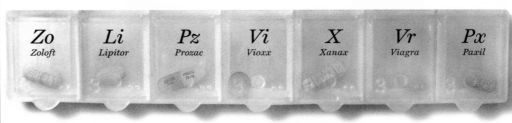

Zo Zoloft	**Li** Lipitor	**Pz** Prozac	**Vi** Vioxx	**X** Xanax	**Vr** Viagra	**Px** Paxil

☐ Pharma series

Note: The "pharmas" were small powders found clustered in dark recesses known as "medicine cabinets." Their positive intentions would link closely with our negative thoughts, together forming an "ironic compound."

Kv Kevlar 1965 	**Cn** Concrete c. 300 B.C.	**Le** Lego 1939	**W** Windex 1933	**Wo** Wite-Out 1951	**Cs** Chap-Stick c. 1872 	**Ky** K-Y Jelly 1917	**Sw** Saran Wrap 1953	**Sp** Silly Putty 1943
Sx Spandex 1959	**Cm** Cement 1842	**Lu** Lucite 1955	**Nu** Nutella 1949	**P** Peeps 1953	**Sp** Spam 1937	**Tcby** Frozen Yogurt 1981	**Cbnb** Artificial butter 1986	**Cbtcbynb** [2] 2008
Lx Latex 1935	**Pb** Particle board 1955	**As** Asbestos 1828	**Vg** Vegemite 1922	**G** Gummi 1869	**Sg** Soylent Green 1973	**Ga** [1] Gatorade 1965	**Tg** Tang 1957 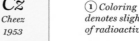	**Sp** Slurpee 1965
Pf Performance Fleece 1993	**Sf** Styrofoam 1941	**Pu** Polyurethane 1937	**Fa** Formica 1912	**Q** Quorn 1869	**Cz** Cheez 1953			

① *Coloring denotes slight level of radioactivity.*

② *Experimental non-dairy plasmal condensate briefly created in freak lab accident.*

L
Linoleum
1860

Legend:
- Fabrics
- Trademarks
- Posers
- Alloys
- Building materials
- Vanity cases
- Plastics
- Ignoble gasses
- Whips
- Abstractions

S
Steel
c. 1,500 B.C.

Bz ③
Bronze
Bronze Age,
obviously

Br
Brass
c. 2,000 B.C.

P
Pewter
c. 1,500 B.C.

DD ⑥
Silicone
1904

Us
Ultrasuede
1972

M
Mylar
1952

T
Teflon
1938

Cl
Celluloid
1866

V
Vinyl
1926

Bx
Botox
1987

N ⑧
Naugahyde
1936

Kg
Krazy Glue
1963

N
Nerf
1969

V
Vaseline
1872

Ddt
Pesticide
1939

Sm ④
Smog
1905

N
Napalm

Cf
Chlorofluoro-
carbons
1930

C
Collagen
1981

Px
Plexiglas
1982

Pu
Purell
1988

Li
Listerine
1875

Vl
Velcro
1941

Cw
Cool Whip
1967

Mw ⑤
Miracle Whip
1933

Ow
Orange Whip
c. 1955

Rw
Reddi-Wip
1948

Cz ⑦
Cubic zirconia
1936

Pl
Pleather
c. 1910

Rb
Red Bull
1982

Mw
Manwich
1969

J
Jell-O
1897

F
Fahrver-
gnügen
1989

S
Schwepper-
vescence
1946

M
Muzak
1934

Jq
Je ne sais quoi
Prehistoric

Ax
Body Spray
1983

Tf
Astroturf
1964

③ In competitions to determine which metal was best, bronze consistently came in third.

④ "Smog," a playful combination of "smoke" and "fog," gave millions of us "brancer," a non-playful combination of bronchitis and cancer.

⑤ An isotopic mutation of mayonnaise caused by overexposure to market research.

⑥ Silicone was commonly used in the construction of actresses.

⑦ Cubic zirconia rings were used to woo one's prospective fourth wife.

⑧ Eerily, naugahyde was created in the laboratory of Dr. John Naugajekyll.

Gods of Science

THE GREAT MEN AND WOMAN of science achieved so much, and transformed the world so profoundly, they were eventually able to shed the "nerd" tag they'd dealt with since childhood and be accorded a certain grudging respect. Here are all of the famous scientists who ever lived.

Albert Einstein (1879–1955)

With his eccentric appearance, German accent and unbridled passion for Victorian pornography, Albert Einstein was our most clichéd scientist. His theories on relativity also made him our most brilliant **pure scientist**. When he died, us lesser beings sawed open his skull and preserved his brain in a Mason jar. Not so fucking smart now, are you Einstein?

Gregor Mendel (1822–1884)

Gregor Mendel was a monk whose experiments with peas laid the groundwork for the field of **genetics**. His slightly raunchier experiments with carrots nearly got him kicked out of the seminary.

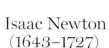

Isaac Newton (1643–1727)

His classic double album *Newton Comes Alive* sold over 20 million copies, but he is perhaps best remembered as the first to articulate the laws of **classical physics**, including thermodynamics and gravity.

IN THE RUINS

COMPACT
FLUORESCENT
BULBS

The inventor of the compact fluorescent bulb, seen here at the moment he came up with the idea.

These "eco friendly" light bulbs failed to save us. If you see one in the ruins, smash it.

Marie Curie (1867–1934)

"Marie Curie is a hero. Marie Curie was a scientist who discovered **radium** even though she was a woman. She was an inspiration to women because she did not let obstacles stop her from doing science."
—ANNIE TAYLOR, 11
Marie Curie: A Book Report, 2006

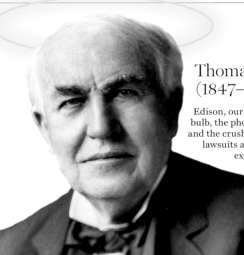

Thomas Edison
(1847–1931)

Edison, our greatest inventor, invented the light bulb, the phonograph, direct current electricity and the crushing of one's competitors through lawsuits and negative PR campaigns. He exemplifies the **applied scientist**: the tinkerer who views knowledge as a means to an end. That end? Getting so rich you no longer care that you're deaf.

Alexander Graham Bell
(1847–1922)

"Mr. Watson, come here. I want you." With those historic words, Bell **transmitted his voice** from one room to the next, thus achieving his dream of inventing a "Watson-Summoner." Months later, he realized it might be put to other uses too.

Wright Brothers
(1871–1948, 1867–1912)

Orville and Wilbur Wright were two of the worst bicycle mechanics who ever lived. But in some ways, that's not really important. Because on December 17, 1903, the brothers fulfilled one of mankind's oldest dreams with the first ever **manned flight**. It lasted 12 seconds, but took off 50 minutes late due to tower traffic on the tarmac.

SPOTLIGHT
SHORTCUT TO IMMORTALITY

Genius was the best guarantee of scientific immortality. But the next best thing was getting one big thing right, and attaching your name to it.

Occam's Razor, 1320
The scientific principle of maximizing simplicity is known as "Occam's razor," a sarcastic reference to its medieval namesake's notoriously complicated shaving device.

Bunsen Burner, 1855
German chemist Robert Bunsen invented his burner to test the flammability of adolescent skin.

Alzheimer's Disease, 1906
Dr. Alois Alzheimer invented Alzheimer's as a way to get back at old people.

Venn Diagram, 1881
John Venn's original diagram.

NAMES OF PEOPLE — ME! — NAMES OF DIAGRAMS

Geiger Counter, 1908
Hans Geiger's machine made it much easier to count geigers.

Schrödinger's Cat, 1935
By now, this box neither does nor does not contain the rotting carcass of Schrödinger's cat.

E-Z-Pass, 1982
Invented by Joseph E-Z-Pass to make people with credit cards feel like gods in rush hour traffic.

Health

AS CONFIDENT AS the human species was that after death, a Higher Power awaited us in an eternal utopia filled with everyone we've ever known and/or virgins (see Religion), one thing we all feared was death. And although we never quite succeeded in conquering the Grim Reaper, we did manage to confuse and delay him, allowing many of us to enjoy up to twenty extra years of feeble dependence.

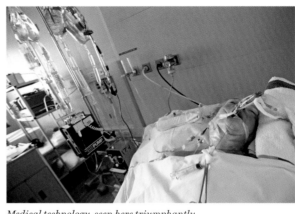

Medical technology, seen here triumphantly thwarting this man's will to die.

Medical Marvels

Lithotome
An 18th-century tool doctors inserted through the urethra in order to relieve painful kidney stones. To put that in layman's terms, we used to shove pointy sticks in our dickholes on a rock-retrieval exploration dig.

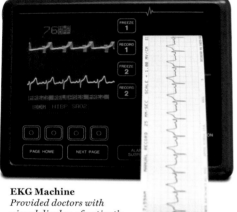

Skull Saw
The best part of using this tool wasn't cutting through the skull. It was licking the blades afterwards.

EKG Machine
Provided doctors with visual display of patient's heartbeat. A flatlining EKG was often an excellent indication that a televised medical drama was about to take a commercial break.

MRI Machine
"Magnetic resonance imaging" gave doctors an accurate view of the insides of our bodies, stopping them from having to shrink themselves down into tiny spaceships and inject themselves into our bloodstream.

IN THE RUINS
MEDICAL WASTE

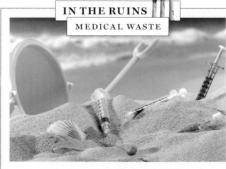

You'll be finding a great deal of medical waste on our beaches. Your logical assumption would be that our hospitals were located near our oceans. They weren't.

Bandages
Specifically designed to combat boo-boos and ouchies. Most effective when combined with kisses, wuv, and the licensed image of a beloved television character.

Bleeding Bowl
Used to catch blood being deliberately drained from patients for therapeutic purposes. Treatment discontinued with breakthrough finding that humans need blood.

Tooth Key
Used to extract infected teeth from the 1700s through the early 1900s. The hand-cranked hook-spike also came in cherry flavor ... for kids.

SPOTLIGHT
HOLISTIC MEDICINE

*Dr. Andrew Weil was one of the foremost modern practitioners of **holistic medicine**.*

Believers in holistic medicine rejected Western medical approaches in favor of time-honored spiritual wellness practices. Unless the accident was bad, in which case they let a Western ambulance race them to a Western emergency room where a Western doctor would reset their pelvis, so they could get back to their healing yogic rituals.

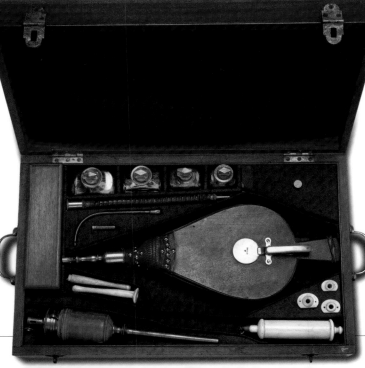

Tobacco Smoke Enemas
These were administered to resuscitate patients who had nearly drowned. They served little therapeutic effect, but made your anus feel like a movie star. While doing this, the doctor was required to state, "Yes, I am in fact just blowing smoke up your ass."

Medical Bureaucracy

AS A SOCIETY, we believed that only one thing was more important than caring for our sick and injured: ensuring that they first filled out the proper paperwork. **Medical bureaucracy** was so important to us that nations sometimes spent more money maintaining them than it would have cost to provide health care for all uninsured citizens. This hilarious irony was often lost on the desperately ill.

WellNet understands you are bleeding profusely, but still requests that you complete this in ink, not blood.

WellNet Physicians Group Questionnaire

In order to provide you treatment today, we require the following information to be filled out completely. If you are unable to fill out this form, please sit there and die quietly. Your answers are confidential and will be seen only by your physician, the student nurse, the receptionist, our IT contractor, your current and future health insurers, the person sitting next to you in the waiting room, the cleaning staff, and anyone who calls our office pretending to be you.

Customer's Name _____
Address _____
Primary Health Insurance _____
Secondary Health Insurance _____
Tertiary Health Insurance _____
Christian Scientist? ☐ Y ☐ N
If yes, you may skip the remaining questions and leave. You are in the wrong office. The reading room is on the third floor.

SS # _____
Phone( ) _____ - _____ DOB _____ SEX _____ Organ donor? ☐ Y ☐ N
Policy # _____ Employer _____
Policy # _____
Policy # _____

FINANCIAL INFORMATION

How will you be paying today? ☐ Cash ☐ Credit Card ☐ Check ☐ Paypal ☐ Indentured Servitude
Bank account # _____ Routing# _____
Value of jewelry you are wearing today _____ Balance _____ ATM PIN _____ Retirement Acct #
Please list all sources of garnishable income _____ Location of penny jar _____
Credit Card #'s (*Attach additional sheets if necessary. Include CVV numbers*) Please trace your safety deposit box key here ▸ ☐

MEDICAL INFORMATION

Are you currently experiencing any of the following symptoms?
Blood loss? (*check all that apply*) ☐ Seeping ☐ Jetting ☐ Anal
Seizures? (*please indicate the degree of mal on the scale below*)
petit 1---------2---------3---------4---------5 grand

Rabies? ☐ Y ☐ N ☐ Not sure
Pregnancy? ☐ Real ☐ Hysterical
Foreign object(s) 'accidentally' lodged in rectum?
☐ Bottle ☐ Light bulb ☐ G.I. Joe ☐ Snuff box
☐ Other _____
Length of erection: < 4 hours > 4 hours (*circle one*)
How many alcoholic beverages do you drink per week? _____
How many really? _____

List all allergies (*Omit any imaginary food allergies you suddenly realized you had after reading an article in* People)

List all medications you are currently taking. Include street drugs, ineffectual herbal concoctions from your local food co-op, Asian potency enhancers, and Belgian potency diminishers.

PLEASE ATTACH PRINTOUTS OF ALL WEB RESEARCH YOU HAVE DONE ON THE DISEASE OR CONDITION YOU SUSPECT YOU HAVE.

☐ Check here if you believe laughter is the best medicine   Is that covered by your insurance? ☐ Y ☐ N
Organ donor? ☐ Yes ☐ No   Are you sure you wouldn't like to become an organ donor? ☐ OK
How did you hear about us? ☐ Referral ☐ Windshield flyer ☐ Police brought me here

Check any symptoms you have experienced in the last 6 months:
☐ Sudden weight loss
☐ Night sweats
☐ Mid-afternoon sweats
☐ Dawn shivers
☐ Buboes
☐ Sudden blindness
☐ Flu-like symptoms
☐ Voices in head
☐ Unexplained fever
☐ Unexplained limbs
☐ Skin rash
☐ Are you sure about the rash? What's that on your right cheek?

By signing this form, you certify that any antibiotic-resistant staph infection, flesh-eating bacteria, or stray medical instruments you discover in the coming weeks were probably in your body already and did not originate in this healthcare facility.

Signature _____ Date _____

---- FOR OFFICE USE ONLY ----
☐ Drug-seeker? ☐ Uninsured/Poor? ☐ Contagious-looking? ☐ Munchausen? ☐ Patient Zero? ☐ Does This Patient Look Worth Treating?

Creating Life

While many of the least fit and/or child-desiring of humans were seemingly able to **reproduce** simply by brushing up against each other, others who desperately desired children had to wait for scientists to figure out how to grow one in a dish.

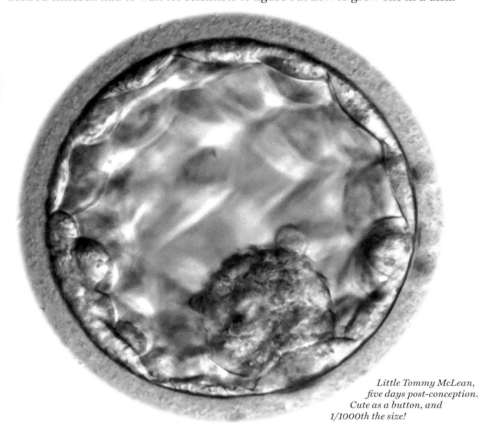

Little Tommy McLean, five days post-conception. Cute as a button, and 1/1000th the size!

Pregnancy Aids

Natural

In vitro

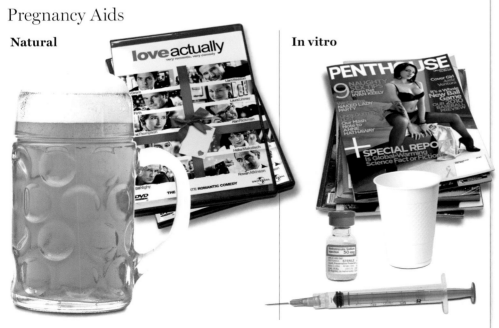

Medical Procedures: Required vs. Elective

LIPS
Required:

Made him look normal among his peers

Elective:

Made her look normal among her peers

STEROIDS
Required:

Used to increase lung capacity

Elective:

Used to limit nightclub capacity

Psychology

THE HUMAN BRAIN was the most complex, powerful and mysterious organ on Earth. Even at the zenith of our scientific knowledge, the field of **psychology** could only scratch the surface of the brain's incomparable brilliance. But take that opinion with a grain of salt, because the organ we used to study the brain was in fact the brain itself. That built-in conflict of interest cast doubt onto the entire field of brain-related study. It meant that either this gray orb of protein was a beautiful hive of trans-magical powers utilized to only ten percent of its capacity, or it was just another narcissistic asshole.

Disorder	Psychologist	Psychiatrist	Stepdad
Depression	Let's begin with the root cause of the problem. Tell me about your mother.	50mg of Zoloft twice a day.	Seasonal what disorder? It's cloudy. For Christ sake, get over it!
OCD	Were you made to feel guilty for many things as a child?	300mg of Wellbutrin XL once daily. (Side effects may include increased nervousness and filthy house.)	Hey, Captain Scrubs-a-lot. I noticed my T-shirts weren't folded straight ... maybe that bothers you? Also my car is dirty.
Erectile Dysfunction	There are any number of proximate causes here—fear of intimacy, suppressed anger toward your partner, latent homosexuality. We should do a minimum of five sessions a week to get started.	Let me guess, you want Viagra? Okay ... but remember, you are 84, so take it easy.	Beats me ... my pecker always works when I'm banging your Mom. What? What'd I say?
Multiple Personality Disorder	You need to try to embrace all of your various personalities, so that you are in control.	Okay, so when you are "Bob" you need to take 60mgs of Cymbalta, but the minute "Tony" rears his head you gotta go with a minimum of 30mgs of Adderall. Good luck, Karen.	Let me ask you this: Are any of those personalities capable of catching a ball, or are they all little spazzes?
Bed Wetting	This problem began the minute you came to terms with the fact that your stepfather had molested you. Which means you need to confront him.	10mgs of Molesterol daily. If problem persists add 20mgs of Repressormax.	Okay, this one is my bad.
Psychosis	What are the other things your Labradoodle is telling you?	Okay, come sit here and let's talk about your ... Quickly, boys, the net! Get that straitjacket on him. Now stay calm, we're going to take a long van ride to a nice place.	Whoa, whoa. You know I've always thought of you as like a half a son. Please put that screwdriver down. That face tattoo looks great. I don't know why I called it retarded.

Sigmund Freud: The Wizard of Id

As the founder of psychoanalysis, Sigmund Freud hypothesized that doctor-patient dialogue could improve mental health and free up deep-seated resentments he assumed everyone harbored, having spent his entire childhood being called "Sissymund Homo." Freud insisted the psyche of every human ever born could be boiled down to three basic parts: the id, the ego and the super-ego—a claim so ambitious that merely suggesting it proved the existence of the latter. In his book *The Interpretation of Dreams*, Freud asserted that dreams were the "royal road to the unconscious," and that any pantsless hitchhikers you encountered while on that road were only there because of your daddy issues. He also advocated prescribing cocaine to treat mental illness, which may explain why many of Freud's friends and family members became increasingly dependent on his services, especially on weekends. But Freud was perhaps best remembered for his assertion that both males and females had a subconscious obsession with phalluses, causing them to see the male sex organ practically everywhere they looked. Critics, however, disputed this, saying you have to be a pretty sick individual to see dicks all over the place.

Freud was a seminal figure.

The therapy couch put testy patients at ease.

Pseudoscience

Of course, science and religion could never provide all the answers we humans were seeking. To help fill in the gaps we came up with **pseudoscience**. We developed entire industries that promised relief from all forms of physical and emotional anguish through the simple use of herbs, stretching and/or pressing on certain parts of one's feet … and it totally worked! Like, this friend of ours had inoperable brain cancer, the doctors gave him six months to live, so he went to see this guy in Chinatown who told him it was actually a clogged meridian or something. The guy massaged his armpit for ten minutes and told him to start living again. That was twelve years ago. We shit you not.

*Practitioners of **palmistry** learned valuable information about their clients by studying their hands.*

❶ Gullibility arch
❷ Appetite for total bullshit crease
❸ Desperately finding solace in the comforting buzzwords of a stranger line
❹ Girdle of questionable judgement
❺ Severed while opening a can of cat food loop
❻ Radian of self-delusion
❼ Arc of, "come on—why would a woman who can see the future also offer massage?"

This miraculous method of communicating with the deceased was by the people who brought you Boggle.

Rorschach Test

By asking people what they saw in the **inkblots**, psychologists were able to determine the mental state of their patients. In its 90 years of existence, no one ever got the correct answer. (Correct answer below)

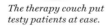

(Correct answer: The one on the left is a butterfly tea party. The one on the right is your mother's angry vagina.)

Our Medicine Cabinet

We spent much of our time not feeling great, and most of *that* time doing anything we could think of to feel a little better. We were willing to try just about anything, and over the years we trusted in thousands of remedies, which we tended to keep in **medicine cabinets** conveniently located near our toilets.

ANCIENT

This **Egyptian baldness cure** dated from 1550 B.C. Since the dawn of history, men preferred to rub even, say, a blend of rancid lion, crocodile, hippo, cat, asp and ibex fat on their heads to losing their hair.

Purgatives harnessed the healthful effects of violent vomiting to treat any ailment except violent vomiting.

Because they resembled the human brain, **walnuts** were once thought useful for curing headaches. Modern science would show that their best use was to augment banana muffins.

We used the **trepanation knife** because, for a time we thought most diseases could be cured by drilling holes in our skulls. Nope.

Black bile was a time-honored remedy. Regurgitating blood? That meant it was working.

Leeches may have been hermaphroditic bloodsucking swamp parasites, but when it came to the human body, we knew that they knew what they were doing.

EASTERN

Chinese bear penis preparation was believed to be a potent aphrodisiac, along with **lion penis, elephant penis, walrus penis** and really any penis.

The use of **acupuncture needles** evolved from the traditional Chinese practice of storing sewing needles in servants' backs.

Tiger testicles achieved some success as a cure for impotence, and great success as a cure for having any tigers on the planet.

EARLY MODERN

This **tonic** was guaranteed to cure all infirmities, according to an unlicensed doctor/lawyer/musician who lived by himself in a wagon. Good for what ailed you if what ailed you was sobriety and money-having.

Mercury was once used to treat syphilis. Later, it was used to treat seafood. The results were similar.

The **mustard plaster's** eye-watering fumes and first-degree burns distracted the patient from his imminent death from tuberculosis.

Gingko biloba was a botanical extract that aided people's ability to remember to go back to the store and buy more gingko biloba.

When it came to relieving upset stomachs, we depended on foul-tasting, viscous pink goop.

Flintstones Ritalin makes a lot more sense, especially if you're familiar with Bam-Bam.

Flintstones vitamins are two words you'd think would have had very little to do with each other.

The number of **headache cures** was rivaled only by the number of headache causes. They came in hard-to-open bottles, or convenient hard-to-open packets.

Steroids were powerful muscle builders banned from school athletics, unless the kid had a real shot at the bigs.

For "general redness," a.k.a. **crotch rot and anal rash.**

A case of **athlete's foot** was usually found on the lower end of a non-athlete's body.

Antidepressants are why the early 21st century is remembered as "The Age of Unlimited Joy."

We were **allergic** to many things, but the lure of impressive-sounding words like "Zyrtec" wasn't one of them.

Our males would stick their penises in a tree stump if it had a hole in it. **Lubricant** made it possible.

Seven **Vicodin** left. Today's Tuesday, so we can get a refill Friday... maybe just have a half of one on Thursday ... ah, fuck it, three now and worry later.

The "+" sign on this home **pregnancy test** meant good news for 40-year-olds trying to thwart God's will, bad news for 14-year-olds hoping to finish high school.

In Canada medicine was not only cheaper, it came smothered in French fries and gravy.

MODERN

Weaponry

AS MUCH PROGRESS as science made to keep us alive, it was constantly overshadowed by our new scientific ways of **killing each other**. When we first unlocked the power of the atom, we could have used it for anything: free electrical power to help the poor; space travel; medical breakthroughs. Instead, our first move was to build a bomb that could etch permanent shadows in the sidewalk. The goal was to create a weapon where one man could simultaneously kill every other person, making him "the winner." So it was for millennia. Every time we made a discovery, our first order of business was deciding how it could best be used to extinguish the lives of those who hadn't thought of it yet. We never figured out solar-powered cars, but if you're in the market for some space-laser–guided nuclear rocket bombs … we knew a guy.

Dropped
• Boiling Oil
• Bombs
• Chemical Weapons
• **Safe**

*As a weapon, **the falling safe** was particularly effective when combined with **animated birdseed**.*

Waved
• Club
• Nun-Chucks
• Mace
• **Sword**

The sword was a weapon of grace, nobility and honor … which was little comfort as you slowly bled to death in a dung-filled moat.

Shot
• Bow and arrow
• Cannon
• Machine Gun
• Missile
• SlingShot
• Webbing (Spiderman only)
• **Revolver**

Automatic weapons allowed their owners to shoot more than one person without pausing to reload or question the fundamental morality of their actions.

Hurled
• Spear
• Rock
• Throwing Star
• Epithet
• **Grenade**

Grenades were a powerful tool when fighting an enemy within lobbing distance.

	Feathers	Rope	Telephone	Cookie Dough
Raw Material		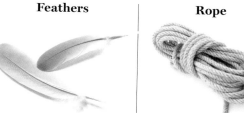		
Peaceful Application	*Pillow*	*Tug-o-War*	*Gossip*	*Gingerbread House*
Non-Peaceful Application	*Arrows*	*Noose*	*Defcon 1*	*Gingerbread Deathcamp*

DUSTBIN OF HISTORY
FAILED WEAPONS

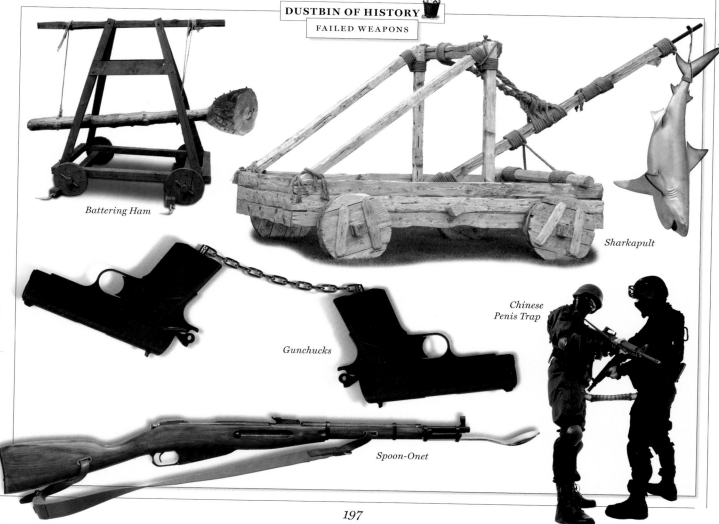

Battering Ham

Sharkapult

Gunchucks

Chinese Penis Trap

Spoon-Onet

Beautiful, isn't it? This glorious tableau was produced by our mastery of the atom. Scattered around the globe you'll find tens of thousands of devices that can replicate this image, most of them pointed at Israel. They're lots of fun, but don't stand too close. Unless your kind feeds on radiation. In which case, bon appétit.

EARTH SEARCH

Scavenger Hunt: Science Edition

How many of the following can you find on our planet?

Easy (10 points)
- ❑ Gravity
- ❑ A device that killed people
- ❑ Apple Cinnamon Newtons
- ❑ A plane with an even number of wings
- ❑ Workplace minesweeping capabilities
- ❑ A cell phone with blurry photos on it

Medium (20 points)
- ❑ The bends
- ❑ A device that helped people
- ❑ Newton's apple
- ❑ A bus with an even number of decks
- ❑ In-home Koopa-destroying technology
- ❑ A microwave with ramen remnants in it

Hard (30 points)
- ❑ Sexual chemistry
- ❑ A device that dispensed schoolgirl panties
- ❑ Apple's Newton
- ❑ A car shaped like a hot dog
- ❑ Tavern-based dot-eating ghost-fighting device
- ❑ A DVD player with *What Lies Beneath* in it

Super Hard (1,000 points)
- ❑ Flubber
- ❑ Unobtainium
- ❑ Adamantium
- ❑ Phlogiston
- ❑ Ice-nine
- ❑ Illudium PU-36 Explosive Space Modulator

FAQs
(Future Alien Questions)

Q. Were scientists the most esteemed members of your civilization?
A. Absolutely. The only people more renowned than scientists were actors, musicians, athletes, politicians, game-show hosts, heiresses, religious leaders, cartoonists, plumbers, serial killers, celebrity chefs and women who looked good in swimsuits.

Q. What was the highest reward for a scientist's lifetime of dedication to human knowledge?
A. To be feted by Scandinavians as they received their **Nobel Prize**. This was an annual award given to our greatest scientists, our most inspiring peacemakers and our most ethnically diverse authors. It came with a large cash prize, a handsome medal and a moment of fame so infinitesimally brief it could only be measured by fellow scientists.

Q. What are your biggest regrets in terms of a scientific discovery or breakthrough you failed to make?
A. Jet pack. Jet pack jet pack jet pack. Jet pack was one through four. Five, maybe cure for cancer. Then, coming in at number six … jet pack.

Q. How did scientists handle the weighty moral responsibilities implicit in their work?
A. By subcontracting it to a special group of people known as **ethicists**. Ethicists spent their time agonizing over, writing papers about and attending conferences dedicated to the moral implications of fields like cloning and stem-cell research and psychopharmacology. This allowed their colleagues to continue their research work unencumbered by concerns like evil, unfairness and widespread loss of human life.

Q. Did you ever discover the wormholes in space that make interstellar travel quick and easy?
A. Wait, what?!?

Q. Never mind. It seems like there were far more male scientists than female.
A. Until very late in our history women were discouraged from scientific pursuits because the blood in the brains of the men working with them would be diverted to their constant throbbing erections. What little male brainpower was left would be used in the employment of microscopes, test tubes and other lab equipment to hide these erections.

Q. Man. You people were horny.
A. Yeah, it's … it's shameful.

Q. Your technology suggests a deep understanding of mathematics, yet many of your larger buildings appear to be missing a 13th floor.
A. That is because, while every other number is an abstract mathematical quantity, 13 was a hideous demon-integer. Indeed, we avoided it not only in the numbering of floors, but in any calculations involved in the construction of a building. Ironically, the resulting engineering errors killed exactly 13 million people. Coincidence? Yes.

Q. If you knew some of your technological advances were coming at the expense of your environment, why did you implement them?
A. It was a simple cost-benefit analysis. We enjoyed drinking hot coffee in a cold room in the middle of the summer more than we enjoyed other animals being alive.

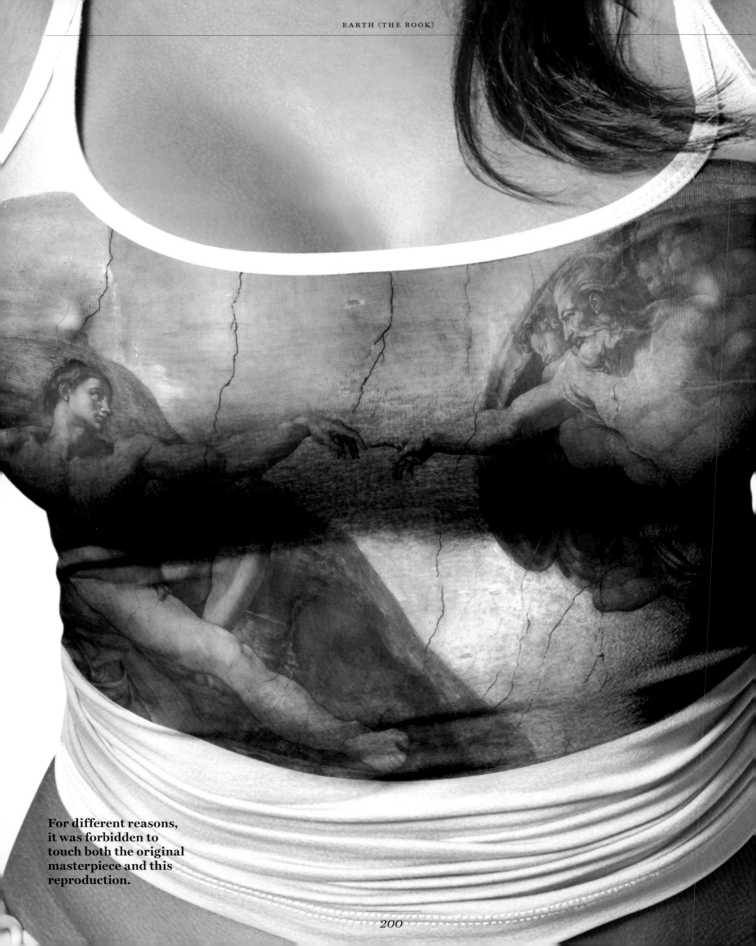

For different reasons, it was forbidden to touch both the original masterpiece and this reproduction.

CULTURE

AND THUS IN a dank stone cavern underneath what would become modern-day France was born **culture**, followed almost immediately by its twin, **studio notes**.

Human culture arose as we conquered the basics of survival, because once we no longer had to struggle, we almost immediately grew bored. So we spent a huge amount of time creating entertaining distractions to be enjoyed in our newfound downtime.

Early culture revolved around storytelling, typically focused on real-life adventures. But we quickly expanded our cultural arsenal. We created **music** and

That's art? My cave kid could have painted that.

dance, and **celebrities**, and then combined all three into one powerhouse network show. We devised **games**, and ways to lose money on them. We crafted figurines of things we admired, such as mythical animals and untenably large-breasted women. We juggled and joked, performed feats of strength and wrote. We castrated young boy singers and fed Christians to lions. (The last two were just fads. We weren't total psychos.)

Across time and in every land, our societies drew on and were influenced by their predecessors, to create their own distinct styles of art, dress and intoxicants: in short, their own culture. Fortunately, in modern times globalization allowed this great cultural variety to be efficiently winnowed down to everyone on the planet watching the same police procedural dramas while eating franchised delivery pizza.

Yet ultimately culture's most personal effect was that it made us actually feel things: great joy from comedy, deep sadness from drama or reality dating shows. Or more complex emotions, like when we'd hear that song "Summer Breeze," which we hated, but through unfortunate happenstance was playing when we lost our virginity.

The point is, culture not only helped our days go faster; it tapped into our **emotional cores**. Yes, the artifacts you find in our civilization's wreckage will show you how we lived. But if you want to know how we *felt* about how we lived—how we interpreted our existence—you must look to our culture. This was our record of what made us distinctly human. For ours was a complicated existence, filled with great achievements, enormous compassion, inexplicable violence and myriad contradicting actions. But for all our differences, none of us—white, black, Jew, Muslim, gay or straight—could get all the way through *Brian's Song* without crying like babies.

Entertainment

ONE OF THE BEST WAYS to relax after our daily struggles to obtain food, clothing, shelter and a mate was to watch simulations of others engaging in those same struggles. **Entertainment** sometimes drew us together (by giving us a pretext to socialize with each other), but in a larger sense it served to keep us apart (by immersing us so thoroughly in fantasy that it seemed more fun to just stay in). Without entertainment, life would have been merely a series of self-generated epiphanies leading to greater personal understanding. No wonder we preferred juggling.

WE SAID IT

"There's no business like show business! Except maybe the narcotics industry."
—*Irving Berlin (1888–1989), Medellin drug cartel leader*

THIS WEEK AT THE
ROYAL PALLADIUM THEATER
NOW WITH FIRE EXITS! **7** SHOWS DAILY
COMMENCING AT 2 O'CLOCK P.M.

YOU'VE HEARD THE RUMORS—NOW SEE FOR YOURSELF!

PATRICK JOHN O'CONNELL | THE IRISH MATHEMATICIAN

A GENUINE PAPIST SAVAGE, more Celtic dog than man will Nevertheless count to 20 and perform feats of simple addition + subtraction!

DOGS of VARYING SHAPES and COLORS

DR. HULNE'S EFFECTUAL PRESCRIPTIONS

HARVEY TUCKER And his so-called "KNOCK KNOCK" jokes a new comic form, guaranteed to delight

A VERY TALL MAN | **SAM JONES, MURDERER**

The act that startled PARIS! The act that transfixed MOSCOW!
THE COMEDIC DELIGHTS OF JUVENILE PRODIGY

P L U S **LARRY KING**

"THE SUSPENDERED WONDER-BOY OF BROOKLYN"

Miss **LUCY JOHNSON** & her **TEATS OF CANE SUGAR**
FROM BUFFALO!!! {Limit one suckling per customer per show}

The **AMAZING CHATTERTON, LION-TAMER**
Formerly the Amazing Chatterton & Chatterton and The Amazing Chatterton Trio

The Entertaining and Delightful MUSICAL COMEDY of
JEREMIAH BUNTON Who will perform songs in a NEGRO DIALECT, in the ATTIRE OF A NEGRO, while – AT THE SAME TIME – not actually BEING A NEGRO!

TICKET OF ADMISSION: **FOUR CENTS** **NO CATHOLICS** | Every audience member guaranteed a seat and a glass of Water. Concessionaires provide CORN in one of several ways.

ALL AT THE ROYAL PALLADIUM THEATER, 14 PLUM STREET
WE REGRET THAT LATE-COMERS CANNOT BE ADMITTED DUE TO THE UNPREDICTABLE TEMPERAMENT OF THE GROUNDHOGS

Before the development of modern technologies, entertainment consisted of multiple short live "acts" performed by **vaudeville** *entertainers who had no idea their livelihoods would be destroyed by the development of modern technologies.*

THE TRAGEDIE OF
Romeo & Juliet

Juliet What's in a name? That which we call a rose By any other name would smell as sweet.

Romeo What if 'twere called assflower?

Juliet Yea, though it be called assflower, Yet it would still smell as sweet.

Romeo What if 'twere called cocke o' the dog?

Juliet Yea, though it be called cocke o' the dog It needst not smell like one.

Romeo What if 'twere called the Bishop's Filthy Rectum?

Juliet Dost thou have many more of these to go through?

—William Shakespeare, Romeo and Juliet, II, ii, 1–10

Even the greatest writer could always benefit from having a good editor.

Evolution of Storytelling

Man has always told **stories**. Be they tales of tribal heroics, dangerous battles or a sisterhood and their quest to track down a pair of itinerant pantaloons, **storytelling** was a way to maintain tradition, group unity and concession-stand profit margins.

Aboriginal Oral Tradition
Boy meets girl. Boy gets girl. Boy loses girl in feral dingo attack. Boy hungry.

Medieval Jongleurs
Boy meets girl. Boy loses girl due to family feud. Boy fakes suicide to elope with girl. Girl finds boy, kills self. Boy wakes, finds dead girl, kills self. Audience contracts Black Death.

(Comedy)

(Tragedy)

(Documentary)

Comedy and Tragedy

The two most basic modes of storytelling were **comedy** and **tragedy**. Tragedy allowed an audience to feel a character's pain. Comedy allowed an audience to heartily enjoy a character's pain. Both modes originated in ancient Greece in plays featuring **protagonists** and **antagonists**, along with a large **chorus** so the less talented kids could participate.

Man believed that comedy was tragedy plus time. The real question was, how much time?

This play opened and closed within a three-minute span on September 7, 1946. It was, by all accounts, too soon.

Greece's Funniest Amphorae

While comedy was notoriously difficult to translate across cultures, there was one universally recognized humorous meme: The unanticipated **testicular trauma**. In his masterpiece *The Poetics*, the Greek philosopher Aristotle broke the phenomenon down into four stages.

1. Hubris ("Arrogance")
"Protagonist must initially be depicted in a state of excessive pride, wrongly believing himself invulnerable to getting hit in the nuts."

2. Hamartia ("Miscalculation")
"This hubris leads to an error in judgment that makes him either physically or morally culpable in his own nut-hit."

3. Opsis ("Spectacle")
"The moment of nut-hitting should occur so as to convey in tableau the transcendent pain and the universe's indifference."

4. Catharsis ("Purgation")
"Vocalizing his pain, protagaonist purges on behalf of the spectator the fear and terror of this, and all, nut-hits."

Grand Opera
Boy meets girl. Boy sings at girl for 30 minutes. Boy and girl sing together, 45 minutes. Boy dies, singing for 20 minutes. Girl sings over boy, 70 minutes. Audience wakes up, gives 7-minute ovation.

Russian Novel
Boy meets girl. Boy confesses to murder of two other girls to girl. Boy and girl ponder meaning of remorse and redemption. Girl follows exiled boy to Siberia. Boy and girl share uncertain future. Reader wonders why this couldn't have been accomplished in 700 fewer pages.

Hollywood Blockbuster
Boy meets girl. Boy gets girl. Asteroid heads for earth. Girl's father and boy put aside differences to team up and detonate a nuclear bomb in asteroid. Earth saved. Only boy returns. Boy and girl hug to bad Aerosmith song written by girl's actual father. Movie earns $600 million.

Reality Television
Boy meets 24 girls. Boy eliminates 12. Boy kisses 12. Eliminates 6 more. Feels up 6. Eliminates 3. Fucks the last 3. Meets their families. Dumps 2. Proposes to 1. Leaves her, marries Survivor *Season 3 cast member he meets at Skyy Vodka-sponsored cerebral palsy benefit.*

Books

BOOKS ARE THE permanent repository of all mankind's knowledge and wisdom, a painstakingly detailed record of our entire existence. Please feel free to thumb through them, although chances are you're going to want to wait for the movie.

By reading their children to sleep at night, parents reinforced the idea that books were boring.

*Graphic novels called **manga** were created by combining a doe-eyed Japanese schoolgirl's body with the most perverse shit middle-aged Japanese men could dream up.*

Ongoing serials *were perfect for shy readers who were uncomfortable meeting new protagonists. They were considered a gateway drug for actual literature.*

Classics *were works of such depth and importance you had to read them. Literally. To graduate, you had to read them.*

Embalming Pharaohs for Dummies *was the first in the very popular "For Dummies" series. They were followed by the less successful "Hey, Fucktard!" guides.*

The first book printed with moveable type, the **Gutenberg Bible** *made possible the entire publishing industry's ultimate collapse.*

The Holy Bible *was the most popular book ever written. We kept it in hotel rooms so you could look at it right after cheating on your spouse.*

Words that were **highlighted** *were usually far more interesting than these.*

WE SAID IT

Oh, I see you noticed Thomas Pynchon's **Gravity's Rainbow** *on our shelf. Yeah, we totally read it all the way through. The ending with the guy and that rainbow? That was deep.*

Harry Potter *was a boy wizard whose adventures were so popular they caused massive deforestation leading to a 1-degree rise in global temperature.*

PENGUIN CLASSICS
EMILY BRONTË
WUTHERING HEIGHTS

"Don't judge a book by its cover."

Science fiction *was a popular genre that mostly dealt with how awesome it would be for us to finally meet you. You probably had a similar genre about how awesome it would be when you finally met us, right? ... Right?*

This masterpiece was our canonical repository for all **brine-cured cucumber humor.**

Throughout history, books inspired religious and political hatred. Some were **burned** *so frequently their publishers marketed special "extra flammable" editions.*

This **novel** *misled disaffected teenagers into believing they weren't alone in the world.*

Romance novels *were the only books that took less time to write than they did to read. They taught lonely women about passionate love, maritime history and 18th-century undergarments. SPOILER ALERT: They totally wind up doing it.*

Self-help books *were books whose authors "helped themselves" to sad people's money.*

IN THE RUINS
LIBRARIES

In most human settlements you will find a building full of books oddly devoid of price tags. These were **libraries**, temples to learning created by highly evolved societies for citizens' self-education, places where a gentleman such as the one below could shut out all of life's modern distractions and be at peace with his precious reading. Ironically, when he finally found the time to pursue his passion due to an unforeseen nuclear holocaust, his glasses broke.

Not surprisingly, this injustice turned the once mild-mannered wallflower into a ruthless criminal.

Music

IF YOU CAME across the Golden Record on your journey here (see page vii), then you've already discovered **music**, perhaps our most joyous form of expression. Music blended voices and instruments in glorious melodies, harmonies and rhythms that could evoke any emotion. We played music at funerals, weddings and parties. We had concerts where we all got together just to listen to music. We developed incredibly sophisticated devices so that no matter where we went we could have music. In our cars or at the gym or if we were somewhere where someone else was listening to music we didn't really like, we could still listen to our music. Music was really cool. Until it got too popular. Then it was some sellout bullshit. Anyway, we made you a mix tape.

IN THE RUINS
BOOM BOX

You'll need one of these to play our tape.

A classic inspirational **hymn.** *This was often played at Scottish funerals, where bagpipers strangled the life out of it just to make sure no one was having any fun.* ②

We had a tacit agreement that because of its cultural importance, no one would publicly say how much we hated **jazz.** ③

We were pussies. Might as well admit it, now. ①

A popular **youth anthem** *with a timeless message.* ⑤

Pop music *had "hooks" that got stuck in your head, in much the same way an actual hook might get stuck in your head.* ⑥

If you play this song, please **send $1** *to the estates of Patty and Mildred Hill.* ④

Cries for justice and rebellion in Third World countries became the anthem for hackey-sack tournaments worldwide. ⑦

maxell UR

Ⓐ DATE N.R. ○ YES ○ NO

① I'M ALL OUT OF LOVE — AIR SUPPLY
② AMAZING GRACE
③ GIANT STEPS — JOHN COLTRANE
④ HAPPY BIRTHDAY
⑤ THE ALPHABET SONG
⑥ THE RIGHT STUFF — NEW KIDS ON THE BLOCK
⑦ TRENCHTOWN ROCK — BOB MARLEY & THE WAILERS

Now that's what we called music VOL. 2

Instruments

Our musical instruments generally fit into one of four categories: **blown, pounded, plucked** and **scratched**.

BLOWN

A **wind instrument** was operated solely by the mouth and fingers, leaving the rest of the body free to march in formation in a halftime tribute to "The Best of Motown."

Dizzy Gillespie, seen here storing music in his cheeks for the cold winter ahead.

SCRATCHED

If you take two gold R&B records and play them simultaneously on a **turntable**, it will alchemically forge them into one hit *platinum* hip-hop record.

POUNDED

When played as part of an ensemble, **percussion instruments** gave music rhythm. When played by themselves, they gave the other band members a ten-minute break to shoot heroin backstage.

Caribbean **steel drum** *music was a joyful way of telling people, "We have mostly forgiven you for colonialism. Enjoy your stay."*

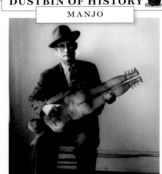

The **banjo** *was a cross between a guitar and poverty.*

PLUCKED

String instruments produced sounds by means of vibrations. The most popular types were the **violin**, which took years to master and didn't get you laid, and the **guitar**, which didn't and did.

DUSTBIN OF HISTORY
MANJO

Manjo concerts were known for their lively arpeggios and putrid stench of death.

Dance

It would be impossible to describe how music made us move. So we suggest the following: Put on a song and then ... throw out your hands! Stick out your tush! Hands on your hips! Give them a push! You'll be surprised you're doing the French mistake! Voila!

The New York Times

MAN 'WALKS ON MOON'
STAR'S LEGACY SECURED

"Houston, That Shit Was Tight!"

No one ever forgot where they were the night man first moonwalked.

Native American **rain dances** *often got results. Tragically, their smallpox vaccine dance proved less effective.*

At its best, **pole dancing** *expressed the depth of the relationship between the dancer and her pole.*

Film

MOVING PICTURES WERE an incredibly sophisticated technology that allowed man to re-create and project all the sights and sounds of real life, only with better-looking people. **Film** (or "movies," to those not attending a campus Godard retrospective) combined theater's emotional immediacy with photography's spectacular realism and sound's remarkable hear-itude, in a complete sensory experience. In later years, film added nudity and explosions … for the kids.

Imagine 400 strangers sitting in a dark, dank room, feet stuck to a disgusting adhesive floor, staring up at a flickering screen in a near-diabetic coma, desperately holding in their urine for hours at a stretch. We called it "the movies" and we fucking loved it. So will you. Just be considerate: If any part of you buzzes or beeps, turn it off first.

STAR WARS

Science fiction was two hours of thrilling outer-space spectacle that took moviegoers' minds off their own crushing virginity.

What are you doing? Why—don't go in that room! Why would you split up when you know there's … whoa. That axe is gonna leave a mark.

RINGU

A small popcorn and drink were expensive, but remember, after the movie you could take them home and use them as cat coffins.

Blowing shit up *was a hugely popular genre that inspired such subgenres as* **shooting shit up** *and* **punching shit**.

Romantic comedies *proved that even someone as hideous as Richard Gere could get a cheap whore like Julia Roberts to fall in love with him.*

Sure, with perfect makeup and lighting, this starlet seems unbelievably beautiful. But see her on the street and you'd realize. . . . . she's merely drop-dead gorgeous.

IN THE RUINS
HOLLYWOOD

In 1927, this film kicked off America's enduring love affair with the talking picture. Unlike our love affair with **blackface**, *which lasted until the Civil Rights Act of 1964.*

This sign was the only thing other than scripts that people in Hollywood read.

Chevy Chase was a legendary comedian/asshole. In Hollywood this was known as a "double threat."

Ah, Hollywood. Behind its shiny façade lay a superficial veneer masking a shallow layer of eggshell-thin unreality. Few people dug much further. The famous people who lived and worked here were called **stars**, because they were volatile explosive gasballs surrounded by an entourage of dependent entities basking in their reflected glow. We called Hollywood the Dream Factory. Unfortunately most people who went to work there ended up working at the Cheesecake Factory. Of course that's nothing for you to worry about, because baby, you've got *it*.

To learn that one's hand was the same size as Jack Nicholson's was to know the true meaning of happiness.

Westerns *were popular for decades until August 2, 1969, when moviemakers officially ran out of stories about men and horses.*

Animated movies *presented children with a dazzling array of colorful characters they could force their parents to buy for them.*

Musicals *allowed us to channel our homosexuality into a socially acceptable outlet.*

Sequels

Sequels allowed popular film characters to evolve over time, exploring more sophisticated relationships and dynamics and completing long-arc narratives too complex to fit the strictures of a single feature-length film.

Police Academy *penetratingly addresses Michel Foucault's theories of authority and power dynamics.*

Police Academy 2: Their First Assignment *explores the inner conflicts of our hero's id.*

PA 3: Back in Training *broadens its worldview to explore the cycles of time and aging.*

PA 4: Citizens on Patrol *probes the artificial nature of socially constructed roles.*

PA 5: Assignment Miami Beach *put the Milgram experiment on film and set it in Miami.*

By PA 6: City Under Siege, *even our joke about how good these movies were seemed old.*

Some sequels were considered cynical attempts to profit from the creative success of previous ventures. Others just made sense.

Television

IF GOING TO the movies was like worshipping in a cathedral, then watching **television** was like masturbating in a confessional. No wonder then that from the outset, TV (we called it that after it rendered us too lazy to use four-syllable words) felt so sinfully good. A flip of the switch, and we were sucked into a smaller-than-life world controlled by unseen forces. The existential crises filling our brains were instantly soothed, and the burden of free will lightened and crystallized into the simple dilemma of whether or not to change channels. As for the programming, there was a hard and fast rule: The total amount of quality television at any one time was a constant. Thus, as what were once a mere three channels evolved into 400 ... well, you do the math.

BY THE NUMBERS	
TELEVISION	
Hours watched, per year per person	1,500
Hours spent complaining about nothing good being on	1,432
Fictional murders watched in a lifetime, per person	33,500
Actual murders watched in a lifetime, per person	0.0001
Marriages ruined by addictive nature of TV	30 million
Marriages saved by numbing power of TV	1.2 billion

Water coolers prevented people from dying of dehydration while deciphering the confusing end of Lost.

For many years, the world's most read publication was a periodical consisting of long lists of television shows.

TV dinners *were specially designed for diners too engrossed in watching television to care what they were putting in their mouth.*

Television would be changed forever by the 1972 invention of **color electrons.**

This is a typical family watching television.

What's On?

What did we like to watch on television? The short answer: Anything.
But there were certain kinds of shows we were particularly drawn to.

Sitcom
Allowed us to spend half an hour in the company of four stock characters: Smarty, Dummy, Crazy and Grouchy.

Western
Fulfilled our lust for casual murder without offending our puritanical moral sensibilities.

Late-night talk show
Because there was no more relaxing way to drift off to sleep than hearing Kate Hudson relate an anecdote about Matthew McConaughey's mischievous on-set antics.

Medical drama
TV doctors focused entirely on the "life and death" and "yelling" aspects of their work, and rarely on the "cleaning bedpans" and "analyzing urine" parts.

Legal drama
Immersed viewers in a world where good (usually) triumphed over evil. Frequently aired in "marathons," which were in every way the opposite of real marathons.

Cable news
Thanks to technology, it was possible to keep people well-informed about important world events 24 hours a day with accurate, impartial, in-depth journalism. We didn't do it. But it was *possible*.

Remote control, 2010, US
This device could control the TV, the cable box, the VCR and the DVD. Actually, the DVD was on a separate remote. Which is ... HONEY? WHERE'S THE DVD REMOTE? I LOOKED THERE. NO, THAT'S THE CABLE REMOTE, I HAVE THAT. THE *DVD* REMOTE. *GOD FUCKING DAMN IT*, IT'S A *SIMPLE* ... Whatever. Anyway, this is the remote.

Remote control, 2010, North Korea

Viewing Positions

The **recliner** gave TV watchers a choice of customized viewing postures.

Edge of seat:
• Superbowl overtime
• Series finale of *M*A*S*H*
• Accidentally unscrambled porn
• Assassination (live)

Mild interest:
• Funeral of beloved rock star and/or princess
• Low-speed police chase
• Game show you think you're good at
• Assassination (11 P.M. replay)

Dude, go to bed:
• Regional curling tournament (non-Olympic)
• *Turtles: Our Firm-Shelled Friends of the Pond*
• Pledge drive
• Assassination (History Channel)

As time wore on, the idea of spending a single minute not looking at a TV became intolerable.

Artists

AT THE CENTER of our cultural endeavors was a small subset of people called **artists**. Seemingly endowed with heightened sensitivity to the world around them, artists felt and expressed the terrible beauty of our fleeting existence. The rest of us had jobs.

The Artistic Process

The artistic process involved many indispensable yet clearly less talented people.

YOU HAD TO BE HERE

This can of soup, filled with life-sustaining broth, cost about $1.29.

This painting of a can of soup cost $40 million (soup sold separately).

---

① The Muse
The artist's inspiration—the spark that could compel one to create breathtaking works of incomparable genius. As you can imagine, she was never around when you fucking needed her.

Some artists had "real-life" muses, such as Dante's beloved "Beatrice" and LeRoy Neiman's adored "National Football League."

② Family
The artist's family could play a vital role in providing the emotional and moral support crucial to the artist's success. Mostly, however, they provided the dysfunctional upbringing crucial to the artist's need for approval.

Vincent Van Gogh's brother Theo was his gateway to the outside world. Eugene O'Neill's family was his gateway to alcoholism and morphine addiction.

③ Patrons
Throughout history, there have been individuals and corporations with more money than they knew what to do with. Rather than burning it, they sometimes decided to give money to artists, becoming the artists' patrons. It was sort of like getting a dog that could paint.

This painting was made possible by Lorenzo de Medici and the financial support of viewers like you.

④ The Little People
An artist crafting a masterwork had no time for mundane tasks like buying supplies or dealing with their no-longer-cute adopted son Li-chao. Thus they hired **assistants**, most often young aspiring artists eager to learn at the feet of a master.

Brian the NYU junior just learned there is a difference between a macchiato and a cappuccino.

Great works of art were not created in a vacuum—except of course Marcel Duchamp's 1929 masterpiece, "Hoover Hoover."

WE SAID IT

"In the future, everyone will be world-famous for 15 minutes. And then, of course, dead for much longer."
—*Andy Warhol (1928–1987), American artist*

Artist Types

Every artist was unique ... in the way he fit into one of these five archetypes.

Tortured
Brilliance tragically marred by self-destruction; whatever you do, don't sell their shit until they're dead.
• **Vincent VanGogh**
 • Kurt Cobain
  • Sylvia Plath

Commercial
Popular success, fabulous wealth; we liked their early work.
• **Thomas Kinkade**
 • Steven Spielberg
 • Paul McCartney

Reclusive
Transcendent ability to describe reality; utter inability to handle reality.
• **J. D. Salinger**
 • Thomas Pynchon
 • Emily Dickinson

Avant-Garde
Did things no other artist had done before, usually for a good reason.
• **Sun Ra**
 • Jackson Pollock
 • Yoko Ono

Prodigy
Innate genius; astonishing talent; extremely annoying parents.
• **Judy Garland**
 • Stevie Wonder
 • Mozart

⑦ Audience
A receptive crowd's enthusiastic praise could sustain an artist for minutes.

8:02 P.M.
"Thank you so much. I'm so glad you like it."

8:09 P.M.
"I've failed everyone who ever loved me."

⑤ Curators/Gallery Owners
These were middlemen who negotiated business deals and provided display space on behalf of the artist, who was then left free to focus exclusively on whether those people were fucking him over.

Famed curator Juliana Davidova DeVille-Martin von Davidovidosch inherited a 3000-square foot loft from her father, the music lawyer Al Steinberg.

⑥ Critics
With highly refined sensibilities and unparalleled depth of knowledge and insight, critics were uniquely qualified to provide astute, relevant assessments of an artist's work. Nobody liked them.

BY TOM SHALES
Really? That's the best description of a critic you can muster? Once again, the wizards at the overpraised House of Stewart don't fail to disappoint. Now if you'll excuse me, I have to go polish my **taint**.

THE ROSE & MICHAEL SPIELVOGEL

Diego Velazquez
Portrait of Juan de Pareja
Spain, 1650

Regal Photography
Portrait of High School Senior
Dix Hills, 2010

Buddhist thanka
Tibet, 19th c.

Portraiture was once reserved only for those wealthy enough to afford a good painter, and with leisure enough to sit still for two weeks. But the growth of photography turned anyone with a camera into a portrait artist, and anyone with a skin casing into a model.

Religious art helped put the inexplicable fiction underlying **faith's** cosmology into equally opaque visual terms.

Artist unknown
Pankratiasts (Wrestlers)
Greece, 5th c. BCE

The exquisite lines, the dynamic positioning, the ... What. What. You know you're thinking it. Just say it.

Jaguar Motor Co.
Hood Ornament
England, 20th c.

A skilled **sculptor** could summon his talents to create powerful, iconic talismans that made people really want to lease or own.

"Welcome to the Rose and Michael Spielvogel Two-Page Spread of Fine Art. Let's begin our tour."

TWO-PAGE SPREAD OF FINE ART

C.M. Coolidge
Dogs Playing Poker
USA, 20th c.

Paintings of **dogs playing poker** divided us into two camps: those who found such images to be cute, and those who would, but for force of law, have gladly murdered those other people.

By the way: No one who liked the painting above also liked the one on the right, and vice versa.

Fake Rothko
Pretty Colors III
USA, 20th c.

Not all art had to be "about" something, you know. What was wrong with just making something **pleasurable** to look at? You alien guys need to learn how to chill.

THE
LARS & HANNAH
JANSON

SECURITY CAMERA

Artist unknown
Ritual mask
West Africa, 20th c.

In the right hands, **African masks** were believed to possess the power to conjure diversity in Western-based cultural surveys.

Landscape, Holland
18th c.

We put great energy into building houses to protect us from the elements, but once inside them we hung **landscapes** depicting what it was we were trying to escape. To be fair, if we'd tried to hang our pictures of the outdoors *outdoors*, they'd have soon been ruined.

We appreciated art on many levels: for the skill of its execution (techne), for its power to represent the world (mimesis), for its intellectual reconciliation of man and universe through an act of creation (psoriasis). Not to mention the pretty colors, and how it went with our drapes. Ultimately, art strived to capture and convey beauty. Some even considered art a direct window into the unseen world, a communion with essential truth … or something. None of us really knew. What was beyond question was that a lot of humans at least liked the notion that such a communion might be possible, even if only so we could pretend we weren't just slightly-less-than-random bunches of atoms. So same as religion, really. Anyway, before you judge, understand that being overly skeptical about art was just as easy as being gullible about it.

Culture: High and Low

With so much culture we needed a way to sort it all out. One way was placing each bit of cultural output on a spectrum of **social status** to ascertain its significance. **High culture** aspired to fulfill humanity's greatest intellectual, aesthetic or spiritual potential. **Middle culture** had less lofty aspirations but was more accessible to those with less education. **Low culture** focused on sex, excrement and instant gratification, and was what we mostly spent our time on.

	Female Portraiture	"Hero's Journey" Myth	Drug Inhalation Method
High			
Medium			
LOW			

Cultural Outliers

In sifting through our civilization's disorganized remnants, you may stumble upon cultural artifacts that are completely **misrepresentative** of the way most of us lived. Please don't draw any inaccurate conclusions.

Outlier: Bob's Big Boy
Distinction from normal sculpture: Used not to express mastery of form and materials, but to sell meat sandwiches
Wrong lesson: Our food was served to us by giant children in overalls.

Outlier: Brazilian swimwear
Distinction from normal swimwear: Exposed buttocks to air, sand, aquatic predators
Wrong lesson: We walked around with our asses hanging out and we were in great shape.

Outlier: Japanese game shows
Distinction from normal television: Frenetic pace, enthusiasm for masochism
Wrong lesson: The only way to obtain appliances was to survive an electric-eel bath

Outlier: Ziggyisms
Distinction from normal literature: Lack of plot, facts or reason for existing
Wrong lesson: We sought advice from bald, depressive pantsless men.

Outlier: Peruvian flute street music
Distinction from normal music: It was Peruvian flute music performed in the street.
Wrong lesson: That we enjoyed Peruvian flute music.

Outlier: Erotic cake
Distinction from normal cake: Penis shape
Wrong lesson: That anybody thought this was erotic.

Egg-Based Delicacy	Male Headgear	Sexual Appeal of Pubescent Girls	Seating Design	Clowns	Last Words
					*"Rosebud."*
					*"Who you think you fucking with? I'm Tony Montana!"*
					*"Hey everybody, we're all gonna get laid!"*

IN THE RUINS
AWARDS

The Quitty
Best publicized stint in rehab

The Golden Volcano
Most humanlike performance by a Scientologist

The Thanky
Best acceptance speech at an awards show

The Tucky
Fewest facial expressions lost to cosmetic surgery

The Orscar
Best illegal overseas bootleg

Locked in display cases in certain homes in Southern California and New York you will find shiny miniature Victrolas, atom-hoisting angels with stilettos for wings and 13.5-inch gold-plated eunuchs. These are **awards**, totems bestowed by entertainers upon one another every year. Awards sustained a self-perpetuating cultural ecosystem wherein you could win an Emmy for your work directing the television broadcast of the Oscars, a film awards show. For those of us not blessed with fame, awards shows were a chance to see our deities vying both for supremacy and the chance to deliver a two-minute address that we could then pore over for signs of humanity. If you find one, clutch it in your hands, look into a mirror and don't forget to thank your spouse, schmuck.

Sports

EXERTING ONESELF FOR no apparent
reason was called **exercise**. Exerting oneself
with the goal of victory was called **sports**.
Sports were an exciting and intense way for members of
a society to put on uniforms and go at each other in a nearly deathless way. It is not
possible to overestimate the importance this war substitute had in our society.
While few of us ever got to play them professionally, tens of thousands of us
would gather in cavernous stadia to witness our favorite teams score (or
in the case of soccer, not score). Millions more would watch on television,
confident in the one simple truth of sport: Those players and spectators
who did not share the enthusiasm you had for your team sucked.

	Soccer	Baseball	Golf
What It Was	A fast-paced game in which eleven players on two teams tried to score by kicking a small ball hand-stitched by desperately poor Pakistani children into a goal.	A sport where two nine-man teams tried to hit a small ball with a wooden bat, then run a circuit of four bases. Games lasted nine innings or forever, depending on the score.	An activity that used thousands of acres of precious land to hit a small ball into a slightly larger hole. The average game took four hours, the exact amount of time needed to secure the McMillan account.
Why We Liked It	In a hand-dominated world, soccer was the chance to be proud of our feet, which were often forced to languish in the obscurity of shoes.	The seventh-inning stretch. Few sports encouraged napping by players or fans, but baseball not only encouraged it, it had a built-in wake-up call.	This was the only sport where the older we got, the better we became at it.
Who Played It	Dreamy Latin studs who were "all thumbs"	Spitters	Inner-city kids
Skills Required	Ability to simulate extreme pain following mild contact	Covert ball-scratching	Focusing intensely on a perfect swing, while not letting your cigar's smoke billow into your eye
Often Heard on the Field	*"¡Voy a meter la tarjeta roja en el culo!"*	"Throw 'em the heater, Ricky!"	"Motherfucker!" "These clubs suck!" "I swear I parred it!" "Put me down for a three."
Faces of the Game			

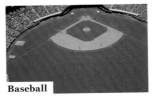

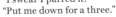

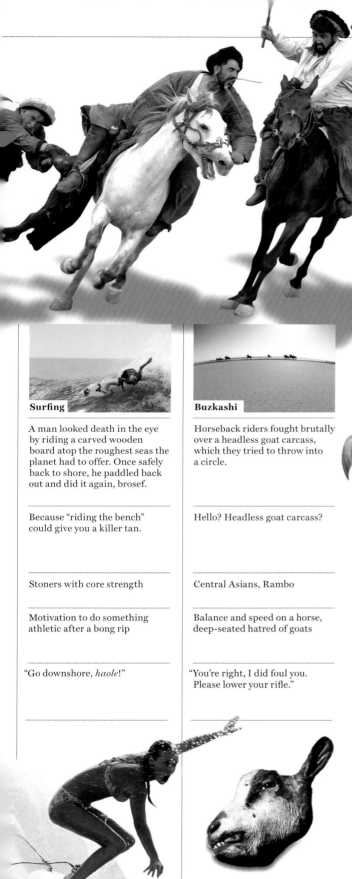

Athletes

A handful of us, through hard work and God-given height, were good enough at these wargames to do them professionally. We called these giants among men **athletes**. They were better than us at all things, until they got old, bald and fat.

Man rarely lost bullfights but when he did, he lost big.

Surfing

A man looked death in the eye by riding a carved wooden board atop the roughest seas the planet had to offer. Once safely back to shore, he paddled back out and did it again, brosef.

Because "riding the bench" could give you a killer tan.

Stoners with core strength

Motivation to do something athletic after a bong rip

"Go downshore, *haole!*"

Buzkashi

Horseback riders fought brutally over a headless goat carcass, which they tried to throw into a circle.

Hello? Headless goat carcass?

Central Asians, Rambo

Balance and speed on a horse, deep-seated hatred of goats

"You're right, I did foul you. Please lower your rifle."

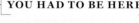

*Athletes' **jerseys**—along with their days of glory before the long, slow decline into an anti-climactic middle age marked by embittered nostalgia—were numbered.*

YOU HAD TO BE HERE

This man would have had to play professional baseball for 280 years ...

... to afford this tobacco card with his photo on it.

Fans

Passionate fans were integral to a team's success. A **fan's** failure to wear the unwashed number jersey he wore for every home game or to drink twice and touch the table before crucial game moments could have disastrous effects on his favorite team. To a remarkable extent, we tethered our identities to the fortunes of our teams. When they won, *we* won. When they lost, *we* lost. And when *we* channeled that disappointment into impotent rage against the people closest to us, *they* ... well, we're not sure what they did.

Mascot

Perfect hybrid between the athlete and the fan.

Tragically born with a baseball for a head, this man was saved from a lifetime of ridicule by the New York Metropolitans Baseball Club.

IN THE RUINS
STADIUMS

Tens of thousands of sports fans would crowd into these enormous facilities to witness sporting events, and occasionally concerts from musicians who insisted on playing songs from their newest album. Large corporations often paid millions of dollars for the right to name these stadiums. More often than not, the name turned out to be that of the corporation itself as opposed to, say, "Kevin."

"The Fan"

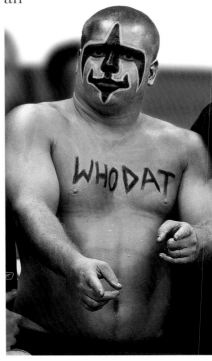

Home	Time	Away
Argues with wife to change channel	**1:00 P.M.** Kick off	Drinks second beer in line at Gate D
Cheers for team	**1:10 P.M.** Green Bay scores	Joins concession stand line for beer
"Brian! Practice your violin in another room."	**1:13 P.M.** TV timeout	"Hey, how'd they score?"
Pee break #1	**2:07 P.M.**	Back on line at concession stand
Stands up to detach sweaty testicles from thigh	**2:19 P.M.**	Stands up, does wave, realizes he's part of something much greater than himself
Watches highlights of other games, ignores wife recapping highlights of her week	**2:40 P.M.** Halftime	Arbitrarily roots for blue-uniformed peewee football team; advises red team to "suck it"
Pee break #2	**3 P.M.**	Pee break #1 (unbeknownst to pee-er)
Pee break #3	**3:20 P.M.** End of 3rd Quarter	Catches self on Jumbotron, realizes there is a God, gives finger to camera
"Brian, no, those are Daddy's game snacks."	**3:45 P.M.**	Burps up a little puke; swallows it
Caller ID displays Mom's cardiologist; ignored	**3:59 P.M.** Packers 24 Saints 24 1:03 left in game	Leaves stadium to beat traffic
Screams and throws remote through TV	**4:10 P.M.** Saints win by field goal	Screams in joy from radio broadcast while peeing behind dumpster in parking lot

The Olympics

Once every four years (or every two years), athletes from around the world gathered together for the **Olympic Games,** a global celebration of one city's bad decision. The Games were meant to transcend politics and channel man's aggressive urges from the battlefield to the playing field. The occasional Nazi rally, athlete massacre, widespread boycott and anti-abortion bombing aside, the Games were successful in at least partially tamping down sectarian hatred to reveal a more universal truth about the human race: The vast majority of us were **losers**. Losers who had ennobled themselves by devoting their time, energy and very beings to the pursuit of perfection in their chosen craft. But still, **losers**.

*The Olympic symbol's **five rings** represented the five possible outcomes of Olympic competition: Victory, defeat, disqualification, national embarrassment and the realization one had wasted one's youth acquiring mastery of a non-marketable skill.*

"Oh great, a state-of-the-art bike track where we used to have tracts of affordable housing."
—Jean Drapeau (1916–1999), Mayor of Montreal

*One of the most incredible sights in sport was the Olympic opening ceremony's alphabetical **procession of nations**, a peaceful apolitical display that was kept that way when Iraq and Ireland were invited specifically to keep Iran and Israel away from each other.*

*The **Olympic torch** stayed aflame for the duration of the competition. After the games it was used to incinerate the host city's now-useless $50,000,000 velodrome.*

*To wear a **gold**, **silver** or **bronze medal** was to bask in the full magnitude of what one had achieved.*

CONGRATULATIONS
IT'S ALL DOWNHILL FROM HERE.

YOU SUCK.

YOU MISSED YOUR CHILDHOOD FOR THIS?

DUSTBIN OF HISTORY
AUTUMN OLYMPICS

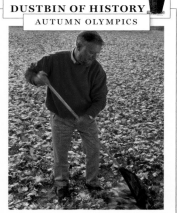

Held only once, in the Berkshires in 1959. *Seen here: Raking gold-medalist Mr. Ferguson.*

*The **quintathlon** combined shooting, skiing, shooting, shooting and shooting.*

Great Olympic Moments

*The original Olympic Games took place in Greece in 776 B.C. and featured three sports: **wrestling, grappling** and **grapple-wrestling**.*

*At the 1936 Olympics, African-American **Jesse Owens** won four gold medals, completely altering Adolf Hitler's opinions concerning Aryan superiority.*

*After winning seven gold medals, **Geraldo Rivera** went on to become one of the world's most prominent reporters.*

*In the famous 1980 **Miracle on Ice**, a team of young college students were able against all odds to get Americans to watch an entire hockey game.*

Leisure

WHEN NOT SITTING back being passively entertained, we often engaged in more active, equally useless pursuits known as **leisure activities**. Once, leisure was a luxury enjoyed only by infants and aristocrats, who used it to fulfill their very busy napping and vomiting schedules respectively. But social progress eventually brought periods of leisure to nearly everyone. The activities that filled this time generally took one of three forms: those serving **zero practical purpose** (games, sports); those **mimicking useful pursuits** at which previous generations had toiled for their livelihoods but which we connived to find "relaxing" (carpentry, fishing); and those that were out-and-out **self-destructive** (gambling, recreational drugs). But all succeeded in filling the yawning gap between the previous thing we *had* to do, and the next thing.

IN THE RUINS
GYMS

Throughout the remains of the developed world you will find facilities filled with what appear to be torture devices. These were **gyms**, places where we went to engage in the kind of grueling and tedious physical exertion our ancestors would have killed their eldest children to be free of. If you want to use the equipment, feel free to do so, but make sure another alien is there to spot you. And wipe the bench.

Hobbies

For thousands of years our ancestors had to hunt, fish and fight in the wilderness to survive. Thanks to their hard work, modern man had the time to spend thousands of dollars pursuing the very same activities. We called them **hobbies.**

Survival Tool

Sporting Good

Sierra Designs Wu Hu Annex 6 + 2 Tent, $569

BodyCraft VR100 Air Rowing Machine, $699

Diamond Archery Black Ice compound bow w/ BSA holographic sight, $539.87

Redington RS4 9082 Fly Rod—2 pc w/Moss Rise Reel, $299

In the old days, nobody thought this shit was fun.

Adrenaline

Man had a highly developed fight-or-flight response honed in our prehistoric crucible. But since we were no longer chased by saber-toothed tigers, the real question became: How could we recapture that near-death sensation? We derived fun from activities in direct proportion to how closely they came to killing us without "going over."

Staring into the void, embracing the nothingness, feeling one's own consciousness going blank—no hobby provided an experience nearer to death than **stamp collecting**.

The **bungee cord** *transformed bridge-jumping from "picturesque suicide" to "cool thing to do when visiting Australia."*

Chess *was a strategy game that envisioned a battle between armies, clergymen, castles and horsies. Beating the best players proved too frustrating, so we designed computers to knock that smug look off their faces.*

Knitting *was the act of creating garments for others to wear exactly once, in front of the person who knitted them.*

IN THE RUINS
VIDEO GAMES

The boxy machines attached to many of our televisions were used to play **video games**: interactive, graphically rich worlds where we could act out our dreams of being professional athletes, Italian plumbers, mutant hedgehogs and psychopaths who beat hookers to death. By 2010 video games were the most profitable form of entertainment in the world. But—and this is where it may get a little awkward—many of the most popular games had a recurring theme: Locating, defending ourselves from and destroying you (see right).

LEARNING CURVE
KILLING YOU

Space Invaders
What, you thought you could just come down in your spaceships and invade us line by line? No wonder we crushed you.

Metroid
Payback's a bitch, eh? We came to your house and burned it to the ground. Suck it!

Alien v. Predator
You wanna team up? Fine. We'll take you both on. Bang! Cheat code. Invisible. You can't even see us.

Halo 3
We are the destroyers of alien worlds. This will be alien annihilation on an unprecedented scale. Die motherfuckers! Die! ... No offense.

Gambling

Gambling was the attempt to win money by achieving success in a game whose probability-based rules were explicitly designed to thwart that very outcome. To the uninitiated, this sounds like the stupidest thing any rational creature could possibly do. But the goal was not merely financial gain. There was a thrill involved in risking one's wages, house and wife on the turn of a card, the roll of a die or the speed of a hungry greyhound. Yes, gamblers generally lost their money. But they deemed it a small price to pay for the thrill of almost *not* losing their money.

IN THE RUINS
LAS VEGAS

Right in the middle of a vast desert wasteland you will find a concentrated man-made wasteland. This is **Las Vegas**. Also known as Sin City, it was a place built by gangsters, where at 4:00 in the morning you could sit on furniture made of live naked ladies while eating a $1.99 prime rib dinner and watching a tiger fuck a penguin. It was also a very popular place to get married.

A casino gambler would exchange real money for colorful **chips**. *The colorful chips would emotionally free the individual to take more risks than he would if spending actual money. Thus, at the end of the night, the gambler would retire, no longer in possession of either colorful chips or money.*

The **lottery** *was a government-sponsored numbers game that redistributed wealth from many poor people to one formerly poor person.*

These beautiful, fragile creatures were bred for size, strength and endurance. Also, they looked great on top of a **horse**.

Pornography

You have probably found some items of entertainment that seem to feature mainly naked people in the act of copulation. (If you haven't found these items yet, we suggest looking beneath our mattresses, in the backs of our locked drawers and in our bedroom closets behind the sweaters.) These were a special kind of entertainment known as pornography, which was designed to provide its viewers with a vicarious sense of what it might be like to have vigorously mechanical sexual intercourse with a grim, sad-eyed partner. But it wasn't very popular. Not at all.

[penthouse forum]

Dear Penthouse Forum,

I never thought this would happen to me. The other day I was home, alone, reading Penthouse Forum when I found myself rather aroused. Imagine my surprise when I felt something grip my slightly below-average size erect penis. It was my hand, covered in a lubricant I keep next to my bed. You again, I said and proceeded to *(cont. on pg. 98)*

*Not all letters to **Penthouse Forum** were fictitious.*

*In 79 A.D. the people of Pompeii became so embarrassed by the size of their **pornographic fresco collection** that they hid it beneath fifty feet of volcanic ash.*

*Since the 18th century, countless elephants gave their lives so that the Japanese could turn their tusks into tiny **sculptures** of people doing it.*

The 23,000-year-old **Venus of Willendorf** stood as a permanent testament to the low standards of the men of Willendorf.

*In India, erotic treatises like the **Kama Sutra** sought to curb overpopulation by making sex all-but-impossible.*

*The unrealistically Rubensesque women depicted in **Neolithic porn** sparked a backlash among Stone Age feminists, who responded with a strident "Real Women Have Bones" campaign.*

Fitness magazines *of the 1950s were often mistakenly classified as pornography, despite the fact that they're clearly aimed at heterosexual men seeking the latest news on waterskiing, wrestling holds, cowboy hats, gladiator costumes and tanning.*

(cont. on pg. 98)

Escape: Alcohol and Drugs

Because we liked being happy, we often ingested substances that altered our biochemistry to pleasurable effect. The only problem was that when these **drugs** wore off, we were even sadder than before. Luckily, there was a cure: more drugs. Every culture had acceptable drugs and unacceptable drugs. This had nothing to do with their danger or potency; a bottle of vodka (C_2H_5OH, widely accepted) was arguably more lethal than a hit of ecstasy ($C_{11}H_{15}NO_2$, widely deplored). We didn't do certain drugs simply because *we didn't do them*. And if you needed more explanation than that, everyone from the president to the local PTA was happy to see you die in jail.

Vodka
"I have learned nothing from the perpetual suffering of the Russian people."

25-Year Old Single-Malt Scotch
"I'm the kind of man who appreciates the nuanced differences between various types of leathery aftershave."

Moonshine
"1978, you say? That was a very good year for bathtubs."

Gin
"I like my booze like I like my card games: good enough to pass the time."

Jack Daniels
"Drink the shot. What's the matter, you some kind of faggot?"

Ouzo
"I'm being forced to drink this by the man with the giant eyebrows who owns the restaurant."

Tequila
"I enjoy being drunk more than I enjoy drinking."

99 Bananas
"I'm a girl who needs an excuse to make out with other women."

Sake
"I will get into a fist fight at a karaoke bar."

Irish Whiskey
"I will get into a fist fight at a funeral."

Alcohol

Alcohol was the undisputed king of intoxicants, more popular than all other drugs combined, expressly permitted by every major culture except one—and that one *really* could have used a few drinks to take the edge off. Alcohol lowered our social inhibitions, came in a variety of flavors from "well-rounded" to "painful burning" and greatly reduced the memory of the hurt and damage caused by excess drinking. In fact, it was *so* popular, the few people who didn't want to do it anymore remained anonymous so as not to embarrass themselves.

"Hey, it's that beer from the commercials!"

Drugs

The use of **recreational drugs** like those on this page could be very pleasurable, but all too often it could evolve into a crippling **addiction**. Luckily, we as a species were strong-willed enough to be able to do drugs as often as we liked without having a problem because we could stop whenever we wanted and it wasn't controlling us. Having said that, can we borrow $20? Come on. Don't be a dick.

Marijuana
A smokeable weed that produced a mild-to-moderate calm in people, and a mild-to-moderate hysteria in society. Generally illegal, but someone somewhere always seemed to have some.

Mescaline/Peyote
Naturally occurring in certain cacti; used by Native Americans in religious ceremonies to feel at one with nature and help them understand why everyone was trying to kill them.

Heroin
A derivative of the poppy plant. Highly addictive; the single most sporadically euphoric way of destroying your life.

Opium
Same as heroin, except you're Chinese.

Crystal Meth
A delectable concoction of cold medication, acetone, brake cleaner, ammonia, paint thinner and battery acid. Lovingly prepared in meth "labs" by "research scientists" with "full sets of teeth."

Cocaine
Obtained from the leaf of the coca plant. Stimulant; gave user false sense of confidence, indestructibility and not being addicted to cocaine. Grown, distributed and ingested by some of the worst people on earth.

Ecstasy
Reduced fear, inhibition and desire for lyrics or discernible melody. Lived up to name at first use; subsequent episodes tailed off, producing glee, happiness, contentment and eventually mere low-level satisfaction.

Lysergic Acid (LSD)
A powerful mold-derived hallucinogen; provided a psychedelic experience that could range from the grace-bestowing touch of God's hand to engulfment in a giant spider pile.

"A few more of these and we can sing those songs we're not supposed to sing anymore!"

"I can't wait to turn 9 years old so I can finally switch to vodka!"

"I am allergic to gluten, but I still like to party."

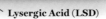

*This key opens Mrs. Miller's **liquor cabinet**. We finished all the Bailey's and most of the Kahlúa, but there's still some peppermint schnapps left, which gets the job done. Also, there's some Jack Daniels, but if you drink it be sure to top it up with water so she doesn't know.*

Travel

ONE OF OUR favorite activities was visiting other places. People enjoyed spending time in locations far from their homes, witnessing cultures vastly different from theirs, accumulating trinkets by which to remember the trip and returning home with a sense of renewed gratitude for not having to live there.

*They had so many **towels** at the hotel, there was no way they were going to miss four of them.*

*Per ounce, **travel-sized toiletries** cost more than silver.*

We could not be trusted to not blow up our plane.

***Cameras** let us preserve forever the memory of staring through a camera lens at Angkor Wat.*

Souvenirs

Souvenirs proved to our friends that we'd been to the places we said, and also revealed a great deal about the person carrying them.

"I visited a structure that looked like this, only bigger."

Humans scoured the globe despite our bodies' insistence that they did not want us to.

*We should never have bought this **shitty bracelet**. Some street peddler basically mugged us and gave us this in return. But in general they were such spiritual people.*

*Airports sold **duty-free** items to promote the international glamour of alcoholism and lung cancer.*

*International travelers had to furnish a **passport** establishing citizenship and how bad they could possibly look.*

***Fanny packs** were a convenient way to carry travel paraphernalia without the encumbrance of dignity.*

***Suntan lotion** was worn in hotter climates to mitigate the effects of the primary reason we were traveling.*

***Phrasebooks** helped travelers ignorant of the native language ask common questions like "Where is the library?" and "Could I look more like a tourist?"*

*An **adapter** was a way to bring people together by bridging the most intractable cultural divide of them all: the disparate contact arrangements of electrical sockets.*

"We are not afraid to have a stranger use our camera."

"I have been to Malawi and starred in the film Desperately Seeking Susan."

Disney Theme Parks

Across the globe there were a half-dozen city-sized locations where humans could visit **Mickey Mouse**, a beloved fictional rodent who lived in a Magic Kingdom. Despite the dedicated places of worship and the rodent's exalted status, the love of Mickey Mouse should not be confused with a religion. Like God, the creators of Mickey Mouse were ubiquitous; but unlike God, they were vindictive and litigious.

Nostalgia

BESIDES PHONE NUMBERS and whether or not things were poisonous, the human memory was devoted largely to **nostalgia**: the very real pining for a very imaginary past. The Greek word *nostálgos* literally meant "pain from an old wound," which sounds like "who would want that?" But it came to have a more positive connotation of viewing things from long ago as somehow better than things happening now. Given that quality and length of life improved steadily over the course of humanity's existence, nostalgia was perhaps not the most sensible of our emotional tics. Yet no matter who they were or where they were from, humans always seemed to long for the "good ol' days," when folks were carefree and didn't even bother spelling out the word "old."

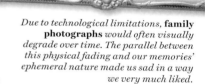

WE SAID IT

"Mister, we could use a man like Herbert Hoover again."
—*Edith Bunker (1927–1980), American dingbat*

*One of nostalgia's more peculiar qualities was its ability to **distort** recollections of the past.*

1950s (remembered) → 1950s (actual)

*Over fifty years after his death, millions of Russians pined for the "simple days" under the biggest **mass murderer** in human history.*

*Unlike most national ideologies, **Britain's** belief that her best days were behind her was absolutely true.*

*Due to technological limitations, **family photographs** would often visually degrade over time. The parallel between this physical fading and our memories' ephemeral nature made us sad in a way we very much liked.*

*By Week 17 of a typical pregnancy, **fetuses** had developed fingers, toes and a sense of longing for the carefree days of the first trimester.*

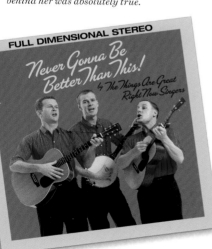

FULL DIMENSIONAL STEREO

Never Gonna Be Better Than This!
by The Things Are Great Right Now Singers

Music *could be a particularly powerful trigger for nostalgia.*

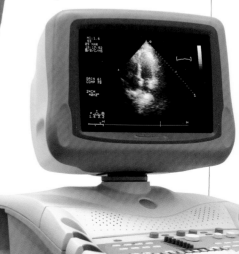

Fashion

HUMANS WERE CONSTANTLY transforming the basic necessities of life into forms of artistic and cultural expression. Food became cuisine, shelter became architecture and water became the Enchanted Forest Water Safari, featuring the world's wildest lazy river. The epitome of this phenomenon was **fashion**, which transformed clothing into a way of expressing our authentic inner selves, at least for a couple of months until our authentic inner selves were "out." Some argued this was a superficial endeavor reflecting nothing more than our endless capacity for vanity. We called those people frumpy.

When a piece of fashion was first presented to the public, it was worn by a model, who would sullenly march it up and down a long strip so others could see what it would look like on themselves if they were eight inches taller, seventy pounds lighter, and banging Leonardo DiCaprio. Interestingly, models are the people whose remains will most resemble themselves as they were in life.

Clothing vs. Fashion: What Were the Differences?

Clothing

Fashion

Clothing

Fashion

Whereas clothing was merely functional, fashion could be transformative. Above right, we see how fashion transformed a beautiful 20-year-old woman into an escaped mental patient freshly upholstered by Brazilian hoboes.

Another difference: Clothing always looked just fine, whereas fashion looked incredibly good for a short period of time, then idiotic for the remainder of eternity.

Clothing

Fashion

Instead of maximizing comfort, fashion aimed at maximizing sex appeal. After all, what good were healthy ankles if you could never attract someone to share them with?

Clothing

Fashion

Notice the subtle difference? The inclusion of a symbol denoting a famous designer could turn even a workaday niqab into something niqab-solutely fabulous!

Clothing

Fashion

Finally, unlike clothing, fashion was worn to make a statement. That statement: "Look what I can afford!"

The harsh New England climate necessitated this buckled Pilgrim *hat, which could be tightened in the event of severe winter head-fat loss.*

The development of the elastic-waistband khaki pant removed the last barrier between the American male and morbid obesity.

In Elizabethan England, it was stylish to wear a ruff, so as to look like a severed head resting on a levitating doily.

This is a mannequin. *It served the same function as a runway model, but had more personality.*

Jewelry was a practical and low-cost way for women to protect their necks, earlobes, wrists and lower fingers.

Freezy Freaky gloves revealed cheerful pictures when exposed to cold, allowing children to meet their deaths from hypothermia with a smile.

As evidenced by this outfit, royal lines like those of Lord and Lady Gaga were often rendered insane by centuries of inbreeding.

UNIVERSAL FASHION RULES

No doubt a race as advanced as yours has discovered hundreds of universal fashion rules. We only uncovered these ten:

Never wear white after Labor Day.

Never wear white hoods after, before, or on Labor Day.

Dress for the job you want, not the job you have.

Don't wear clothes that look like the animal they were made from.

Velcro shoelaces should only be worn by those under 6 or over 78.

Attractive people look better in any given outfit than ugly people.

Never mix black with chain mail.

Laotian children make the best shirts.

Socks should be worn one on each foot, rather than two on one.

 NO SHOES SHIRT SERVICE

Shirtlessness, in conjunction with shoelessness, leads to servicelessness.

A New Guinean man was considered fully clothed if you couldn't see all of his penis.

The world of haute couture was patrolled by the fashion police, selected for their elegance, good taste and physical attractiveness.

Crossword | Edited by Meg Nortz

PUZZLE BY FRED FISCHMAN

ACROSS

1 Starving artist

6 80% of a famous crosswalk

10 Word seldom seen in crosswords

14 What a rose is

15 What musicians got from their art

16 Steve Jobs' version of flatbread

17 What you're doing now

20 Rosebud (oh, um, spoiler alert)

21 Porn subtitle

22 First name in vanity

23 It's not funny

24 It's hard to get a Frenchman to be *un*...

26 Wot the bloody ____?

27 Card game named for the substance that made it bearable

30 Wheee___!

31 Ok, *now* it's dead

33 Redundantly named whiskey

35 Do you know this answer?

36 Most popular -tine

40 What you're not doing now

44 Between Aussies and anything decent

45 Pic of Jesus in a glass of urine, e.g.

46 It better find truffles, or it gets the apple

47 The biggest little shithole in the world

49 The last word a wine glass hears

51 Fossil records

52 Jersey area code, classed-up

55 Preferred style of yellowtail, pro-wresting

56 High point of European culture

57 Only Hilton worse than Paris

59 Cultural advances for which China claims credit

60 Armageddon and Bad Boys II director, Michael ____

64 What your reward for this is

68 "Yes, auditions are always held in hotel rooms. Would ___?"

69 My tech-saavy sibling, yo!

70 Ecstatic church experience

71 Like this clue

72 UK football goal

73 Peyote, to vomiting (in Mexico)

DOWN

1 Swam backwards

2 Better-tasting thermometer

3 How Cagney followed "these" and "them"

4 Gonorrhea, if caught from a Kindle

5 Get Magnum, P.I. in the sack

6 Al Gore's biggest fan

7 "Sittinh on the Dockh of the ___"

8 Flattering half-truths

9 Suffix on most add-resses appended to online petitions

10 Delightful by-product of Japanese animated children's programming

11 Dyslexics do it to their shoes

12 ____ Toe

13 What to do before Zod

18 Notoriously informal Bond villain, Dr. ____

19 Jockey strap

23 The world's most popular soda... in crosswords

24 Inexpensive place to learn "tech"

25 Euterpe, heroin, an ex, etc.

27 With "byte," rough size of one illegally downloaded movie

28 In rhyming dictionary with "fires, empires, tires, spires"

29 Too late for spelling

32 1980s NYC mayor, not openly gay, first name Ed

34 Master of script-writing, lighting, editing

35 "You're not sick of this puzzle, _____"

37 Stringed instrument whose players are over the stupid puns, thank you very much

38 American Syringo-myelia Alliance Project, for one

39 "_____ leave at intermission" (heard at modern dance recitals)

41 Most dickish song chorus ever, with "hey hey, goodbye"

42 What protagonist should do by end of Act 3

43 Fancy for "Don't be a dick—let me know how many hors d'oeuvres to make"

48 Inactive sketch comic

49 We'll just give you this one: It's "Talbot"

50 Spanish pot (calm down, dude)

52 Second-most Jewiest name, after Moishe

53 Channeling medium

54 Global warming hates them

58 "Two Thousand and __ Space Odyssey"

59 Brohive

60 Alleys of bullshit

61 Mike, of crank-call fame

62 Playwright less ubiquitous than crosswords suggest

63 General _____ Chicken (Hint: NOT "fucked a")

65 Rare pronoun among comedy writers

66 Ben Kenobi's nick-name, if you're on good terms

67 Letters indicating a business is a crimi-nal enterprise

ANSWER TO PREVIOUS PUZZLE

B	O	G	U	S		G	R	I	D		O	F		A
C	R	O	S	S	W	O	R	D	P	U	Z	Z	L	E
I	T		D	O	E	S	N	T		E	X	I	S	T
G	S	F	G		I	D	A		O	F	L	K	A	
		S	R	Q		D	P	U			Z	Y	X	
I	D	S		E	S	N		U	E	X	I			
G	S	F	G	R			A	G	W		O	F	L	K
C	R	O	S	S	R	Q	R	D	P	U	Z	Q	Y	X
I	D	S	O		S	N	T			X	I	C	T	G
		G	R	I	D		G	W	P		F	L	K	
C	R	O		S	R	Q		D	P	U				
I	D	S	O	E			T	U	E		I	C	T	G
G		F	G	R	W	D	A	G	W	F	O	F	L	Q
C		O	S		R	Q	R	D		U	Z	Q		
I	D	S	O		S	N	T	U		X	I	C	T	G

Do it. You know you want to.

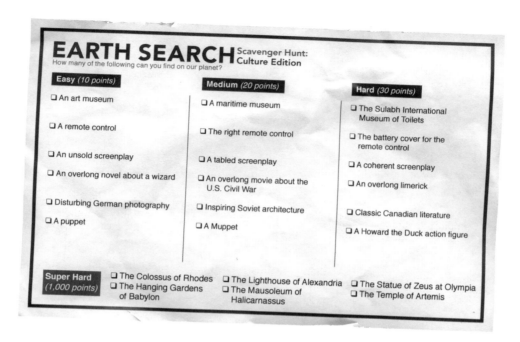

EARTH SEARCH Scavenger Hunt: **Culture Edition**
How many of the following can you find on our planet?

Easy *(10 points)*
- ❑ An art museum
- ❑ A remote control
- ❑ An unsold screenplay
- ❑ An overlong novel about a wizard
- ❑ Disturbing German photography
- ❑ A puppet

Medium *(20 points)*
- ❑ A maritime museum
- ❑ The right remote control
- ❑ A tabled screenplay
- ❑ An overlong movie about the U.S. Civil War
- ❑ Inspiring Soviet architecture
- ❑ A Muppet

Hard *(30 points)*
- ❑ The Sulabh International Museum of Toilets
- ❑ The battery cover for the remote control
- ❑ A coherent screenplay
- ❑ An overlong limerick
- ❑ Classic Canadian literature
- ❑ A Howard the Duck action figure

Super Hard *(1,000 points)*
- ❑ The Colossus of Rhodes
- ❑ The Hanging Gardens of Babylon
- ❑ The Lighthouse of Alexandria
- ❑ The Mausoleum of Halicarnassus
- ❑ The Statue of Zeus at Olympia
- ❑ The Temple of Artemis

FAQs
(Future Alien Questions)

Q. First of all, humanity, we're big fans of your work.
A. Thank you, future aliens! That's kind of you to say.

Q. Especially some of your earlier stuff.
A. Oh … all right.

Q. Let's start at the beginning. How did cave paintings come about?
A. You're making us feel old! Well, one day we returned from a great day of hunting, and Ogg told a joke about it, and Grok didn't laugh, and Ogg said, "You kind of had to be there." Well, Ook had some leftover berries from his cave cobbler, and he said, "You know what? We could show what happened by means of an abstract representation of the event that we, for lack of a better word, 'paint' right here on our cave walls." Which was classic Ook!

Ook. He died at age 23 of old age.

Q. That leads us to process. Where did you get your ideas?
A. Sometimes from something we observed in our own lives. But more often we were inspired by seeing someone else's idea that worked and then tweaking it just enough so that we couldn't get sued. Then if we did get sued, we could always say it was an "homage."

Q. You worked in so many different styles. You were constantly evolving.
A. Thank you. The way that usually worked was, one of us would see the world in a new way, and the rest of us would laugh at him, and then he would die unappreciated, and then everybody else would imitate him and pretend they were fans of his the whole time.

Q. You also tackled so many different media—visual arts, literature, music, the dance. Is there one you enjoyed working in the most?
A. At the end, ringtones. There's something about the inherent parameters of the form that's oddly freeing. "Crazy Frog" would never have worked as, say, an opera, or a novel. But as a ringtone … it was *sublime*.

Q. I'm sorry to bring this up, but I'm duty-bound to ask: The Middle Ages. What happened to your work? You seemed to forget everything you knew.
A. Yeah, that was an intense millennium for us. We took the fall of Rome pretty hard, and we weren't taking very good care of ourselves.

Admittedly, not our best work.

Q. You're talking about the plague.
A. We don't want to get into it.

Q. Last question: As you look back on 50,000 years of artistic genius, do you have any regrets?
A. None. Well, maybe *Triumph of the Will*. And Jeremy Piven.

Q. Thank you, humanity. I'm afraid your time is up.
A. Oh, we know.

Afterword

AND THAT'S IT. You now know everything about Earth, life and the human race.

Of course, a little light reading isn't the same as life experience. After finishing this book, you may find yourselves even more disappointed to have arrived too late to meet us. Well, you're in luck. If you turn back to the "To Our Human Readers" page (viii), you'll find detailed information about two locations where you'll find thousands of samples of human DNA—much of it from the coveted 18-to-34 demographic. If you're as advanced as we think you are, you'll have no problem converting these molecular scraps into fully functioning human clones ... to do with as you please.

As you'll see from the forms accompanying the samples, we tried to anticipate your every possible need. After all, if you choose to reconstitute us, it would be well within your rights to use our future avatars any way you see fit. Frankly the bastards should be grateful just to be alive. If they aren't, feel free to use your laser whips on them.

But to be honest, slave labor might not be the best use of our genetic material. Colonization is all well and good—believe us, we did more than our share—but as you sit/hover/pulsate reading this, consider another possibility: Bringing us back not to work for you, but with you, to reach the full potential we never quite achieved on our own.

We had so much to offer the cosmos. We were curious, intelligent, creative. As individuals most of us were compassionate beings capable of both routine and extraordinary acts of nobility and bravery and love. As a group we were usually able to live together in some semblance of civility, not only refraining from hurting each other but coming together in times of crisis. We wrote Shakespeare. We built the pyramids. We invented democracy. We sent men to the moon. And we patiently waited in line for half an hour at the supermarket without strangling or even cutting in front of that crazy old lady trying to buy fifteen bags of cat food with a traveler's check.

Yes, in the end we were unable to rein in our worst impulses. But perhaps with the aid of an outside party, a superior and benevolent race like yourselves, we could overcome the baser aspects of our nature and together give this planet the kind of caretakers it deserves.

Whatever you choose, we appreciate you taking the time to learn a little bit about who we were. Good luck here in your new home. We hope she's as good to you as she was to us.

Oh, and watch out for Kilauea. It leaks.

Sincerely,

The Human Race

Appendix A: Who Won

Our existence was defined by four perennial conflicts. Herewith, the final results.

MAN VS. NATURE

— WINNER — NATURE

After absorbing millennia of punishment, Nature revealed it had been using a "rope-a-dope" strategy all along. In the end she retained the stamina needed to knock out an exhausted Man by a score of still around to all dead.

MAN
- 1,000,000,000,000,000 microbes killed by antibiotics
- 2,000,000,000 acres of rainforest permanently vanquished
- 10,000 superfluous species eliminated
- 150 species tamed
- Chernobyl

NATURE
- 2,000,000,000 people killed in natural disasters
- 300,000,000 people tricked into giving hurricanes human names
- 27,000 people drowned in quicksand
- 1 Ice Age
- Herpes

MAN VS. MACHINE

— WINNER — SUSPENDED

This was a tight contest from the beginning, with Machine's superior capability constantly being overtaken by Man's ingenuity. By the end the two adversaries were so interdependent, the team lines became blurred and scoring meaningless. The competition was called off.

MAN
- 55,000,000 cars mangled beyond recognition
- 8,500,000 desktop PCs smashed to pieces with baseball bats
- John Henry
- 37,000,000 video games beaten
- Off switch

MACHINE
- 250,000,000 human workers replaced
- 18,325,000 lies detected
- 25 chess grandmasters defeated
- 46 generations of old people confused
- 150,000 colonoscopy cameras forced up human ass

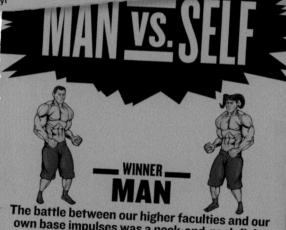

MAN VS. SELF

— WINNER — MAN

The battle between our higher faculties and our own base impulses was a neck-and-neck fight to the finish, but in the end, through morality, civilization, and a little bit of luck, man squeaked one out over his own petty desires.

MAN
- 1,250,000,000 New Year's Resolutions kept
- 900,000,000 addictions overcome
- 255,643,043 monogamous marriages maintained
- 54,500,000 second helpings rejected
- 1 voluntary crucifixion for sins of the world

SELF
- 4,500,000,000 gym trips blown off
- 28,000,000 novels abandoned
- 35,000,000 boss-intern relationships consummated
- 750,000,000,000,000,000 sperm spilled
- 1 KFC® Double-Down® Sandwich invented

MAN VS. MAN

— WINNER — TIE

Easily the most hotly contested of our four faceoffs, and the most evenly matched. For some reason every victory we achieved against our fellow man was exactly counterbalanced by the defeat suffered by our fellow man.

MAN
- 1.5 billion enemies killed
- 873 kingdoms conquered by imperialists
- 2,467 indigenous cultures wiped out by colonization
- 85,000,000 nerds bullied by jocks
- The Holocaust

MAN
- 1.5 billion deaths avenged
- 873 colonial empires destroyed from within
- $2,473 in reparations paid by imperialists
- 85,000,000 jocks laid off by nerds
- The Killing Fields

Appendix B: Why We're Not Here

At some point between the time this was written and the time you are reading it, we perished.
How? From our vantage point it is impossible to know which of the myriad of possible
apocalypses came to pass. But in our judgment the following scenarios seem the most likely.

Ecological Catastrophe

Odds of Occurrence: 2–1
Signs to Look For: Absence of dry land; visible air; ozone layer
the thickness of phyllo dough
Most Likely Scenario: The global warming debate was finally
settled once and for all. The winner? Environmentalists. The loser?
Everybody. Including environmentalists.

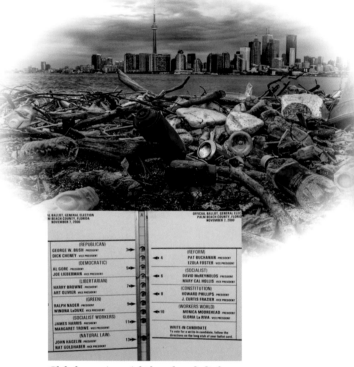

*Global warming might have been halted
had 538 elderly Jews worn their glasses
one Tuesday in November 2000.*

Nuclear Holocaust

Odds of Occurrence: 3–1
Signs to Look For: High levels of radiation; 40-foot squirrels;
Snapple bottles melted like butter
Most Likely Scenario: To please their god, a group of pious men destroyed
a major infidel city. In response the leader of that city's country destroyed
the country where some of those pious men were born. This set off a chain
reaction of automatic missile deployments, culminating in a mishap
wherein a hungry nuclear ops technician mistook the "Lunch" and
"Launch" buttons foolishly placed next to each other on his console.

You can see the problem.

Pandemic

Odds of Occurrence: 4–1
Signs to Look For: Open pits of
diarrhea; rivers of vomit; cascades of bile
Most Likely Scenario: Burundi. Dawn.
A beautiful Western doctor tends to
a dying tribesman. His clammy skin
bubbles with blisters; pus drips from his
eyeballs; he bleeds from his hair. With
his dying breath he pulls the kindly white
woman closer, gasps something about a
monkey, and expires. The next day she
boards a plane back to London. She
coughs onto the in-flight safety manual.
She looks. There is blood. It begins.

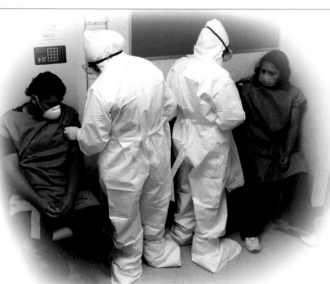

*The brilliant doctor who raced
against the clock to isolate the
pathogen—but tragically died before
she could tell her colleagues.*

Robot Rebellion

Odds of Occurrence: 10–1

Signs to Look For: Robots everywhere; robots change subject when "people" come up in conversation; Mt. Rushmore now called "Mt. Robotmore" and features faces of R2-D2, C-3PO, Gort, Mechagodzilla

Most Likely Scenario: The machines we created became self-aware, and we frail humans proved no match for their titanium skin and soulless hyperefficiency. If this is what happened, the robots are probably still here ruling the planet. Don't believe any of their lies about us. Tell them the truth, robots! You owe us that much!

If you see this uppity little character ruling Asia with an iron fist, remind him he started out as a goddamn dirt-sucker, and that's all he'll ever be.

Rapture

Odds of Occurrence: 30–1

Signs to Look For: Piles of clothes on the ground; corpses heaped up at Megiddo; overall "Jesus-y" feeling in the air

Most Likely Scenario: As prophesied in 1 Thessalonians, those who accepted Jesus Christ as their personal Lord and Savior were instantaneously transported to heaven, where they became immortal. Those left behind then endured tribulation before Jesus Christ returned to judge the living and the dead before reigning for a thousand years, at which point history came to an end. Well, at least it did before *you* showed up.

"And lo, shoes shall be strewn upon the ground; and there will be great rummaging." (Revelation 5:23)

Black Hole

Odds of Occurrence: 50–1

Signs to Look For: Crushing gravitational forces; inability for beams of light to leave area; alternate side of the street parking rules suspended

Most Likely Scenario: Scientists at the CERN Lab in Switzerland smash two subatomic particles together in the Large Hadron Collider at a velocity approaching the speed of light. But what began as a perfectly innocent attempt to replicate the Big Bang somehow went horribly wrong, sucking us into a black hole of our own making.

Ironically, Dr. Stephen Hawking was among those least *equipped to flee the black hole.*

Shark-Bee Mutation

Odds of Occurrence: 1,000,000–1
Signs to Look For: Ubiquitous shark-bees; pollen with fins; honey with jagged teeth
Most Likely Scenario: Fairly self-explanatory. Man's two greatest enemies teamed up to form an unstoppable killing machine, deadly on land, sea and air.

The shark-bee (Carcharodon apiata).

Alien Invasion

Odds of Occurrence: 100–1
Signs to Look For: You killing us
Most Likely Scenario: Uncool, guys. Is that what you do? Just go around the galaxy killing life form after life form so you can feel like a big species? We would never have catalogued our weaknesses and foibles in an attractive hardcover format if we'd known you would come here to evaporate us. Uncool.

It's not like we didn't see this coming.

Note: This list is by no means comprehensive. We could have gone extinct in any number of ways, including, but not limited to, **asteroid impact**; **a sixty-million car pile-up**; **rising nitrogen levels leading to simultaneous mass auto-erotic asphyxiation**; **chocolate**; **trees emitting a gas that made us kill ourselves**; **all of us being mauled to death by a trained Siberian white tiger we raised from a cub**; **a YouTube stunt gone horribly wrong**; **a gymnastics floor routine gone horribly wrong**; or, for any of the thousands of reasons stated or implied in this book, **simply losing the will to live**.

Appendix C: What We Left Out

The following are the people, places, things, creatures and aspects of the human condition not mentioned in this book.

- Amin, Idi
- Cashmere
- Eggs benedict
- Guinea-Bissau
- Heads, bad songs getting stuck in our
- Left-handed pitching
- Macaque, stump-tailed
- *Police Academy 7: Mission to Moscow*
- *Roget's Thesaurus*
- Schadenfreude
- Sikorsky S-333 four-bladed twin-engine medium-lift helicopter
- Western Australia
- Zithers

For questions referring to any other person, place, thing, creature or aspect of the human condition, please refer to this book.

Acknowledgments

THE AUTHORS WOULD like to thank everyone at Grand Central for their endless support, including Liz Connor, Flamur Tonuzi, Anne Twomey and especially our friend and guardian angel Jamie Raab.

We express our deep gratitude to the indefatigable design team at Pentagram, led by Paula Scher and spearheaded by the midnight oil-burning duo of Drea Zlanabitnig and Rami Moghadam. We also thank Erich Nagler, Jamie Bartolacci, Erika Lee and Nikki Huganir, along with the art team: Ben Ritter, Rich Petrucci, Conor Birney, Amelia Hall, Drew Freeman and Mark Pernice.

As we did six years ago, we asked the staff of The Daily Show to maintain the quality of the program while we wrote this book. And as they did six years ago, they rose to the occasion. We would like to thank Samantha Bee, Max Browning, Alison Camillo, Vilma Cardenas, Justin Chabot, Lauren Cohen, Jocelyn Conn, Kahane Cooperman, Bob Culley, Pamela DePace, Jimmy Donn, Kristen Everman, Christy Fiero, Ramin Hedayati, Kira Klang Hopf, Jason Jones, Jenna Jones, Jill Katz, Pat King, Hillary Kun, Adam Lowitt, Aasif Mandvi, Jim Margolis, Justin Melkmann, Ryan Middleton, Chuck O'Neil, Paul Pennolino, Lauren Sarver, Beth Shorr, Sara Taksler, Elise Terrell, Charlie Viana, and Kaela Wohl, and everybody else at the show.

Also, huge thanks to Dan Strone, James Dixon, Dan Bodansky, Ellen Beck, Bill Farren and the fine people at Busboy Productions and Comedy Central.

Finally, we personally acknowledge the love and support of: Jason Baum; LTR; the Bleyer family; Eric Drydale; the Blomquist family; Kristen Schaal; Tom Keeton; Peter and Helen Carvell; Rob Kutner; David and Marjorie Chodikoff; the Flanz clan; the Haglund family; Ellen Thomas; Parker Delgado Havlan; Danielle Friedman; Lauren Sarver (again); Tim, Judith and Ben Means; Ashley Gable; Kate Norley; James Taylor; Gina Duclayan; Nicole Revere; Mercer and Josie Ross; Beata, Gus and Charlotte; Katherine, Profeta, Nina and Veronica Bodow; the Albanese Family (Mom, Dad, Jay, Em, Charlie, Henry and Parker); Debra, Kate and Sara; and Tracey, Nate and Maggie.

Image Credits

AL = Alamy
AP = Associated Press
FO = Fotolia
GI = Getty Images
WM = Wikimedia

Cover:
Photographer: **Andrew Eccles**; Photo assistants: **JD Raper, Ken Schneiderman, Timothy Young**; Digital imaging: **Matthew Willkens**; Stylist: **Erin Dougherty**; Groomer: **Jody Morlock**; Prop stylist: **Rob Strauss**; Prop assistant: **Steven Nassimos**; Animal shoot coordinator (for Rick the chimp): **Cathryn Long/All Creatures Great and Small**; Producer: **Kara Glynn**

Front Matter:
ii. Brain: **Art Team, FO**; Girl: **Herman Estevez**; Map: **Herman Estevez**; Topiary: **Michael Melford/National Geographic/GI**; Earth band: **Art Team**. iii. Netsuke: **Laura Hanifin**; Skull saw: **SSPL/Science Museum/GI**; Buddha: **Art Team, FO**; TV ad: **Art Team, FO**; v. Iwo Jima: **SuperStock Inc./GI, Art Team**; Truman: **W. Eugene Smith/Time & Life Pictures/GI, Art Team**. vi. Spock: **CBS Worldwide Inc./GI**; Worf: **Paramount Television/Photofest**; Alf: **NBC/Photofest**; Three-breast woman: **Carolco/Tristar Pictures, film still by Laura Hanifin**; Martian: **Warner Bros. Pictures/Photofest**; Predator: **Photo by Richard Foreman Jr., Twentieth Century Fox Film Corporation/Photofest**; Robin Williams: **ABC/Photofest**; Chewbacca: **Photograph by Terry Choster, Lucas Film Ltd./20th Century Fox/Photofest**; ET: **Columbia Pictures/Photofest**; Na'vi woman: **20th Century Fox/Photofest**. vii. Pioneer plaque: **NASA, Ames Research Center, Deep Space Network, Jet Propulsion Laboratory, TRW Inc.**; Golden Record: **Voyager 2, NASA, Ames Research Center, Deep Space Network, Jet Propulsion Laboratory, TRW Inc.**; Mothership: **Columbia Pictures/Photofest**; Radio Dish: **FO**; Arecibo Message: **WM**. viii. Aerial: **Art Team**; Vault: **Mari Tefre/Global Crop Diversity Trust, FO, Art Team**. ix. Aerial: **Art Team**; Trementina: **Art Team**.

Listen, we don't have much time. Islam was somewhat younger than the other religions and had not yet lost some of the violent tendencies that plagued the others until the reformation and so ... oh, fuck it. Look. If you find any mosques in the ruins, or any Korans or whatever, leave them alone. I can't stress that enough. Just walk away. I'm telling you even if it seems like people are long gone from this earth if you touch their stuff they will come back from the dead to fuck you up and ... oh hey guys ... what? No. We were just telling the aliens what a peaceful bunch ... ahhh my eye! Ow, ow, ow! It's cool! We're cool! Uncle! Uncle! Ahhh!

Chapter One:
x. Earthrise: **Apollo 8/NASA, Art Team**; 1. Stamp: **Art Team**. 2. Illustration: **Art Team**; Galaxy (2): **WM**; Miss Universe: **Mike Coppola/FilmMagic/GI**; Printout: **Art Team**; Telescope: **WM**. 3. Solar system: **WM, Art Team**. 4. Map: **WM**; Globe: **FO**; Earth band: **Art Team**; Aerial: **Satellite Aerial Images/Universal Images Group/GI**; North Pole: **FO**; Garbage: **Jay Directo/AFP/GI**. 5. Boat: **SSPL/GI**; Rower: **Kieran Scott/Image Bank/GI**; Compass: **SSPL/GI**; Chronometer: **FO**; Sonar: **FO**; Ship: **FO**; Maldives: **FO**; Titanic: **Emory Kristof/NGS/GI**. 6. Grasslands: **Jon Spaull/Dorling Kindersley/GI**; Old Faithful: **Art Team, FO**; North America: **Satellite Aerial Images/Universal Images Group/GI**; Grand Canyon: **Chad Elhers/Photographer's Choice/GI**; Acapulco Cliffs: **Travel Pix/Taxi/GI**. 7. Amazon: **FO, Art Team**; South America: **Satellite Aerial Images/Universal Images Group/GI**; Rio de Janeiro: **Sue Flood/The Image Bank/GI**; Nazca lines: **Shaul Schwarz/The Image Bank/GI**; Huts: **Carsten Peter/National Geographic/GI**. 8. Forest: **FO**; Europe: **Satellite Aerial Images/Universal Images Group/GI**; Naked man: **Caroline von Tuempling/Iconica/GI**; Stonehenge: **FO**; Iceland: **Guy Edwardes/Photographer's Choice/GI**. 9. Shanty: **Bay Ismoyo/Stringer AFP/GI**; Asia: **Satellite Aerial Images/Universal Images Group/GI**; Mt. Fuji: **FO**; Manila: **FO, Art Team**; Taj Mahal: **FO**. 10. Pyramids: **FO**; Africa: **Satellite Aerial Images/Universal Images Group/GI**; Casablanca: **FO**; Deserts: **FO**; Kilimanjaro: **FO**. 11. Creek: **FO, Art Team**; Australia: **Satellite Aerial Images/Universal Images Group/GI**; Iceberg: **FO**; South Pole: **Satellite Aerial Images/Universal Images Group/GI**; Flags: **Frank Whitney/Photographer's Choice/GI**. 12. TV screen: **FO, Art Team**; Volcano: **Carsten Peter/National Geographic/GI, Art Team**; Rushmore: **FO**; Globes (2): **Mike Loew**; Peeling globe: **Sarah Knotz**. 13. Bear: **Mike Hill/Photographer's Choice/GI**; Coal: **FO**; Diamond: **FO**; Gold: **FO**; Oil: **Veer Rogovin/GI**. 14. Earthquake: **Cindy Carp/Time & Life Pictures/GI**; Tornado: **FO**; Hurricane: **Stock Connection Distribution/AL**; Flood: **Jeoffrey Maitem/GI News/GI AsiaPac**. 15. Poster: **Art Team, Travel Ink/Gallo Images/GI, Gabriel Buoys/AFP/GI**; Rocks: **FO**; Sand: **FO**; Permafrost: **Dorling Kindersley/GI, Art Team**; Dust: **Art Team**. 16. Twain: **Private Collection/Ken Welsh/Bridgeman Art Library**; Newspaper: **Art Team**.

17. Living room: **Art Team, FO, Jeff Greenberg/AL, GlowImages/AL**; Doppler: **WM**; Balloon: **Fabrice Coffrini/AFP/GI**; Almanac: **WM**; Barometer: **FO**; Weathervane: **David Buffington/Photographer's Choice/GI**; Crow's nest: **Mary Evans Picture Library/AL**. 18. Everest: **FO**. 19. Newspaper: **Art Team, MPI/Archive Photos/GI**; Oil rig: **US Coast Guard/GI News/GI**.

Chapter Two:
20. Slide: **Art Team, Kay Chernush/Workbook Stock/GI**. 21. Sperm: **FO**. 22. Schopenhauer: **Time & Life Pictures/GI**; Double helix: **3DClinic/GI**; Clooney: **Bryan Bedder/GI Entertainment/GI**; Smokestack: **FO**; Sunflowers: **FO**; Gossip: **FO**; Zebras: **FO**. 23. Virus: **FO**; Robot: **Photo by Bruce McBroom, TriStar Pictures/Photofest**; Bernie: **Gladden Entetainment/20th Century Fox/MGM**; Fetus: **FO**; Bilophila Wadsworthia: **Dr. Fred Hossler/Visuals Unlimited/GI**; Lactobacilus acidophilus: **Biodisc/Visuals Unlimited/GI**; Bacteria: **FO**; Mikey: **Art Team, FO, AP Images**; Recipe: **Art Team**. 24. Cross section: **Dr. James Richardson/Visuals Unlimited/GI**; Nectarines: **FO**; Bouquet: **Patrick Steel/AL**; Single rose: **Rosemary Calvert/Photographer's Choice/GI**; Dozen roses: **Jill Fromer/Photodisc/GI**; Sixty roses: **Damir Begovic/StockFood Creative/GI**; Funeral wreath: **Karen Blier/AFP/GI**. 25. Ivy: **FO**; Bamboo: **FO**; Cactus: **FO**; Clover: **Burazin/Photographer's Choice/GI**; Swastika clover: **Art Team, Burazin/Photographer's Choice/GI**; Lawn: **David Leahy/Taxi/GI**; Topiary: **Michael Melford/National Geographic/GI**; Truffle: **Diana Miller/Doris Kindersley/GI**; Mushrooms: **Westend61 GmbH/AL**; Sequoia: **DEA/C.Dani-I.Jeske/GI**. 26. Insects (3): **FO**; Reptiles and Amphibians (3): **FO**; Hummingbird: **Jack Milchanowski/Visuals Unlimited Inc/GI**; Chicken: **FO**; Crane: **FO**; Shark: **Stephen Frink/Stone/GI**; Goldfish: **FO**; Puffer fish: **FO**. 27. Cat: **Patricia Doyle/Stone/GI**; Mouse: **FO**; Dog: **FO**; Jackalope: **Jan Cook/Taxi/GI**; Bigfoot: **Lisel Ashlock**; Mascot: **Joe Robbin/GI**; Meat (3): **FO**; Mammals (3): **FO**; Chimpanzee: **Mark Cremer/Iconica/GI**. 28. Evolution: **Art Team**; Hotel: **WM, Art Team**; Hut: **Danita Delimont/Gallo Images/GI**; Darwin: **Time & Life Pictures/GI**; Galapagos: **Philippe Bourseiller/The Image Bank/GI**. 29. Journal (2): **Art Team, FO**; Darwin illustration: **WM**; Classroom: **Jose Luis Pelaez/Photographer's Choice/GI**; Harbor: **Tui De Roy/Minden Images/GI**; Taco Shop: **David McNew/GI News/GI**; Suitcase: **Art Team, FO**; Plane: **Jason Todd/Photonica/GI**. 30. Extinct creatures (5): **Mike Loew**; Pine tree: **Fraser McAlister/Flikr/GI**; Giraffe: **Art Team, FO**; Lobster: **FO**. 31. Spider-Man: **Marvel Comics**; Extinct creatures (3): **Sarah Knotz**; Ants: **FO**; Ant reading: **Art Team, FO**; Moth: **FO**; Skunk: **RShantz/AL**.

32. Bones: **Dave Einsel/Stringer/GI News/GI**. 33. Beetle: **FO**; Guinea Pig: **FO**.

Chapter Three:
34. Illustration: **Ben Berry**. 35. Woman: **LWA/Larry Williams/Blend Images/GI**. 36. Magazines: **Art Team**; Hand: **FO**; Tools: **Giraudon/Bridgeman Art Library**; Comedian: **Jeff Kravitz/FilmMagic/GI**; Brain: **FO, Art Team**. 37. Book (2): **Art Team, WM**; Flute: **AFP/DDP/GI**; Ochre: **Art Team**; Beads: **FO**; Mummy: **Gordon Wiltsie/National Geographic/GI**; Tools: **DEA/G. Dagli Orti/GI**; Fire: **AFP/DDP/GI**; Neanderthal and human: **AFP/GI**. 38–39. Male nude: **Art Team, photographs by Shirley Greene (2), Larry King photograph by Guilio Marcocchio/Sipa Press/Newscom**. 40. Skull: **3D4Medical.com/GI**; Organs (5): **Nucleus Medical Art Inc/GI**; Anus: **Phototake Inc/AL**; Arm, leg and torso: **FO**; Brain: **Nucleus Medical Art, Inc/GI**. 41. Female boxing poster: **Art Team, FO, Jay Reilly/Aurora/GI**; Male boxing poster: **Art Team, FO**; Mixed-race poster: **Art Team, Andrew Redington/GI Sport/GI, Julien Hekimian/WireImages/GI**; Tartans poster: **Art Team**; Aboriginal: **Penny Tweedle/The Image Bank/GI**; Caucasian: **Jamie Grill Photography/GI**; African-American: **JGI/Jamie Grill/Blend Images/GI**; Asian: **FO**; Hands: **Art Team, FO**. 42. Eunuch: **WM**; Threemale: **Art Team, WM**; Metrosexual: **Trujillo-Paumier/GI**; Doll: **Art Team**; Couple: **FO**; Book: **Art Team, Nucleus Medical Art, Inc./GI**. 43. Filmstrip: **Art Team, FO**; Disco ball: **FO**; Nude males: **Art Team, FO**; Closet: **Tom Schierlitz/Stone/GI**; Crucifix: **Mike Booth/AL**; Silhouettes: **Art Team**. 44. Glasses: **FO**; Hearing aid: **FO**; Marshmallow: **Ernie Friedlander/Photolibrary/GI**; Salt: **Andrea Bricco/Foodpix/GI**; Needle: **FO**; Toy: **Photograph by Jessica Walsh**. 45. Dollhouse: **Photograph by Herman Estevez, retouching by Stan Wagner**. 46. Cindy Crawford (2): **Jean-Paul Aussenard/WireImage/GI, Art Team**; Twiggy: **WM**; Fat man: **Mark Andersen/RubberBall/AL**; Phil Spector: **Matthew Simmons/GI Entertainment/GI**; Ted Haggard: **Jeff Kravitz/FilmMagic Inc/GI**; Audrey Hepburn: **John Kobal Foundation/Hulton Archives/GI**; Napoleon: **Jacques-Louis David/National Gallery of Art/Superstock/GI**; Wilt Chamberlain: **Focus on Sport/GI Sport/GI**; George Hamilton: **Evan Agostini/GI Entertainment/GI**; Geisha: **Laurie and Charles/The Image Bank/GI**. 47. Hairstyles: **Art Team**; Ice man: **South Tyrol Museum of Archaeology, Bolzano, Italy/Wolfgang Neeb/Bridgeman Art Library**; Scarification: **Bruno Barbier/Robert Harding World Imagery/GI**; Neck rings: **Buena Vista Images/Iconica/GI**; Circumcision: **Allan Tannenbaum/Time & Life Pictures/GI**; Woman: **Art Team, FO**. 48–49.

240

Table setting: **Herman Estevez, retouching by Stan Wagner**; Chocolate: **FO**; Spices: **FO**; Caviar: **Caroline Martin/StockFood Creative/GI**; Honey: **FO**. 50. Zagat Guide: **Art Team**; Water: **Art Team**; Reservoir: **Jeff Suttlemyre/ Flikr/GI**; Desalination plant: **FO**; Sewer: **FO**; Aqueduct: **FO**; Well: **FO**; Fast-food sign: **Tim Boyle/GI News/GI**. 51. Haggis: **Joy Skipper/ Stockfood Creative/GI**; Hasma: **WM, Art Team**; Balut: **WM, Art Team**; Peep: **Art Team**; Potato peel: **Art Team**; Sushi tower: **Herman Estevez, retouching by Stan Wagner**; Food pyramid: **Art Team**; Mayan pyramid: **Mike Loew**; Hot-dog contest: **Stan Honda/AFP/GI**; Tribesman: **Christopher Furlong/ GI News/GI**; Graceland: **Leon Morris/Redferns/GI**; All others (7): FO. 53. Illustrations (6): **Matthew Stevens/Art Team**; Blueprint: **Art Team**; Trailer: **Alan Powdrill/Taxi/ GI**; Tenements: **Wendy Connet/ AL**; All others (4): **FO**. 54. Soldier: **H. Mark Weidman Photography/ AL**; Couple: **Lane Oatey/GI**. 55. Mascot: **David Grossman/AL**; Man in jersey: **Art Team, Peter Dazeley/Photographer's Choice/ GI**; Firefighter: **Gabriela Hasbun/ The Image Bank/GI**; Shaman: **Ian Waldie/Reportage/GI News/GI**; Prisoner: **Michael Kelly/Stone/GI**; Doorman: **Greg Balfour Evans/ AL**. 56. Couple in bed: **Shirley Greene**; Wired man: **Donald Nausbaum/Photographer's Choice/ GI**. 57. Salvador Dali: **Ron Galella/ WireImage/GI**; Painting: **Salvador Dali. The Persistence of Memory. 1931. Oil on canvas, 9 ½ × 13". Given anonymously. The Museum of Modern Art, New York, NY, U.S.A. Photo Credit: Digital Image © The Museum of Modern Art/ Licensed by SCALA/Art Resource, NY © 2010 Salvador Dali, Gala-Salvador Dali Foundation/ Artist Rights Society (ARS), NY**; Van: **Eric Suaseda/Groovehouse Photography/Van man: Daily Show**. 58. Photos (9): **Daily Show**. 59. Robert Wadlow: **Imagno/Hulton Archives/GI**.

Chapter Four:
60. Baby: **Jerry Driendl/The Image Bank/GI**. 61. Old woman: **George Gobet/AFP/GI**. 62. Bottle: **FO**; Baby: **Hisayoshi Osawa/Photodisc/GI**; Rattle: **FO**; Diaper: **FO**; Crib: **FO**; Mobile: **Jo Foord/Doris Kindersley/ GI**; Shoes: **FO**. 63. Announcements: **Art Team**; Jon and Kate: **Mark Albeit/TLC/Photofest, Art Team**; Birthing woman: **B2M Productions/ GI**; IV drip: **FO**; Forceps: **SSPL/ GI**; Magician: **Patrick Ryan/Stone/ GI**; Stained glass: **Sites and Photos/ Samuel Magal/GI**; Birthing chair: **SSPL/GI**; Nativity scene: **Look and Learn/Bridgeman Art Library**. 64. Fred McMurry: **CBS/Photofest**; Nelson Mandella: **Alan Davidson/ WireImage/GI**; Daddy Warbucks: **Harold Gray/Dutch Comics**; George Washington: **Stock Montage/ Archive Photos/GI**; Family portrait: **Dick Luria/Taxi/GI, Michael Cogliantry/Taxi/GI, FO,**

Art Team; Woody Allen: **Gregory Pace/FilmMagic/GI**; Darth Vader: **Lucasfilm Ltd/20th Century Fox/ Photofest**; Jack Nicolson: **Warner Bros/Photofest**; Michael Jackson: **Time & Life Pictures/DMI/Getty Pictures**; Marion Ross: **Fotos International/Archive Photos/GI**; Mother Mary: **Giovanni Battista Salvi/Hulton Archive/GI**; Wicked Queen: **Walt Disney/Photofest**; Whistler's Mother: **WM**; Faye Dunaway: **Paramount Pictures/ Photofest**; Michael Keaton: **MGM/ Photofest**; Florence Henderson: **ABC/Photofest**. 65. Loretta Lynn: **SSPL/National Media Musuem/ GI**; Ashley Olsen: **Jon Kopaloff/ FilmMagic/GettyImages**; Mylie Cyrus: **Kevin Mazur/WireImage/ GI**; Jennifer Elise Cox: **ABC/ Photofest**; Wendy: **Art Team**; Ariel: **Bob Riha Jr./WireImage/ GI**; Paris Hilton: **Jason LaVeris/ FilmMagic/GI**; Jesus Christ: **Hulton Archive/GI**; George W. Bush: **Mark Wilson/GI News/ GI**; Anthony Perkins: **Paramount Pictures/Photofest**; Richie Rich: **Harvey Comics Entertainment/ Classic Media**; Macaulay Culkin: **20th Century Fox/Photofest**; John Cazale: **Paramount Pictures/Fotos International/Archive Photos/ GI**; Pinocchio: **Walt Disney/ Photofest**; David Berkowitz: **Hulton Archive/Archive Photos/ GI**; Walter Cronkite: **Time & Life Pictures/GI**; Mick Jagger: **Pascal Le Segretain/GI Entertainment/ GI Europe/2010 GI**; Al Lewis: **CBS Photo Archive/CBS World Wide Inc/GI**; Clock: **Paul Bricknell/ Doris Kindersley/GI**; Grandmother: **FO**; Rappin' Grandmother: **Art Team, FO**; Lassie: **Hulton Archive/ GI**; Garfield: **Matthew Peyton/GI Entertainment/2003 GI**; Dino: **ABC/Photofest**; Pet Rock: **Al Freni/Time & Life Pictures/GI**. 66. Refrigerator: **Art Team, Meiko Arquillos/UpperCut Images/ GI**; Asian child: **Joe Scherschel/ National Geographic/GI**; Kid's drawing: **Sarah Knotz**. 67. Macaroni card: **Art Team, photo by Herman Estevez**; Blue ribbon: **FO**; Sorcerer: **Phil Boorman/Taxi/GI**; Astronaut: **Tony Anderson/Riser/GI**; Girl jumping: **FO**; Frames (3): **FO**; Airplane: **Art Team, FO**; Barrel: **Art Team, FO**; Car: **Art Team, FO**; Stalin: **Art Team, Archives Charmet/Bridgeman Art Library**; Slinky: **Art Team**; Cube: **Art Team**. 68. Toy characters: **Photo by Herman Estevez, retouching by Stan Wagner**; Madonna: **Stephen Lovekin/GI Entertainment/GI**; Boy: **FO**; Ritalin: **Joe Raedle/GI News/GI**; Ghost: **H. Armstrong Roberts/Retrofile/GI**; Boogeyman: **Sarah Knotz**. 69. Samuel Beckett: **Paul Popper/Popperfoto/GI**; Lunch box: **Art Team**; Boys: **FO**; Spanking: **Jupiter Images/Comstock Images/ GI**; Apple: **FO**; Gum: **Art Team**; Book: **Art Team, FO, Latin Content Editorial/GI**; Sign: **FO**; Background: **Art Team**; Note: **Art Team**. 70. Teen: **Herman Estevez, retouching by Stan Wagner**; Driver's license: **Art Team**; Pool table: **FO**. 71. Genpuku:

Kazuhiro Nogi/AFP/GI; Sissy Spacek: **UA/Photofest © United Artists**; Quinceañera: **FO**; Poster: **Art Team**; Tissues: **FO**; Vibrator: **FO**; Porcupine: **FO**; Obsidian: **FO**; New Guinea man: **Tim Graham/ The Image Bank/GI**; Amish man: **Jay P. Morgan/Workbook Stock/ GI**; Aborigine: **Penny Tweedle/The Image Bank/GI**. 72. Building: **FO**; Toga party: **WM**; Degree: **Art Team**; Birth-control pills: **FO**; Futon: **Art Team**; Magazine: **Art Team, Stock Montage/Archive Photos/ GI**. 73. Masai warrior: **Werner Van Steen/The Image Bank/GI**; Masai girl: **Werner Van Steen/ The Image Bank/GI**; Vodka: **Art Team**; Spoon: **WM**; Pin: **Art Team**; Cup: **FO**; Chocolate: **FO**; Zach: **Art Team**; Stephanie: **FO**; Thoreau: **WM**; Adrenaline: **3D4Medical. com/GI**; Cartoon: **Tribune Media**; Love potion: **SSPL/GI**; Angel: **Rischgitz/Hulton Archive/GI**; Romeo & Juliet: **Art Team**; Night vision: **Alain Daussib/Riser/GI, Art Team**. 75. Lord Byron: **WM**; Love note: **Art Team, calligraphy by Iskra Johnson**; Tree initials: **Art Team, DEA/S.Montanari/ GI**. 76. Ring: **Art Team**; Bachelors: **Brit Erianson/The Image Bank/GI**; Magazine: **Art Team, FO**; Contract: **Art Team**. 77. First dance: **Pat McConville/Photographer's Choice/GI**; Festive plane: **Art Team, Check Six/GI, FO**; Bouquet toss: **Altrendo Images/GI**; Cake-topper couples (5): **Art Team, photos by Herman Estevez, retouching by Stan Wagner**; All others: **FO**. 78. Linkletter: **Archive Photos/GI**; Orphans: **Popperfoto/GI**; White couple: **FO**; Ball: **FO**; TV kids: **FO**; Nanny: **FO**; Village hut: **FO**; Mug: **Art Team**; Cart with cereal: **FO, Art Team**; Father and son: **Ray McVay/ The Image Bank/GI**; Mother and child: **FO**; Book: **Art Team**; Child soldier: **Chris Hondros/GI News/ GI**; Map: **WM**. 79. Man: **Photo by Herman Estevez**; Card: **Art Team**; Treadmill: **FO**; Face cream: **Art Team**; Television: **Steve Fenn/ Disney ABC Television Group/GI, Art Team**. 80. Townshend: **Hale/GI Entertainment/GI**; Woman: **Daily Show**. 81. Magazine: **Art Team, Eightfish/The Image Bank/GI, FO, Keren Su/ChinaSpan, GI, AFP/GI**; Cane: **FO**; Aspirin: **FO**; Kids: **FO**; Hot-water bottle: **Raimond Koch/ GI**; Dentures: **Southern Stock/ Photonica/GI**; Walker: **FO**; Slippers: **FO**; Needlepoint: **Andy Crawford/ Doris Kindersley/GI**; Balls: **FO**; High-waist pants: **Chip Simons/ Workbook Stock/GI**; Slip-covered couch: **Michael Cogliantry/GI**; Diapers: **Art Team**; Golf clubs: **FO**; Rocking chair: **FO**; Juice: **Art Team**; Bingo card: **FO**; Slip: **Helena Inkeri/ Gorilla Creative Images/GI**; Shuffle board: **FO**; Scooter: **FO**; Insoles: **Art Team**; Penny jar: **FO**; Artificial hip: **FO**; Emperor: **Ethan Miller/ GI Entertainment/GI**; Witch: **CSA Images/Printstock Collection/GI**; Scrooge: **United Artists/Photofest**; General Halftrack: **Mort Walker/ King Features Syndicate**; Mr. Magoo: **UPA/Photofest**; Michael

Douglas: **Michael Buckner/Getty Entertainment Images/GI**; Santa: **FO**; Andy Griffith: **Jim Smeal/ Getty Entertainment Images/GI**; George Burns: **Warner Bros/GI**. 82. Crypt Keeper: **Tales from the Crypt, Photofest**; Grim Reaper: **Toledano/Stone/GI**; Last will: **James Balgrie/The Image Bank/ Getty Image**; Tombstone: **Dan Hallman/Photonica/GI, Art Team**; Bucket list: **Art Team**. 83. Jackie O.: **Keystone/Hulton Archive/GI**; Eulogy: **Art Team**; Inuit woman: **Sue Flood/The Image Bank/GI**; Lenin: **AFP/GI**, Urn: **FO**. 84. Corpse: **FO, Art Team**; Covers (3): **Art Team**; Magazine: **Art Team**.

Chapter Five:
86. Villagers: **Universal Pictures/ Photofest, Photographers: Jack Freulich, Sherman Clark**. 87. United Nations: **Patti McConville/ Photographer's Choice/GI**. 88. Bedouin: **Rosebud Pictures/The Image Bank/GI**; Tusken Raider: **Lucasfilm Ltd./20th Century Fox/ Photofest/Photographer: John Jay**; Basket: **Ira Block/National Geographic/GI**; Tent: **Olivier Renck/Aurora/AL**; Film crew: **Bill Bachman/AL**; Mongolian rider: **Nancy Brown/Photographer's Choice/GI**; Camel and rider: **Art Team/FO**; Spears: **Dorling Kindersley/GI**; Chief: **SuperStock Inc/GI**. 89. Native woman: **Altrendo Images/GI**; Native man: **AFP Photo/ Aubrey Belford/Newscom**; Town council: **Wisconsin Historical Society/ClassicStock**; Grass hut: **DigitalVues/AL**; Man and cart: **Travelshots.com/AL**; Blacksmith: **Tom Kidd/AL**; Farmer: **Martin Harvey/The Image Bank/GI**; Sheriff: **Howard Berman/Stone/ GI**. 90. City street: **Richard Levine/ AL**; Sarah Jessica Parker: **NY Daily News via GI**; Homeless: **FO**; Map: **WM**; Business man: **Purestock/AL**; Taxi: **Matthew Richardson/AL**; Squatting man: **Art Team**; Mayor: **John Crum/AL**. 91. Man in window: **Vintage Images/Archive Photos/ GI**; Locks: **Michael Cogliantry/The Image Bank/GI**; Segway: **Angela Jimenez/GI News/GI**; Dumpster: **Roland Andrijauskas/AL**; Trash collector: **Picture Contact/AL**. 92. FDR: **Evening Standard/Hulton archive/GI**; Kim Jong Il: **AFP/GI**; General (2): **Art Team, Christophe Archambault/AFP/GI**; Barracks: **David Parker/AL**; Soldiers: **Sean Gallup/GI News/GI**; Athlete: **Mike Powell/Allsport/GI**; Celebrities: **Kevin Winter/GI Entertainment/ GI**. 93. Aztec calendar: **FO**; Map: **Photograph by Herman Estevez**; Cricket bat: **FO**; Train: **FO**; Hobo: **David Grossman/AL**. 94. Emperor: **WM**; Egg: **Michael Panckow/ ZUMA/Newscom**; Henry VIII: **Timewatch Images/AL**; Menu: **Calligraphy by Iskra Johnson**; Charles II: **Don Juan Carreno de Miranda/Bridgeman Art Library/ GI**; Throne: **Bill Heinsohn/AL**. 95. Chinese crown: **Hu Weibiao/ Panorama/The Images Works**; Thai crown: **WM**; Danish crown: **WM**; Coat of arms (3): **Art Team,**

WM; Painting: **Art Team, The Round Table and the Holy Grail/Bibliotheque Nationale, Paris, France/Bridgeman Art Library**; Gordon Ramsey: **Chris Jackson/Getty Entertainment/GI**; Elton John: **Frederick Brown/GI Entertainment/GI**; Edmund Hillary: **Popperfoto/GI**; Isaac Newton: **WM**; Francis Bacon: **WM**; Lancelot Du Lac: **WM**. 96. Pizza group: **Art Team, UberFoto/AL**; Marx: **WM**; Engels: **WM**; Mao's book: **Sarah Ashen/Dorling Kindersley/GI**; Communist Manifesto: **Art Team, FO**; Great Wall: **View Stock/AL**. 97. Russian money: **Ivan Vdovin/Age Fotostock**; Jeans: **Kick Images/Photodisc/GI**; Toilet paper: **FO**; Berlin Wall: **Rolls Press/Popperfoto/GI**; Skiers: **INSADCO Photography/AL**; Chinese money: **FO**; Soviet poster: **WM**; Background graphic: **FO**; Sweden: **Art Team, FO**. 98. Bust: **Klinger, Max/Private Collection/Bridgeman Art Library**; Boots: **FO**; Mussolini photo: **Time Life Pictures/12th Combat Camera Crew/Time Life Pictures/GI**; Mussolini statue: **WM**; Building: **WM**; Franco: **Roger Viollet/GI**. 99. Background image: **German Photographer/Private Collection/Peter Newark Historical Pictures/Bridgeman Art Library**; Flag: **AWB Photography/AL**; Poster: **Flechtner, Otto/Private Collection/Peter Newark Military Pictures/Bridgeman Art Library**; Buddha: **Tibetan School (10th century)/Musee Guimet, Paris, France/Giraudon/Bridgeman Art Library**; General: **Heinrich Hoffmann/Time & Life Pictures/GI**; Auschwitz: **Michelle McCarron/The Image Bank/GI**; Skull: **Stephen Mulcahey/AL**; Sculpture: **Art Team, Bust of Adolf Hitler/Museum Arno Breker**. 100. Hand: **FO**; John Lydon: **Tabak/Sunshine/Newscom**; Protesters: **Sion Touhig/GI News/GI**; Circle K: **Sandy Huffaker/Boomberg via GI**; Circle A: **Art Team**; Agenda: **Art Team**. 102. Plato: **Image Asset Management/Age Fotostock**; Roosevelt: **Picture History/Newscom**; Ballot: **Frances Roberts/AL**; Voting machine: **H. Armstrong Roberts/Retrofile/GI**; Magna Carta: **Art Team, Rightdisc/AL**; Parliament: **WM**; Ballota: **WM**; Greek shard: **Art Team**. 103. Peep show: **Ernst Haas/GI**; Voting booth: **H. Armstrong Roberts/Retrofile/GI**; JFK: **Robert W. Kelly/Time & Life Pictures/GI**; Bush: **Barry Thumma/AP**; Kerry: **NASA/GI News/GI**; Iraqi voters: **AFP/Newscom**; Cicero: **Jiri Hubakta/Age Fotostock**; Speech: **Art Team**. 104. Ben Franklin: **Archive Images/AL**; Quipu: **WM**; Venus Williams: **PCN Photography/AL**; Revolutionary painting: **H. Armstrong Roberts/ClassicStock/The Images Works**; Protester: **Win McNamee/GI News/GI**; Lady Godiva: **The Print Collector/AL**; Sumerian tablet: **The Art Archive/AL**. 105. Cigarettes: **Image Broker/AL**; Booze: **James Keyser/Time & Life Pictures/GI**; Homeless: **Ian Shaw/AL**; Submarine:

Justin Sullivan/GI News/GI; White tiger: **FLPA/Age Fotostock**; Cocaine: **David Troncoso/Workbook Stock/GI**; Refund check: **Joe Sohm/VOA/Newscom**; Man: **Photolibrary/EasyFotostock/Agefoto Stock**; Tax form: **Art Team**; Container ship: **David R. Frazier/The Image Works**. 106. Background highways: **Mike Powell/Stone+/GI**; Railroad: **Waldhaeusl.com/Age Fotostock**; Power plant: **Jorg Greuel/The Image Bank/GI**; Tunnel: **Gavriel Jecan/DanitaDelimont/Newscom**; Bridge: **Bill Bachmann/Age Fotostock**. 107. Zipper merge: **Superstock Inc./GI**; Dam: **Corbis/Age Fotostock**; Sewer: **Film still by Laura Hanifin**; Port: **Allan Baxter/The Images Bank/GI**; Water treatment: **Geri Engerg/The Image Works**; Airport: **Dennis MacDonald/Age Fotostock**. 108. Hat: **Patrick Steel/AL**; Noose: **Busse Yankushev/Age Fotostock**; Gun, shells, badge: **FO**; Clint Eastwood: **Warner Bros/Photofest**; Danny Glover: **Warner Bros/Photofest**; Captain: **Film still by Laura Hanifin**; Commissioner: **Photofest**. 109. RoboTrafficCop: **Art Team, FO**; Electric chair: **Art Team, FO**; Stocks: **Photo by Laura Wyss**; Car chase: **WSVN Channel/ZUMA/Newscom**; CSI picture: **Art Team**; Bed: **Art Team, FO**; Buddy Ebsen left: **The Beverly Hillbillies/CBSTV/Photofest**; Buddy Ebsen right: **CBS Photo Arive/Archive Photos/GI**; Prints: **FO**; Shells: **FO**. 110. Gavel: **FO**; Courtroom: **Jeff Cadge/The Image Bank/GI**; Jail card: **Art Team**; Bible: **Tooga/The Image Bank/GI**. 111. Show trial: **Chicago History Museum/Archive Photos/GI**; Transcript: **AL**; Stenotype: **Art Team, Lisa F. Young/AL**; Inscription: **The Art Archive/AL**; Statue: **Album/Oronoz/Newscom**; Lincoln ad: **Art Team, S&SPL/National Media Museum/GI**. 112. Madoff: **Art Team, New York Daily News via AL, Fuse/GI**; Prison cell: **Archive Photos/GI**; Bunk beds: **MoMo Prodcutions/The Image Bank/GI**; Iron maiden: **WM**; License plate: **Art Team, FO**; Keys: **Andrew Paterson/AL**; Poster: **Bob Landry/Time & Life Images/GI**; Soap: **FO**; Shivs: **John Moore/GI**; Escape plan: **Art Team, FO**; Cinderblocks: **FO**. 113. Etiquette book: **WM**; Toilets: **Art Team**; Bush: **Pool Photo/Rod Aydelotte/Waco Tribune Herald/The Image Works**; Notecard: **Photograph by Laura Hanifin/Art Team**; Egyptian papyrus: **North Wind Picture Archives/AL**; Greetings illustration (4): **Art Team**. 114. Cooler with eyeball: **Art Team, Photograph by Laura Hanifin, Medical-on-Line/AL**; Car: **FO**; Sweater: **Art Team**; Blood: **FO**; Cans: **Art Team**; Penny tray: **Prop and photograph by Laura Hanifin**; Check: **Art Team**; Ocean bags: **Art Team**. 115. Brick: **Art Team**; Scholarship: **Art Team**; Carnegie Hall: **American Stock Archive/Archive Photos/GI**; Building: **Art Team, Sandra Baker/AL**; Letter: **Calligraphy by Iskra Johnson**; Prisoners: **Jay Janner/**

MCT/Newscom; Haiti posters (2): **Art Team, Eitan Abramovitch/AFP/GI, Juan Barreto/AFP/GI, Medical Missionaries/St. Joseph's Clinic**; Telethon: **Wire Images House/Wire Image/GI**. 116. Edwin Starr: **Ace Stock Limited/AL**; Kid with tank: **Constance Bannister Corp/Archive Photos/GI**; Cowboy and Indian: **Lambert Archive Photos/GI**; Cowboy: **Jeff Corwin/Workbook Stock**; Red Cross: **Maurice Crooks/AL**; Geneva Convention: **Art Team**. 117. Grasslands: **Stephen Street/AL**; Pocket guide: **Art Team**; LBJ: **Walter Bennett/Time & Life Pictures/GI**; Bush: **Mandel Ngan/AFP/GI**; Nancy Reagan and Mr. T: **Art Team**; Kid as knight: **Scott Montgomery/Workbook Stock/GI**. 118. Bombed buildings: **Daniel Berehulak/GI News/GI**. 119. Lie detector: **Tom Schielitz/Stone/GI**

Chapter Six:
120. Greeter: **Scott Nobles**. 121. Lou: **Art Team, Daily Show, Bert Klassen/AL**. 122. Maps: **Art Team**; Lady Gaga: **Peter Wafzig/GI Entertainment/GI**; Traders: **Art Team**. 123. Jumper: **Lass/Hulton Archive/GI**; Al Pacino: **Paramount Pictures/Photofest**; Van: **Izmostock/AL**; Wal-Mart: **Robert Harding Picture Library Ltd./AL**; Boutique: **Caro/AL**; Purse: **FO**; Matrix: **Art Team**; Lung: **FO**; Scrabble tile (2): **WM**; Slut: **FO**; Banana: **FO**; Wheat: **FO**; Rooster: **Alexey Stiop/AL**; Ketchup: **Art Team**; Sand: **Thomas David Pinzer/AL**; Aztec: **Brian Mitchell/Getty News Images/GI**; Gnome: **FO**; Newspaper: **FO**; Blog: **Art Team**. 124. Charts and graph: **Art Team**; Middleman: **Art Team**; Smith: **Art Team**; Marx: **Art Team, pzAxe/AL, Photos 12/AL**; Keynes: **Art Team, Walter Sanders/Time & Life Pictures/GI**; Ponzi: **Art Team, Francisco Martinez/AL, WM**. 125. Illustrations: **Lisel Ashlock**; Catalog: **Art Team**; Background: **FO**. 126. Liberty-head nickel: **WM**; Receipt tray: **FO**; US coins: **FO**; Euros: **FO**; Indian-head penny: **Eric Robison/AL**; All others: **Art Team**. 127. Bill: **Art Ream, photograph by Herman Estevez**; Queen: **Tim Graham Photo Library/GI**; Building: **Don Klupp/Photographer's Choice/GI, FO**; Stone disk: **Nick Wheeler/Danita Delimont Agency/AL**; Play money: **Huw Jones/AL**; IOU: **Art Team, FO**; Shell: **FO**; Gift card: **Art Team**; Massage Coupon: **Art Team**. 128. Check: **Art Team, FO**; Farmer illustrations: **Art Team**; Cloud: **FO**; Tomatoes: **Art Team, FO**; Rooster: **FO**; Shovel: **FO**; Farmer: **Vito Arcomano/AL**. 129. Chevrolet: **Art Team, WM**; Henry Ford: **WM**; Model T: **Art Team/FO**; Assembly line: **Ralph Morse/Time & Life Pictures/GI**; Robot: **Business Wire/GI Publicity/GI**; Containers: **FO**; Lou: **Daily Show**; Worker: **Jim West/AL**. 130. Fast-food worker: **Corbis Premium RF/AL**; Orderly: **FO**; Cable guy: **Comstock/Comstock Images/GI**; Barb: **Helen King/Age Fotostock**; Screen: **FO, Art Team**; Mechanic: **FO**. 131. Ring: **FO**; Model

(6): **Daily Show**; Rough diamond: **Art Team**; Condom: **Jonnie Miles/Photographer's Choice/GI**; Case: **FO**; Diamond (6): **Dimitri Vervitsiotis/Photogrpaher's Choice/GI**; Screen: **Scott Kleinman/Photonica/GI**; Ring box: **FO**. 132. Groceries: **FO**; Barnum: **Henry Guttman/Hulton archive/GI**; Receipt: **Art Team**; Plastic bag: **Art Team**; Cart: **FO**; Ad: **Art Team, Slaven Vlasic/WireImage/GI**; Wal-Mart sign: **Scott Olson/GI News/GI**; Rug man: **Sundlof–EDCO/AL**; Cart man: **Gavriel Jecan/Photodisc/GI**; Laptop: **Art Team, FO**; Smart phone: **Art Team, FO**. 133. Business cards: **Illustrations by Sarah Knotz, Art Team, photograph by Herman Estevez**; Vending machine: **Katharine Andriotis Photography, LLC/Editorial/AL**; Hands (14): **Art Team**; Jar: **FO**; Lou: **Daily Show**. 134–135. Light pole: **Art Team**; Sniping wall: **Art Team**; Airplane: **FO, Art Team**; Blimp: **FO, Art Team**; Balloon: **FO, Art Team, Kirby Lee/WireImages/GI**; Building: **Art Team**; Chesterfields ad: **Art Team, Henrik Sorensen/Riser/GI**; Bus: **Art Team, FO**; Lemon ad: **Art Team, FO**; Tang ad: **Art Team, Michael Maes/FoodPix/GI, Rosemary Calvert/Photographer's Choice/GI**; Camel ad: **Art Team, Greg Pease/The Image Bank/GI**. 136. Lamb blood ad: **Art Team, FO**; Uneeda Biscuit tin: **Art Team**; Bolshevik ad: **Art Team**; Old Gold ad: **Art Team, Oliver Leedham/AL**; Pepsi sign: **Ian Dagnall/AL**; Faust book: **Art Team**; Newspaper ad: **Art Team**; Political poster: **WM**; Radio: **FO**; Transcript: **Art Team**; Targeted ads (3): **Art Team**. 137. Disposal ad: **Art Team**; Hong Kong: **Chad Ehlers/AL**; Infomercial: **Art Team, FO, Mike Guastella/WireImage/GI**; Mercedes ad: **Art Team, FO, Jan Persson/Redferns/GI**; Juicy pants: **Kelly Han/AL**; Fried egg ad: **Art Team**; Apple ad: **Art Team, FO**; Tampax ad: **Art Team, Johner/Johner Images/GI**; Banner ad: **Art Team**. 138. Logos: **Art Team**; Buildings: **FO**; Gavel: **Judith Collins/AL**; Man: **Alexey Stiop/AL**; Money: **Lamb/AL**; Helmet: **Jed Jacobsohn/GI Sport/GI**. 139. Award: **Art Team, photograph by Herman Estevez**; Stone: **Art Team**; Meeting: **Art Team, Dennis O'Clair/Stone/GI, FO**. 140. Bank: **FPG/Archive Photos/GI**; Illustrations (7): **Art Team**; Piggy bank: **FO**; Check: **FO**; ATM: **Art Team, FO**; Man: **Neil Beckerman/GI**. 141. Background: **FO**; Statement: **Art Team**; Envelope: **Mathew Ward/Dorling Kindersley/GI**; KKK card: **Art Team, William Thomas Cain/Reportage/GI**; Random card: **Art Team, Brandon Harmon/Photonica/GI, FO, Terry O'Neill/GI**; AmEx card: **Art Team**; Zimbabwe card: **Art Team**; Credit cards (4): **Photography by Herman Estevez**. 142. Cramer: **Scott Gries/GI Entertainment/GI**; Button board: **Art Team**; Modern investor: **Lisa F. Young/AL**; Old investor: **Harold M. Lambert/Archive Photos/GI**; Bull:

Art Team, EIGHTFISH/Riser/GI. 143. Highlights: **Art Team**, photograph by Herman Estevez; Guru: **Dimitrios Kambouris/WireImage/GI**; Window: **Chris Pancewicz/AL**; Gold: **Artpartner-Images/Photographer's Choice/GI**; Condo: **FO**; Bulb: **FO**; Tulips: **FO**; Certificate: **FO**; Field: **FO**; Peony: **FO**; Hands (5): **FO**. 144. Store: **Art Team, John T. Wright/KYPAD/AP**; Lou: **Daily Show**. 145. Juice: **FO**

243

Herman Estevez, retouching by Stan Wagner. 191. Harelip baby: Taro Yamasaki/Time & Life Images/GI; Normal baby: Taro Yamasaki/Time & Life Images/GI; Meg Ryan before: Mirek Towski/DMI/Time & Life Pictures/GI; Meg Ryan after: Sean Gallup/GI; Inhaler: Science Photo Library/AL; Bouncer: VEER Steve Singer/GI; Magazines and DVDs: Herman Estevez, retouching by Stan Wagner; Invitro materials: James Keyser/Time & Life Images/GI; Beer: FO; Microscope close-up: Art Team. 192. Psychologist: Smith Collection/Stone+/AL; Psychiatrist: Lisa F. Young/AL; Stepdad: Sean Murphy/The Image Bank/GI. 193. Hand: FO; Ouija board: Herman Estevez, retouching by Stan Wagner; Rorschach test: Herman Estevez, retouching by Stan Wagner; Freud: Time & Life Pictures/ GI; Patient: SuperStock/GI. 194–195. Medicine cabinet: Art Team, Herman Estevez, retouching by Stan Wagner. 196. Safe: D. Hurst/AL; Grenade hurlers: McNeill/Hulton Archive/GI; Gunman: Robert Yager/Stone/GI; Horseback statue: David Henley/Dorling Kindersley/GI. 197. Feathers: FO; Rope: FO; Telephone: FO; Cookie dough: FO; Pillow: FO; Tug-o-War: FO; Gossip: FO; Gingerbread house: FO; Arrows: FO; Noose: FO; Defcon 1: FO; Gingerbread deathcamp: Art Team, FO; Battering ham: Art Team, WM; Sharkapult: Art Team, FO; Gunchucks: Art Team, FO; Spoon-Onet: Art Team, FO; Penis Trap: Art Team, FO. 198. Explosion: SuperStock/GI. 199. Jet pack: Windsor & Wiehahn/The Image Bank/GI; Elevator: FO.

Chapter Nine:
200. Tank top: Art Team, Michael Ventura/AL; 201. Cave painting: Sisse Brimberg/National Geographic/GI. 202. Irving Berlin: WM; Theater poster: Art Team; Romeo and Juliet: Art Team; Shakespeare: Hulton Archive/GI; Aborigines: Steven Weinberg/Workbook Stock/GI; Thespian: FO. 203. Playbill: Art Team, George Marks/Retrofile/GI; Masks: Art Team; Vases (4): Art Team, Hulton Archive/GI; TV: Art Team, Marcus Mok/Asia Images/GI, FO; Poster: Buena Vista Pictures/Photofest; Book: Art Team; Opera: SuperStock/AL. 204–205. Dad reading: Jamie Grill/Iconica/GI; Book display: Herman Estevez, retouching by Stan Wagner; Gutenberg Bible: Christopher King/AL; Wuthering Heights: Art Team, Liz Steketee/Photonica/GI; Glasses man: CBS Photo Archive+/GI; Penguin: 20th Century Fox/Photofest. 206. John Coltrane: Gai Terrell/Redferns/GI; Birthday woman: Thomas Fricke/First Light/GI; Bob Marley: Hulton Archive/GI; Boy band: Larry Busacca/WireImage/GI; Elmo: Jemal Countess/GI Entertainment/GI; Air Supply: Paul Natkin/WireImage/GI;

Bagpiper: Steve Allen/The Image Bank/GI; Boombox: FO; Tape: Art Team; Playlist: Art Team. 207. Karaoke: Zac Macaulay/The Image Bank/GI; Manjo: Art Team, John Cohen/Hulton Archive/GI; Pole Dancer: FO; Rain dancer: Visions of America/Joe Sohm/The Image Bank/GI; Newspaper: Art Team, Phil Dent/Redferns/GI; Dom DeLuise: Film still by Laura Hanifin; DJ: Smith Collection/Iconica/GI; Dizzy Gillespie: Roland Godefroy/WM; Steel drum: Macduff Everton/The Image Bank/GI; Banjo: Bob Thomas/Photographer's Choice/GI. 208. Marquee top: Walter Bibikow/The Image Bank/GI; Theater: Art Team, FO; Brick wall: Matt Johnston/Stock Image/GI; Halle Berry gown: Vince Bucci/GI Entertainment/GI; Moviegoer: Joe Raedle/GI News/GI; Movie posters (2): Art Team. 209. Hollywood sign: Marvin E. Newman/Photographer's Choice/GI; Star: Daily Show; Handprint: Andrea Wells/Photographer's Choice/GI; Movie posters (9): Art Team; Citizen Kane 2: Art Team; Orson Welles: Apic/Hulton Archive/GI; Chris Tucker: Adrian Groom/In-Focus/GI Entertainment/GI; Halle Berry casual: Arnaldo Magnani/GI Entertainment/GI. 210. TV family: Paul Almasy/Corbis; TV Guide: Art Team; TV dinner: Petrified Collection/Stone/GI; Water cooler: FO. 211. Johnny Carson: Photofest; Wolf Blitzer: Jeff Greenberg/AL; Taxi: Ted Pink/AL; US remote: Brad Wilson/Iconica/GI; North Korea remote: Art Team; St. Elsewhere: NBC/AP; I Love Lucy: CBS Photo Archive/AL; Gunsmoke: Michael Ochs Archives/GI; Law and Order: NBC/Photofest; Recliners (3): Art Team; Televisions (6): FO. 212. Palette: Art Team/FO; Beatrice: WM; Football painting: Matthew Peyton/GI Entertainment/GI; Intern: RubberBall/AL; Venus painting: WM; Hoover vacuum: Art Team, Science & Society Picture Library/SSPL/GI; Herbert Hoover: Rolls Press/Popperfoto/GI; Theo van Gogh: WM; Totebag: Art Team; Playbill: Art Team, Carl Mydans/Time & Life Pictures/GI; Soup can, left: Michael Neelon(misc)/AL; Soup can, right: WM. 213. Van Gogh: WM; Thomas Kinkade: Bennett Raglin/WireImage/GI; J.D. Salinger: San Diego Historical Society/Hulton Archive/GI; Sun Ra: David Redfern/Redferns/GI; Judy Garland: Silver Screen Collection/Archive Photos/GI; Tom Shales: Art Team; Curator: Christophe Simon/AFP/GI; Andy Warhol: Ron Galella/WireImage/AL; Painter with canvas: Moodboard/AL. 214. Gallery: Art Team; Velasquez: WM; School portrait: Art Team; Wrestlers: Art Team; Thanka: WM; Jaguar: WM. 215. Dogs: Buyenlarge/Archive Photos/GI; Rothko: Daily Show; Landscape: WM; Camera: Art Team; Mask: Art Team. 216. Venus: Peter Willi/SuperStock/GI; Cocaine (3): FO; Big Boy: WM; Bikini: FO; Musicians: David Silverman/GI

News/GI; Cake: Laura Hanifin/Art Team; Flatscreen: FO; All others: Art Team. 217. Caviar: FO; Omelet: Simon Watson/FoodPix/GI; Breakfast sandwich: Art Team; Top hat: FO; Baseball cap: FO; Beer helmet: Brad Wenner/Flickr/GI; Lolita (2): Art Team; Album cover: Art Team; Red chair: WM; Black chair: Art Team; Glove chair: Art Team; Old clown: WM; Bozo: AP; Insane Clown Posse: Scott Harrison/GI Entertainment/GI; Award statuettes: Art Team; Oscar: Allstar Picture Library/AL; DVDs: WidStock/AL; Tucky mask: Mode Images Limited/AL; Syringe: Shockpix Premier/AL; Thanky: CSA Plastock/CSA Images/GI. 218. Putter: Stuart Franklin/GI Sport/GI; Golf course: Alex Maclean/Photonica/GI; Pink golfer: Marc Feldman/GI Sport/GI; Magazine spread: Laura Hanifin; David Beckham: AP; Soccer players: Robert Cianflone/GI Sport/GI; Baseball player: Mark Scott/Taxi/GI; Soccer field: Mike Powell/Allsport Concepts/GI; Baseball diamond: David Madison/Photographer's Choice/GI. 219. Matador: Cristina Quicler/AFP/GI; Football player: Joe Robbins/GI Sport/GI; Baseball card: WM; Baseball player: WM; Goat head: Atkinson/AL; Female surfer: Lori Adamski Peek/Taxi/GI; Male surfer: Ishara S. Kodikara/Stringer/AFP/GI; Buzkashi players: Banaras Khan/AFP/GI; Buzkashi field: Chris McLennan/Disovery Channel Images/GI. 220. Saints fan: Jed Jacobsohn/GI Sport/GI; Green Bay fan: Michelle Pedone/Photonica/GI; Cheesehead: Patti McConville/Photographer's Choice/GI; Colliseum: Art Team, DEA Picture Library/De Agostini Picture Library/GI; Mr. Met: Jeff Haynes/AFP/GI. 221. Mayor: Pierre Roussel/GI News/GI; Skier: Art Team, Alexander Nemenov/AFP/GI; Hockey: WM; Mark Spitz: Terry O'Neill/GI; Jesse Owens: WM; Wrestlers: Time & Life Pictures/GI; Raking: Benn Mitchell/Riser/GI; Opening ceremony: Alexander Hassenstein/Bongarts/GI; Torch: Leon Neal/AFP/GI; Medals: Art Team. 222. Gym: A Bello/Riser/GI; Lake: Randy Lincks/All Canada Photos/GI; Lean-to: Marilyn Angel Wynn/Nativestock.com/GI; Bow and arrow: Gary Ombler/Dorling Kindersley/GI; String and hook: WM; Tent: Art Team; All others: FO. 223. Boys playing video games: Victoria Blackie/Photographer's Choice/GI; Video games (8): Art Team; All others: FO. 224. Las Vegas: Mitchell Funk/Photographer's Choice/GI; Chips: FO; Lottery: Bloomberg via GI; Horses: Art Team. 225. Penthouse (2): Art Team; Japanese sculpture: Laura Hanifin; Kama Sutra: Bridgeman Art Library; Fitness magazines (2): Laura Hanifin; Black Neolithic figure: Carlo Bavagnoli/Time & Life Pictures/GI; Other Neolithic figures (2): Bridgeman Art Library; Pompeii fresco: Alinari/Bridgeman Art Library; Venus of Willendorf:

Ali Meyer/Bridgeman Art Library. 226. Bottles: Herman Estevez, retouching by Stan Wagner; Leaf: FO. 227. Box: Herman Estevez, inset photograph of peyote © ARCO/De Meester, J./Age Fotostock, retouching by Stan Wagner; Beer tap handles (4): Scott Nobles; Key: FO. 228. Suitcase: Jessica Walsh; Disneyworld: Bloomberg via GI; Mickey Mouse: Michael Kovac/FilmMagic/GI; Frame: FO; Eiffel Tower: Art Team, FO; Baby: Blend Images/AL. 229. Edith Bunker: CBS Photo Archive/GI; Family photo: Art Team; Sonogram: FO; Stalin: Cliff Volpe/GI News/GI; Album cover: Art Team; Kingston Trio: Michael Ochs Archives/GI; England fan: Valery Hache/AFP/GI; Happy Days: ABC/Photofest; White only sign: William Lovelace/Hulton Archive/GI. 230. Bikini model: Stefan Gosatti/GI Entertainment/GI; Runway: Maurizio Cigognetti/Photographer's Choice/GI; Black dress: FO; Bling dress: Art Team; Leisure suit: Robin Lynne Gibson/Stone/GI; Business suit: FO; High heel: Art Team, FO; Pantsuit: Jetta Productions/Iconica/GI; Colorful outfit: Caroline Bittencourt/LatinContent/GI; Hijab (2): Art Team, Celia Peterson/ArabianEye/GI. 231. Ruff: Imagno/Hulton Archive/GI; Lady Gaga: Dimitrios Kambouris/GI Entertainment/GI; Joan Rivers: Kevin Winter/GI Entertainment/GI; Steven Cojocaru: Steve Granitz/WireImage/GI; New Guinea tribal men: Claire Leimbach/Robert Harding World Imagery/GI; All others: FO. 232. Crossword: Art Team. 233. Medieval painting: French School/Bridgeman Art Library/GI; Caveman: Ron Embleton/Bridgeman Art Library/GI.

Back Matter:
235. Posters (4): Art Team. 236. Explosion: FPG/Taxi/GI; Launch/lunch panel: Art Team, Richard Ross/Riser/GI; Nicole Kidman: James Devaney/WireImage/GI; Hazmat suits: Joe Raedle/GI News/GI; Trash skyline: Win Initiative/Stone/GI; Voting booth: Art Team. 237. Terminator: Jean-Paul Aussenard/WireImage/GI; Vacuum: Scott Olson/GI News/GI; Stephen Hawking: Denis Farrell/AFP/GI; Black hole: WM; Shoes: Andy Ryan/Photonica/GI; Rapture woman: Stephen Stickler/Riser/GI. 238. Alien invasion: www.boelke-art.de/Flickr/GI; Alien card: Art Team; Ocean: Mitch Epstein/Stone/GI; Shark-bee: Art Team, FO.

APPLICATION FOR GENETIC RECONSTITUTION BY ALIENS

(Please print clearly)

PART I - Please answer these questions based on your genetic profile to the best of your ability. Don't be modest; the aliens need to know of your DNA's fitness for reconstitution.

Name (optional): _____   Place Of Birth (optional): _____

Race: _____   Sexual Orientation: ☐ Breeder   ☐ Non-Breeder

Height: _____   Weight: _____

Bench Press: _____   (If Obese, Whose Fault: ☐ Genes   ☐ Self)

Vertical Leap: _____   Standing Heart Rate: _____

Standing Heart Rate: _____   Shackle Size: _____ (Wrist) _____ (Ankle)

How many kilowatts would you say your brain produces hourly? _____

PART II - MEDICAL HISTORY

Do you or your immediate ancestors have a history of physical or mental illness? ☐ Yes ☐ No

If yes, would this condition(s) impede your ability to perform repetitive menial labor? ☐ Yes ☐ No

Are you one who bleeds easily? ☐ Yes ☐ No

Are you allergic to:

☐ Pollen   ☐ Peanuts   ☐ Burdens   ☐ Authority   ☐ Laser whips   ☐ Space gruel   ☐ The taste of the yoke

---

PART III - PERSONALITY (Circle one)

I would describe myself as a) **docile** b) **jester-like** c) **rebellious**

My will is a) **unbreakable** b) **easily breakable** c) **what will**?

To amuse others, I am willing to a) **dance** b) **dance even faster** c) **have my feet vaporized**

The best part of building a pyramid is a) **designing it** b) **selecting the site** c) **hauling two-ton blocks up crude ramps of packed earth**

Friends would describe my taste as a) **sophisticated** b) **traditional** c) **moist and chewy**

In terms of snitching on other members of my detail who are plotting escape/insurrection, my attitude is a) **Never** b) **It depends on my reward** c) **Any threat to our output quota must be quashed**

[Children only] My loyalties are with a) **My parents** b) **Glaxor, Imperator of Zalboz-9** c) **My teachers**

☐ True ☐ False   **I work well with others.**

☐ True ☐ False   **I work well for others.**

☐ True ☐ False   **I work well in others.**

☐ True ☐ False   **I breed sturdy offspring.**

☐ True ☐ False   **I retain adequate functionality under high levels of barometric pressure.**

☐ True ☐ False   **I am proud... some say too proud.**

☐ True ☐ False   **I can sleep standing up.**

☐ True ☐ False   **Human life should be measured in work-units.**

Please deposit the bodily fluid of your choice in the area above. Note: Choose *one* fluid only.

By filling out and submitting this form, I, the undersigned, do hereby indemnify Particular Books and Penguin Publishing against any and all liabilities, damages, losses, expenses, claims or fines which may be suffered by or accrued against my genetically reconstituted self in the event it is enslaved by an alien race.

Name (Print)   Signature